Varieties of Things

D0870451

For Graham,
a committed Humean

application of mathematical axioms or rules and other mathematical theorems, without appeal to empirical evidence.

Thus, we have here one clear example of a difference in methodology that marks off one discipline from another that can be exploited in helping to understand what makes metaphysics different from empirical science. Moreover, since few doubt that mathematics yields knowledge that is distinctive and valuable, the example shows that the a priori method is as legitimate a way of arriving at knowledge as is the empirical, or a posteriori one.

Many philosophers believe that this difference in methodology is fundamental to the difference between metaphysics and the empirical sciences. But appeal to the mathematical example to show this is itself problematic. After all, mathematics is a discipline that arrives at knowledge in an a priori way! Analogies between mathematics and metaphysics may help us to see what makes them both different disciplines from empirical science, but generates another problem. Why do we need metaphysics to tell us what there ultimately is when we have other a priori disciplines that can do that? What could metaphysics tell us about reality that these other disciplines could not?

The problematic nature of the mathematical example can actually help us to see that there is another, fundamental, difference between science and metaphysics. This has to do, not with methodology, but with subject matter. We opened this chapter with a characterization of metaphysics that immediately prompted the question, what could metaphysics tell us about reality (fundamental or otherwise) that empirical science could not? We now see that an appeal to differences in methodology alone is not enough to provide a satisfactory answer to this question; it simply prompts a more general reformulation of it. So we can ask, what makes any discipline different from another, once we put methodological differences aside? And one clear answer to this is: subject matter. What makes chemistry a different empirical science from biology is the objects, properties, and phenomena, that fall within its domain. These form the subject matter of the various disciplines, the things about which they set out to obtain knowledge. Chemistry deals with things chemical: with chemical elements, chemical properties, and chemical phenomena; biology deals with things biological: with biological organisms, biological properties, and biological phenomena. All of these things are physical things, but they form different categories of physical things. Likewise, what makes algebra a different a priori discipline from arithmetic, at least on one understanding of the disciplines, is that they deal with different mathematical things, different properties of these things, and different (mathematical) functions that operate on these things.

If metaphysics differs from other a priori disciplines, but not in methodology, then, it is because the subject matter of metaphysics is different. It is different in being far more general than the subject matter of other a priori disciplines. Metaphysics is not concerned with the existence of numbers of particular kinds, such as rational numbers, real numbers, or imaginary numbers, nor is it concerned at arriving at knowledge about these things. Nor is its interest restricted to things that are the objects of study by the a priori disciplines, such as mathematics. As the definition states, it is the study of fundamental reality – and not just some part of it. So, its subject matter includes everything that there is, including everything physical. However, even setting aside differences in methodology, metaphysics is not concerned with the existence of particular *physical* things or kinds of things, nor is it concerned with arriving at knowledge about these things. Its concerns are far more general, and in two ways.

First, its concerns about existence cut across differences between the domains of different disciplines: metaphysics is concerned with the existence of the most fundamental kinds of things, where, by 'fundamental' it is meant, 'of the most general kinds presupposed by other disciplines'. For example, it concerns itself with questions like these: Are there both physical and non-physical things? Are there physical and non-physical properties? Are things (both physical and non-physical) nothing more than 'bundles' of properties? Or are there properties as well as things that have them? Are there mental things? Are mental things just physical things? Are there persons? Are persons just physical things? Or are they physical and mental things?

Second, its concerns are not just about whether things of certain fundamental kinds exist. Its concerns are about what it is for things of these kinds to be of the kinds they are. Just as scientists ask whether items of certain kinds – such as electrons – exist and also what it is for these items to be items of the kinds they are (or, what it is for these kinds to be the kinds they are), so too, with regard to the most general and fundamental kinds of things that are the subject matter of metaphysics, metaphysicians ask whether items of these fundamental kinds exist and also what it is for these items to be items of the kinds they are (or what it is for these kinds to be the kinds they are). So, they don't just ask questions of the form 'Are there Xs?', where the Xs are of the most general kinds presupposed by other disciplines; they also ask questions of the form, 'What is it to be an X?'. Note, however, that these questions are not independent of one another. A satisfactory answer to a question of the form 'Are there Xs?' should require us to have, or arrive at, a very good idea of what it is to be an X. Alternatively, failure to come up with a satisfactory answer to a question of the form 'What is it to be an X?' should make us wonder whether there are Xs at all.

Four features of metaphysics, viewed as the study of ultimate reality, emerge from this brief discussion and characterize it in a way that marks it off, as a distinct and valuable discipline, from others. The first is its concern with questions about the 'real' nature of things, and of what, fundamentally, there really is in the world. As the above paragraph makes clear, the fundamental kinds of things with which metaphysics is concerned are not those whose existence and nature are the concern of other disciplines, whether empirical or a priori, to discover and describe, but are rather ones whose existence and nature are presupposed by those disciplines. The second is its 'intellectual' or a priori nature, where, by 'a priori', it is meant that its subject matter is knowable independently of sensory experience. As Aristotle (and countless others) conceived of it, metaphysics is an intellectual or a priori discipline concerned with questions that cannot be answered by empirical observation and experiment. The third relates to the universality or generality of its concerns, that it is concerned with existence as such, in its most general form, and not, as the particular sciences are, with the existence of things of this or that particular kind.[3] In other words, metaphysics is concerned with questions of existence and reality that are inherently more general than those that occupy the particular sciences and other disciplines, and is in this sense more universal. Psychology may concern itself with human beings as cognitive agents, and geology may concern itself with rocks; but metaphysics concerns itself with all of the things of all of the kinds that there may be, their natures, and their relations to one another. Moreover, it does so without being constrained by the assumptions that inevitably limit the particular disciplines (Irwin 1988; Loux 2002). For example, physics may concern itself with the various kinds of physical things that there are, but it does not question whether there are physical things, and if so, what it is to be a physical, in contrast to a non-physical, thing. However, metaphysics does raise precisely this kind of question.

It is perhaps this third characteristic of metaphysics, more than any other, which may explain its utility in relation to other disciplines, in that the latter proceed on the basis of assumptions that metaphysics makes explicit and attempts to justify. It may also account, at least in part, for the history of disagreement amongst metaphysicians, and the subject's reputation for 'making no progress' with regard to generating an agreed body of information or knowledge. It is relatively easy, one might argue, to adjudicate between competing claims within the individual sciences, because such sciences work with principles or assumptions that they do not themselves question. Within such a framework, there are agreed criteria of how to go about settling such disputes. But metaphysics, it might be thought, by its very nature can appeal to no fixed criteria of this kind to settle its disputes: beyond standards of internal consistency, indefinitely many metaphysical theories can provide equally adequate explanations of our beliefs about the world. (As we shall see in chapter 2, this assumption that metaphysics can appeal to no principles or assumptions that it does not itself question is unwarranted, as is the assumption that there is radical indeterminacy in metaphysical theorizing of a kind that does not obtain in other disciplines such as science.[4] There are, within the discipline of metaphysics, principles and criteria by which to adjudicate between competing ontologies.)

Finally, because the nature of metaphysics is to deal in an a priori way with the most general and fundamental questions of the natures and kinds of things that there are, the propositions of metaphysics have traditionally been conceived as being necessarily rather than contingently true. That is, if true if at all, they concern not only what is the case but also what must be the case. Thus, for example, Aristotle thought that whereas natural science can discover which the substances are, or what things count as substances, only metaphysics can discover what it is to be a substance, so that metaphysical truths about substance, if true at all, *must* be true, and so are presupposed by natural science. And Kant, as we shall see, thought that metaphysics discovers propositions about the world that must be true if experience of the world is to be possible.[5]

Aristotle and Kant shared a conception of metaphysics that embodied all of the above characteristics. However, they differed fundamentally in their views about what metaphysicians can or will discover or come to know. Aristotle believed that we can discover what is beyond experience, and he believed this because he did not recognize the roles that our senses and minds play in shaping what we can know. Kant, in contrast, believed that we cannot discover what is beyond experience, and he believed this because he thought that all of our a priori knowledge – knowledge whose justification is independent of sensory experience – is about, not how the world must be, but how the world must be experienced. This difference will become clearer as the discussion of Aristotle's and Kant's views progresses below.

Aristotle's Conception of Metaphysics

Aristotle conceived of metaphysics as justifying, by reason and logic, fundamental assumptions made by the sciences – commonsensical ones, such as that there are material things – about the natural world. Specifically, its aim is to arrive at knowledge of the highest principles and causes of things. His work provides a conception of metaphysics that takes us some way towards understanding both what it means to say that metaphysics is the study of fundamental reality and why it has a distinctive place amongst other disciplines.

Aristotle held that it is in the nature of metaphysics to study being as such, or, as he puts it in Book IV (Γ.1) of the *Metaphysics*, 'being qua being, and the attributes that belong to this in virtue of its own nature', and he described this study as the science of being. Other disciplines may be concerned with the nature of things of particular kinds, such as trees, and frogs, but they are not concerned with being in general, the kind of being that abstracts from the nature of this or that particular thing, or indeed, of things of this or that particular kind. But metaphysics is concerned with the existence of anything, insofar as it exists at all, or under the aspect of existing. This is not to be understood as the claim that metaphysics has a peculiar kind of subject matter, that of being qua being. Rather, the claim is that metaphysics is a discipline that studies beings, or things that there are, and does so in a certain manner, or in a certain way, namely, just *as* things that are (Cohen 2003). Aristotle thought that other disciplines, such as mathematics and natural science, also study things that there are, but that they do not do so insofar as they are things that are. Mathematics studies things insofar as they are measurable or countable; and science studies things insofar as they change or move. But metaphysics asks and attempts to answer the question, what is required for something – anything – to be, or exist?

Aristotle was concerned both with whether things of certain kinds are ones whose existence is fundamental to the existence of others and with what it is for these things to be what they are, what their natures are. With respect to the latter, he held that there are many different kinds of being, or ways in which things are; for example, the being of substances, the being of properties or qualities of substances, and the being of changes and/or processes to which substances are subject. He believed, however, that some things are ones whose being is more fundamental, more basic, than is the being of others. It was his view that particular substances (such as individual human beings, or individual apples) are the ones whose being is fundamental in that their existence is fundamental to the existence of others, and (in the *Organon*) he distinguishes between primary (or individual) substances and secondary substances (or kinds, such as the kind, *tiger*). The latter are the species and genera into which individual substances fall. The nature of a primary substance is explained in terms of four causes. Briefly, these are (1) the formal cause, which concerns the essence of a substance, that which makes it the thing of the kind that it is, (2) the material cause, which concerns its material constitution, that which composes it, (3) the efficient cause, which concerns how it came into being, or into existence, and (4) the final cause, which concerns its purpose or end. The first two notions, in explaining the essence and constitution of a substance, help to explain what capacities or potentialities it has, whereas the final two notions help to explain how change with regard to a substance is possible.

Aristotle's doctrine of substance forms the core of his metaphysics. His view was that a material substance comes into being through a form being given to matter, somewhat like the way in which the lump of matter from which a statue is carved becomes an individual thing when it acquires the form of a statue. Since every material substance consists of both matter and form, Aristotle rejected the view that the only reality that there is consists of pure forms. Nevertheless, he considered the forms that 'shape' matter to be most important in explaining both what the nature of a substance is and how a substance changes (its highest cause). Further, at one point in the *Metaphysics* VII (Z)–IX(θ), he suggests that the principal subject matter of metaphysics is the nature of substance (VII.1), that substances are basic subjects that are identical with their essences (i.e., with that which gives them their natures), and that the essences of substances are their forms. Further, he suggests that, in engaging in metaphysical enquiry, he is not so much concerned with the perceptible substances, but ultimately with the unperceptible ones, namely, the pure and divine ones that are without matter (Z, ch. 11, 1037a 10–17). Taken together, these claims imply that metaphysics is the science of forms (Irwin 1988, chs 10–12), some of which (like the Unmoved Mover, or God) are 'pure' forms and so are immaterial substances. The Unmoved Mover, in being the first cause of all things, is the highest of all causes.

The result is that two rather different conceptions of what metaphysics can discover are to be found in the work of Aristotle. On the one hand, there is the conception that construes metaphysics as arriving at knowledge, in most general terms, of the nature of substance as a combination of matter and form: the study of the ultimate constituents of each and every kind of individual substance in the experienceable world (each individual being of the kind it is in virtue of its matter being informed by the form it is). On the other hand, there is the conception that construes metaphysics as arriving at knowledge of forms, some of which are 'pure' ones. This is well illustrated by Aristotle's arguments for the necessary existence of the Unmoved Mover (or God), the initiator of all change in the experienceable world that is not itself part of that world, whose existence is knowable only through the intellect. Despite the fact that Aristotle struggled to free himself entirely from the second conception, both conceptions are important to an appreciation of his work, since he believed that a complete philosophy was also a theology.

This conception of metaphysics as first philosophy, we have seen, is of a discipline that studies the general nature of kinds of substances that particular sciences presuppose. Aristotle, however, made an important and controversial assumption about the nature of the subject. In claiming that, whereas natural science studies things that are better known to us, first philosophy studies things that are better known in themselves, he was assuming that it is possible, by the exercise of reason or the intellect alone, to have knowledge of what things are in themselves, without this knowledge being shaped by any perceptual and conceptual apparatus. The eighteenth-century British empiricists, Locke, Berkeley, and Hume attempted to account for our general knowledge of the world on a model of the mind according to which, although the mind has innate powers, it has no innate structures or concepts – that is, no structures or concepts in it from birth. However, this attempt was unsuccessful, and it eventually led to the sceptical philosophy of David Hume. Since then it has become increasingly clear that the role of the human mind and the concepts it employs play a much larger role in the acquisition of knowledge of the world than Aristotle was prepared to acknowledge. What he did not recognize is the roles that our senses and minds play in shaping what we can know; he thought that the human mind is a kind of transparent medium through which we can just 'see' how things are in the world.[6] In his *Critique of Pure Reason*, Immanuel Kant occupied himself almost exclusively with this issue, and his discussion of it led to a new conception of what metaphysics can or will discover, and so of what, by means of it, we can come to know.

Kant's Conception of Metaphysics

As we have seen, Aristotle held that we grasp the truth of metaphysical propositions by means of the intellect alone. But these propositions, concerned as they are with the being of things as they are in themselves, provide us with knowledge of the world; of the ultimate nature of substance and of the Unmoved Mover. So, on this view, the intellect alone can give us knowledge of the real world.

Furthermore, some of these propositions, for example, those concerned with the necessary existence of the Unmoved Mover, are knowable only by means of the intellect because they concern a reality that is supersensible, incapable of being sensed. So the intellect alone can give us knowledge of supersensible reality. This aspect of Aristotle's metaphysics – the aspect that construes metaphysics as providing knowledge of what is beyond experience – contrasts sharply with the conception of metaphysics developed by Immanuel Kant.

Kant did not believe that propositions that purport to describe a reality knowable to the intellect alone could constitute knowledge. He believed that if any proposition is knowable a priori, it could provide knowledge of the world only if it is applicable to the world accessible to sense experience. Kant captured this idea in the notion of a synthetic proposition that is knowable a priori. This is a proposition that is independent of sense experience in that no proposition describing sense experience entails either it or its negation (and so it is a priori), but yet is applicable to – possibly true of – the experienceable world (and so is synthetic). Kant thought that the proposition that every event has a cause is one such proposition. He believed that propositions of this kind form the basis of (in the sense of making possible) substantive knowledge in disciplines – sciences – other than metaphysics, in particular, mathematics and empirical science. But he also believed that metaphysical propositions, if they were to provide real knowledge, must also be of this kind.

So Kant, like Aristotle, believed that metaphysical principles are knowable a priori, are presupposed by all sciences, and have a generality or universality that particular sciences lack. However, by setting limits on what is knowable, he set limits on metaphysical knowledge itself. Metaphysical knowledge, inasmuch as it is possible at all, must concern itself with truths that are knowable a priori but are synthetic. It follows that we can have no knowledge, by means of the intellect alone, of the supersensible.

According to this conception, the main tasks of metaphysics are: first, to identify the synthetic but knowable a priori judgements used in perception and thought about the world; and, second, to demonstrate their indispensability to such perception and thought. Kant claimed that certain synthetic but knowable a priori judgements used in perception and thought about the world were indispensable because (1) they employ certain a priori forms or structures of perception (specifically, space, and time), one, or the other, or both, of which are presupposed by every act of perception but are not themselves the objects of perception, and (2) they employ certain fundamental concepts (which he called 'categories') such as the concept of causality, and the concept of modality, without which thought about and understanding of the world is impossible.[7] He treated the question, 'How is metaphysics possible?' as elliptical for the question 'How is metaphysical knowledge possible?'. His view was that the answer to the latter is to be determined by the results of enquiry into the conditions of knowledge in general.[8] This turns metaphysics into epistemology, thus obliterating Aristotle's distinction between being qua being and being qua known.

Kant's rejection of metaphysics as the study of being qua being, insofar as it involves rejecting the view that it is possible to have knowledge of things as they are in themselves, is a rejection of transcendent metaphysical knowledge; knowledge of a reality that cannot be experienced. His view is that metaphysics is possible only if metaphysical propositions can constitute knowledge; and this in turn is possible only if such propositions employ forms of sensibility and concepts that are applicable to the world of sensory experience. It follows from this that there can be no body of knowledge obtained by the exercise of reason or the intellect alone.[9]

Despite this fundamental departure from Aristotle, Kant believed in the a priori and universal nature of the propositions of metaphysics. And, like Aristotle, Kant worked with assumptions about the nature of the subject. Specifically, he believed that perception and thought about the world require that these two faculties have specific structures which cooperate to yield knowledge; that, within these faculties, are quite specific a priori forms (intuitions and concepts) without which perception and thought about the world would be impossible. To be sure, these forms could not themselves yield knowledge of the world, since they require content, derivable only from sensory experience. But, without the forms of intuition and thought, no knowledge of the world is possible.

Unfortunately, the structure of perception or intuition that Kant assumed supposes that space is Euclidean, i.e., three-dimensional, and that time is Newtonian, i.e., that it is a separate dimension from the spatial dimension, and this does not do justice to the many existing non-Euclidean geometries nor to the concept of four-dimensional space-time. This suggests that empirical study into the nature of space and time might yield truths that are not only incompatible with the propositions of metaphysics but falsify them, thus undermining the claim that the propositions of metaphysics are a priori. Further, Kant argued that 'we cannot think of an object without Categories' – fundamental concepts embodied in certain synthetic a priori judgements about the experienceable world. Yet developments in quantum mechanics in the twentieth century suggest that the 'principle' of causality – that every event has a cause – and the category of causality embodied in it, are not indispensable to thought about the world, which again undermines the a priori status of metaphysical propositions.

There is, however, a way of defending Kant's claims about the necessity of the forms of perception and thought to knowledge about the world against such scientific refutations, thereby protecting the a priori status of metaphysical knowledge. This is to argue that the claims of metaphysics should be interpreted as ones about what is necessary to make experience of the world possible. Thus, for example, we can argue on Kant's behalf that if the concept of Euclidean space is not fundamental to experience of the world, the concept of physical space, whatever that may entail, is fundamental to experience. Interpreted in this way, Kant's position is that metaphysics is compatible and continuous with science in that it aims to identify the fundamental intuitions and concepts presupposed in perception and thought – both commonsensical and scientific – about the world, but will presuppose no particular realization of scientific theory. Its claims will be corrigible, not because it presupposes the claims of some particular scientific theory (as was being claimed above), but rather, because its a priority will not make it immune to error. And why should it? After all, the a priority of a claim has to do with how it is justified, not with whether it is true. What matters to the a priority of metaphysical propositions is not whether they are immune from error, but what sorts of error they might be vulnerable to. If metaphysical knowledge is subject to error, it is not subject to the same sorts of error to which science is subject. Metaphysicians should not be deceived by the senses – but that is because metaphysical knowledge is not sensory knowledge. Still, metaphysicians may be deceived by other sorts of error, such as fallacies in reasoning; its a priority will not protect it from that.

A Working Conception of Metaphysics

We began with a description of metaphysics as the study of fundamental reality, of the ultimate categories or kinds of things that there are in the world. This description is equally true of Aristotle's and of Kant's metaphysics: both are concerned in a very general way with questions of being or existence. Further, both take the method of metaphysics to be a priori. However, Aristotle and Kant differ in their views of what metaphysics, thus conceived, can discover. We've seen that this difference between them is signalled by Kant's rejection of the view that metaphysics is the study of being qua being as opposed to the study of being qua known.[10] Because Kant, but not Aristotle, believed that all knowledge, metaphysical knowledge included, is shaped or informed by the human perceptual and conceptual apparatus, he, unlike Aristotle, believed that we could not have knowledge of things as they are in themselves, and so could have no knowledge of truths about God, causation, and other matters traditionally conceived as metaphysical.

These remarks express a fairly determinate view of the nature and function of metaphysics. By way of helping to develop it further, we shall conclude this chapter by discussing two important distinctions that have figured in recent thinking about the discipline of metaphysics, as raised and examined by a contemporary philosopher, Susan Haack (1976, 1979). Haack raises a number of questions about the aims and claims of metaphysics, specifically with regard to ontology, that part of metaphysics that explores the question of what things or sorts of things there are. Her questions go right to the heart of what metaphysics is and why it has been held in such contempt from the eighteenth century onwards in Western philosophy, from Hume to the Logical Positivists. These thinkers took exception to Kant's view that some synthetic propositions could be known a priori, and so rejected the possibility of metaphysics as Kant conceived of it.[11] Haack's discussion is instructive for a number of reasons, one of the more important ones being that it helps illuminate the relation between metaphysics and our common-sense thinking about the world. But it also leads very naturally to a more fully developed account of the nature and function of metaphysics that we will presume throughout the remainder of this book.

The Strategy

In 'Some Preliminaries to Ontology' (1976), Haack examines Carnap's (1950) distinction between two kinds of questions, 'internal' ones, and 'external' ones. Carnap's purpose is to distinguish certain kinds of ontological questions, which make sense and are capable of being answered relatively unproblematically, from other kinds of ontological questions, which make no literal sense at all. 'Internal' questions are questions that can only be asked sensibly after the adoption of a particular linguistic framework (i.e., interpreted language fragment), and are about the domain associated with that framework. Examples of internal questions that can be legitimately raised and answered are particular questions about an entity of some kind, such as 'Is 5 a prime number?', as well as general, category questions about the existence of items of a given kind, such as 'Do numbers really exist?' According to Carnap, questions of the latter sort, while being very general, can be answered unproblematically 'within', or after the adoption of, a given conceptual or linguistic framework. So, for example, if you were to ask me whether there really are numbers, I, who have adopted the linguistic framework of numbers, could meaningfully reply, 'yes, there are numbers, since 5 is a number'.

Haack takes the form of an internal question to be 'Are there so-and-so's according to L?', where L is a linguistic framework/interpreted language fragment.

'External' questions, on the other hand, are questions that arise prior to the adoption of a given linguistic framework, about the 'reality' of the framework itself. Haack takes them to have the form 'Are there so-and so's (period)?' These are inherently general and fall into two sorts. First, there are questions of a practical kind that we can ask about a given linguistic framework, say, the framework of numbers. We can ask whether it is useful or expedient in some way to use number-talk, or to use number-concepts. (So the question 'Are there really numbers?' actually has two 'senses', an internal one and an external one, both of which can be meaningfully addressed.) Carnap considers this first type of external question to be harmless because, in his view, it is not one whose answer commits any speaker or thinker using the framework to the existence of items corresponding to the terms or concepts in the framework.

However, Carnap maintains that there is a second kind of external question, which does not make any sense at all, and to which we cannot give an intelligible answer. This is a 'framework' question understood, not as a pragmatic question, but as a theoretical one about the 'reality' of the entities in the domain associated with the framework. Thus interpreted, it is a question about the truth or falsity of the framework itself.

Haack argues that Carnap's attempt to show that external theoretical questions are literally meaningless does not succeed. She discerns two main arguments in Carnap's work (principally, in his 1928 and 1950 work). The first has two threads, one focusing on the sense of 'real', and the other focusing on the sense of 'so-and-so's' in 'So-and-so's are real'. Haack disentangles these two threads, and argues that neither establishes that external theoretical questions make no sense.

One thread of argument in Carnap is that only after the adoption of a conceptual/linguistic framework can it make sense to ask what is real and what is not. Haack disagrees. She argues that there is always the possibility of constructing a metalanguage – a language in which there are expressions that enable us to talk about the conceptual/linguistic framework at issue – in which such questions can meaningfully be formulated.[12]

A second thread of argument in Carnap is that prior to the adoption of a linguistic framework, 'so-and-so's' has no established sense. Only a linguistic framework can give it a sense. Here Haack agrees, but wonders how this shows that external theoretical questions are pseudo-questions. Certainly no question about the reality of 'so-and-so's' will be meaningful if 'so-and-so's' has no meaning. But how are we to assess the claim that only a linguistic framework can supply a meaning? If we think of natural languages, every existence question will be relative to a linguistic framework, and no existence question will be senseless. If on the other hand we restrict ourselves to formal languages, then there will be some external existence questions, and the distinction between internal and external theoretical questions will be saved. But saving it requires that we commit ourselves to the highly implausible view that only expressions in formal languages have sense.

The second main argument in Carnap is that we cannot make sense of external theoretical questions by means of the internal sense of 'so-and-so's' in 'There are so-and-so's according to L' and the question whether the sentences of L are true. According to Carnap, the acceptance of a linguistic framework is a pragmatic rather than a theoretical matter, and so carries with it no ontological commitment. If so, this way of attempting to make sense of external questions would be blocked, since accepting L would not be a matter of accepting the sentences of L as true. But Haack points out that in order for Carnap's response to work, one would need to construe him as an 'epistemological pessimist' – one who holds that we cannot know or discover whether theories are true, but only which ones are compatible with the data, and of these, which are preferable on grounds such as simplicity and/or other pragmatic criteria. The problem with this is that Carnap was not in general an epistemological pessimist. She concludes that:

> Carnap's distinction between internal and external questions could be seen as an unsuccessful, but not altogether abortive, attempt to explain how persistence with the question, whether there really are so-and-so's, may be a symptom of controversy about whether they are, really, what they are ordinarily taken to be. (Haack 1976, p. 272)

In 'Descriptive and Revisionary Metaphysics' (1979), Haack revisits the issue of the nature and function of metaphysical enquiry. Here she is concerned, not specifically with the question of how we are to understand ontological questions, but more generally with the question of how we are to understand the nature of metaphysical claims. Her subject matter is the distinction between descriptive and revisionary metaphysics as drawn by Peter Strawson in *Individuals* (1959) and embodied in his work and in Whitehead's *The Concept of Nature* (1930).

Haack's discussion falls into two parts. In the first, she compares and contrasts Strawson's 'descriptive' metaphysics with Whitehead's 'revisionary' metaphysics. In the second, she raises some difficult and important questions about the distinction between these two types of metaphysics and assumptions underlying it.

According to Strawson, descriptive metaphysics aims to describe the actual structure of our conceptual framework, the scheme by which we think about the world. It differs from conceptual analysis only in its generality. Whereas, in one traditional view, the latter is concerned to make explicit the necessary and sufficient conditions for any concept to be the concept it is, descriptive metaphysics is concerned to uncover the fundamental concepts required for human thought about the world to be possible. It aims to:

> lay bare the most general features of our conceptual structure . . . a massive central core of human thinking which has no history . . . the commonplaces of the least refined thinking . . . the indispensable core of the conceptual equipment of the most sophisticated human beings. (Strawson 1959, pp. xiii–xiv)

This conceptual scheme has a core that has remained constant throughout history and is invariant between languages. It is this central core that descriptive metaphysics attempts to uncover. Note, however, that uncovering it is not simply a matter of taking our talk and thought at face value. As Strawson recognizes,

> The structure [which the metaphysician] seeks does not readily display itself on the surface of language, but lies submerged. He must abandon his only sure guide when the guide cannot take him as far as he wishes to go. (Strawson 1959, pp. 9f.)

It seems, then, that the results of doing descriptive metaphysics can surprise us, and can be counter-intuitive to unreflective common sense. The relevant contrast here is that between a description of how we appear to think (i.e., the conceptual structure that we appear to work with), on the one hand, and how we really think (i.e., what conceptual structure we really work with), on the other. Aristotle and Kant are cited as descriptive metaphysicians.

Revisionary metaphysics, in contrast, aims to change or alter our actual conceptual scheme by recommending another, on the grounds that it is more adequate for some purpose other than that which serves ordinary thought and talk about the world, such as the purposes of science. Strawson describes its relation to descriptive metaphysics thus:

> The productions of revisionary metaphysics remain permanently interesting, and not only as key episodes in the history of thought. Because of their articulation, and the intensity of their partial vision, the best of them are both intrinsically admirable and of enduring philosophical utility. But

this last merit can be ascribed to them only because there is another kind of metaphysics, which needs no justification at all beyond that of inquiry in general. Revisionary metaphysics is at the service of descriptive metaphysics. (Strawson 1959, p. 9)

This passage suggests that Strawson views revisionary metaphysics as viable, but only alongside and against the background of descriptive metaphysics. However, Haack questions whether this is Strawson's considered view.

She argues that there is a deep ambiguity in Strawson's work concerning the relation of revisionary to descriptive metaphysics. Although Strawson's 'official' view about the possibility and value of revisionary metaphysics vis-à-vis descriptive metaphysics is modest and conciliatory, there is a persistent strand of thinking in individuals that challenges its credentials to contribute anything of value to metaphysics. This emerges in his discussions of 'our' conceptual scheme, and, within that scheme, of the priority of material bodies and persons over other categories of particulars.

Strawson's claim that 'descriptive metaphysics needs no justification at all', and that 'there are categories and concepts which . . . change not at all' suggests that revisionary metaphysics is not just an alternative to descriptive metaphysics, but one that could never seriously compete with it. His claim that 'persons and material bodies are what primarily exists' suggests that he thinks not only that the concepts of person and material body are fundamental to our thought about the world, but that persons and material bodies themselves are ontologically basic. His claim that the concept of a person is primitive confuses concept with object:

> the meaning of saying that this concept is primitive is that it is not to be analysed in a certain way or ways. We are not, for example, to think of it as a secondary kind of entity in relation to two primary kinds, viz. a particular consciousness and a particular human body. (Strawson 1959, pp. 104–5):

The first occurrence of 'it' in the above quotation refers to the concept, *person*, but the second occurrence plainly refers to persons themselves.

It is hard to see how purely descriptive claims about our conceptual scheme could directly support claims about what kinds of things exist in the world beyond our concepts. But Strawson plainly thinks that they do. This makes better sense if he is understood, not as making onto-logically conservative claims on behalf of descriptive metaphysics, but, rather, as making quite radical ones. Understood conservatively, he is claiming that, for those of us humans who happen to be working with this particular conceptual scheme, the world itself could not but be constituted by particulars, and, of those, persons and material bodies. This leaves it an open possibility that there might be humans who experience and think the world differently, which undermines the move from claims about our conceptual scheme to claims about what kinds of things exist (period). However, understood radically, Strawson is claiming, not just that certain concepts are indispensable to our conceptual scheme, but also that 'we' includes all possible human beings. His claims that 'our' conceptual scheme is without a history and is 'the indispensable core of the conceptual equipment of the most sophisticated human beings' suggest this more radical view that there simply could not be human beings who experienced and thought the world in a fundamentally different way. And that suggests that ours is not just one conceptual scheme amongst many other possible ones (for human beings), but is the only possible one. If so, then the qualification 'for those of us' is otiose, and the move from claims about fundamental concepts to claims about ontologically basic kinds is natural, if contentious. It is contentious because, even if ours is the only possible conceptual framework, it does not follow that non-conceptual 'reality' answers to it.

Haack argues that there is real rivalry between descriptive and revisionary metaphysics if Strawson is construed in the radical way, since the radical interpretation makes it impossible to do revisionary metaphysics. But she wonders whether, on this understanding of 'descriptive' metaphysics, the distinction between it and revisionary metaphysics can ultimately be made out. This is where the difficult questions arise.

Real Metaphysics

Haack ends both of her discussions by posing some questions and suggesting directions in which answers might be found, which are promising and important. First, she suggests that, although Carnap's attempt to distinguish internal and external theoretical questions fails, there is something of value to be salvaged from it. What remains is a distinction between 'straightforward' ontological questions and 'hard' ones. It is possible, Haack suggests, that the hard questions are hard, not because they are about whether items of a kind really exist, but because they are about what it is to be an item of that kind. Of course, sometimes a question of the form 'Are there really "so-and-so's"?' is intended to challenge the assumption that so-and-so's exist at all. But more often than not, it is intended to challenge the assumption that 'so-and-so's' are things of the kind that we thought they were. As she puts it:

> But isn't it, one might ask, simply perverse, not to say downright incon-
> sistent, to admit that two is a number, but to deny that there are numbers?
> . . . the point is that there remains room for dispute about what, exactly,
> numbers are. And those who hold the apparently perverse position of
> admitting that x is a φ but denying that there are really any φs often turn
> out to do so because they hold an unusual view about what φs really are;
> they think that numbers are really logical constructions out of proposi-
> tional functions, for instance, or that physical objects are logical con-
> structions out of sense-data. (Haack 1976, p. 471)[13]

Haack's attitude towards the internal/external questions distinction is
echoed in her discussion of the distinction between descriptive and revisionary metaphysics. Having identified the source of Strawson's radical
view about the nature of descriptive metaphysics as involving commitment to a kind of 'conceptual invariance' thesis with regard to all languages, she points out that whether such a thesis is true is not an easy
matter to determine, since it raises many difficult questions that need
answering. Here are only a few of them:

> What is a concept? How are concepts individuated? What is a conceptual
> scheme? How are conceptual schemes individuated? What is the relation
> between a language and a conceptual scheme? How are languages indi-
> viduated? Who are the 'we' of 'our conceptual scheme'? Is descriptive
> metaphysics possible? Is revisionary metaphysics possible? What could it
> mean to say that one conceptual scheme is 'better' than another? (Haack
> 1979, p. 27)

Haack ends by suggesting how one might begin to answer at least some
of these questions. First, she suggests that Strawson's commitment is to
a 'global conceptual invariance' thesis, and that he takes the connection
between a conceptual scheme and language to be strong rather than
weak: if a language has certain features, then speakers of it must employ
a certain conceptual scheme.[14] She argues that there is some reason to
think that this connection is weaker than Strawson envisages. Second,
she points out that the global conceptual invariance thesis makes it
impossible to do revisionary metaphysics since, if there is no alternative
to 'our' conceptual scheme, it is not possible to produce a more adequate
one, whatever the purposes for which it may be required. Third, she
points out that the individuation of conceptual schemes will require some
criterion for the individuation of concepts, since we will need to know
when it is right to say that a concept has changed, and when it is right
to say that it has been replaced by a new one. She favours a view about
concepts, which treats them as dynamic, rather than static. The dynamic

view can be reconciled with Strawson's 'revisionary' metaphysics, construed in a modest way as offering something viable that can be of use to descriptive metaphysics. The static view, however, encourages the dismissal of revisionary metaphysics as suffering from conceptual confusion. She ends by quoting Geach as paradigmatic of the static view, to which she offers the following response:

> 'at the same time' belongs not to a special science but to logic. Our practical grasp of his logic is not to be called into question on account of recondite physics . . . A physicist who casts doubt upon it is sawing off the branch he sits upon. (Geach 1965, p. 312)
>
> I will reveal my sympathies by urging that we are not on a branch, as in Geach's metaphor, rather, on a raft, as in Neurath's. And if you object that this means we are all at sea, I reply that this is no worse, at any rate, than being up in the air. (Haack 1979, p. 30)

Haack's remarks not only suggest a certain view about the nature and function of metaphysics, but also contain the foundations of a solid, positive account. According to this account, there are genuine, real metaphysical questions, the so-called hard ones, even if there is no useful internal/external question distinction. Some general, category questions about ontology make sense, as do their answers. These questions are best seen as arising 'within' a linguistic framework. Why do they make sense? They do because, although they arise after the adoption of a linguistic framework, they question whether what in the world answers to at least some of the category concepts embedded in it is what we thought answered to them. These are not just questions about what concepts and conceptual structures are embedded in the linguistic framework adopted. They are questions about what the world is like, given those concepts. Of course raising such questions will require using these concepts. But the questions that are raised are not naturally viewed as 'about' those concepts. Nor, principally, are they best viewed as questions about whether anything at all answers to those concepts (although some part of metaphysical thinking will involve questions like these, for certain falsehoods in the framework). They concern the natures of things of certain kinds. According to this view, then, metaphysics is not fundamentally about whether items of this or that kind exist; it is about what it is for items of this or that kind to have a nature, and what that nature might be.

Because this is what 'real' metaphysics is concerned with, it cannot be merely descriptive, for it is concerned not only with whether sentences in a linguistic framework are true, but also with what in the world makes them true when they are. Because its aim is to arrive at our best theory of the world, it will inevitably involve conceptual change. As Haack puts it:

> The [view], with which I sympathize, sees our concepts as the result of a long and continuing evolution, and as containing residues of earlier scientific and metaphysical theories. (Haack 1979, p. 30)

Does this mean that descriptive metaphysics is fine as far as it goes, but revisionary metaphysics is also viable and important? Or does it mean that there really is no distinction between descriptive and revisionary metaphysics, since nothing that we would wish to call 'real metaphysics' – the kind of metaphysics that deals with the 'hard' questions – answers to 'descriptive metaphysics'? Haack would probably say the latter. This is not just because she views concepts as dynamic, whereas Strawson's descriptive metaphysics treats them as static. It is also because, at any stage in the evolution of 'our' concepts, the 'hard' questions will need to both mention and use these concepts in asking what in the world answers to them. We shall need to both mention and use the concept *number*, such as it is, in order to raise and answer the question 'Are there really numbers?' because doing metaphysics partly involves doing semantics. Properly understood, revisionary metaphysics actually incorporates a 'descriptive' element. But, in attempting to arrive at a 'best' theory of the world, it will be concerned to refine and shape these concepts so as to better express that theory. Evolution of concepts in metaphysics is motivated by the need to find better concepts to better express our best theory of the world. So a good descriptive metaphysics is also at the same time a good revisionary one. And there are constraints on what counts as a good revisionary metaphysics.

Let us develop these remarks further. On the present view metaphysics aims to arrive at our best theory of the world – of the fundamental kinds that there are, and what their fundamental natures are – in an a priori, rather than an a posteriori way. Its starting point is just where both Aristotle and Kant thought it was: with our ordinary common-sense and scientific thought about the world. Beginning with this, it attempts to refine and defend the view of the world embodied in such thought, especially common-sense thought, since such thought is the basis for science. Why is refinement necessary? Because our common-sense views about the world generate puzzles, and apparent inconsistencies, which need resolving. Here is just one: material substances – things like apples, human beings, and tables – can change, and can remain the very same things through change. But change involves something's being different from one time to another. So, it seems that material things can be both the same and not the same throughout change. If metaphysics is to defend this – common-sense! – view of material things, it needs somehow to refine that view.

Thus, metaphysics is bound to be, not merely descriptive of our actual thought, but revisionary in at least two ways. First, in attempting to arrive at our best theory of the world, metaphysicians will inevitably 'attempt to produce a better structure' than that contained in our actual thought about the world. This is because the aim in producing our best theory is first and foremost to produce a – or the – true theory. Strawson, who describes the proper aim of metaphysics as descriptive, cites Descartes, Leibniz, and Berkeley, as revisionary metaphysicians. To the extent that they were, their aim in producing a better structure was to produce a better theory of the world, of what kinds of things there are and what their natures are. They thought their theories were better because they better describe the world as it really is.

Since all knowledge is shaped or informed by the human conceptual apparatus, metaphysical knowledge is too. This means that metaphysics is the study of what there is, where this study (like any other study) is shaped and informed by the human conceptual apparatus. Metaphysical knowledge, like all knowledge, is constrained by conditions, some of which concern the psychology of the knower. This does not mean that metaphysical truths do not describe facts in the non-mental world, or that the truths about them are somehow only true 'relative' to our perceptual and conceptual apparatus, any more than that the truths of science are only true relative to our perceptual and conceptual apparatus merely because scientific knowledge is constrained by the psychology of those that discover it. Whether knowledge of facts in the non-mental world is possible depends partly on whether human beings have concepts of the appropriate kinds, and partly on what, if anything, in this world answers to those concepts.

So metaphysics is revisionary in at least this way. But it is revisionary in another way as well. It does not purport to study what there is according to the conceptual framework or frameworks by which we think about the world. It purports to study what, fundamentally, there really is.[15] It is true that, in order to do so, it must make use of concepts and/or categories by which we think about the world. But this does not show that metaphysics is not the study of what, fundamentally, there really is, but is rather the study of what there is according to our conceptual and perceptual framework. At most it shows that how the formulation of questions about what there is, is dependent on what concepts are available to us.

Given this conception of real metaphysics, one begins doing metaphysics by identifying conceptual frameworks. Theories, whatever else they may be, are typically expressed by sets of sentences and are commonly identified in this way.[16] We speakers of English often use sentences of English to refer to objects or other things or phenomena in the world and say things about them. One of the paradigmatic ways in which certain words, namely, singular terms, are used in English and other natural languages is to refer to or to pick out single, individual objects or other things in the world, in order to say things, truly or falsely, about them. However, any speaker of a language that expresses a theory will make use of terms to which no particular ontological significance is attached. So not all words or expressions are taken to refer, or do refer, to anything at all. Matters are more complicated still, since there are expressions in English that have the grammatical, but not the semantical form of a referring expression or singular term, since they do not function to refer to or pick out a single object. Think, for example of the expression 'the sake' in 'She did it for the sake of her country'. The form of this expression is grammatically that of a singular term, like 'the cat'. But no one seriously thinks that the expression 'the sake' refers to an individual thing, a sake, despite its grammatical similarity to other singular terms that are taken to refer to things such as cats. This distinction is what Strawson has in mind when he says that the structure of our conceptual framework 'does not readily display itself on the surface of language, but lies submerged' (Strawson 1950, p. 9; see also van Inwagen 1998a, 1998b; Benardete 1989; and Loux 2002.) Given this, how can we work out what the ontological commitments of a theory actually are?

It has been argued that, in order to determine the ontological commitments of a theory, one needs a criterion of ontological commitment (Quine 1960, 1964a, 1964b; Lombard 1986; Aune 1986). This is a principle for determining just what objects or entities a theory says there are (or what entities must exist in order for a theory to be true). It tells us what features a theory must have in order to be committed to the existence of items of any sort, and it also tells us that the presence of these features is enough, or sufficient, for such commitment. Suppose, for example, that the rather crude picture of reference hinted at above, that all words refer, were one that was presumed by speakers of the linguistic framework of English. Then a criterion of ontological commitment, in attempting to make explicit the ontological commitments of speakers of that framework, would need to be sensitive to that presumption. It might do this by formulating the criterion in something like the following way: a theory T is committed to just those items that are required to be objects of reference of its words. Clearly, given the example above of expressions like 'the sake', the theory of reference presumed here is too crude to be plausible, but for present purposes that is not what matters. What matters is that the criterion of ontological commitment be capable of expressing the ontological commitments embodied in the theory expressed by speakers of English: it must make explicit what may be only implicit background assumptions made by speakers of that linguistic framework. And commitment is both different from, and prior to, the issue of truth. One cannot adjudicate between theories with respect to their truth if one cannot even tell what their commitments are, and so what they take to be true.

A criterion of ontological commitment is capable of serving two purposes. First, it can enable users of it to adjudicate between competing claims, given any particular linguistic framework as to what speakers of that framework are ontologically committed to. Given that speakers of any language will make use of terms to which they attach no particular ontological significance, this purpose would be served even if there were only one conceptual framework, common to all languages. But, second, supposing that there is more than one such framework, a criterion of ontological commitment can enable users of it to discern, amongst them, what their differing ontological commitments are. This latter is a necessary preliminary to choosing between competing theories of the world.

To see this is to see that a criterion of ontological commitment is a meta-theoretical principle; a principle that can be employed by metaphysicians when attempting to determine what there really is by attempting to specify the best theory of what there is. The starting point for metaphysics is our conceptual system embodied in natural language and thought. Applying a criterion of ontological commitment to it, we can see what prima facie ontological commitments are implicit in this system. For example, English contains the noun-phrase, 'goodness sake', and because of the presumption that the objects that a theory says there are are those that are referred to by the noun-phrases employed by it, English speakers appear to be committed to the existence of sakes. Since, however, these are only prima facie commitments, we can exercise a certain amount of freedom in attempting to specify what the real ontological commitments of that system are. Suppose again that the conceptual system embodied in English were to presume the crude theory of reference suggested above. Then a criterion of ontological commitment based on such a theory would assign ontological status to expressions such as 'the sake' and 'Pegasus'. One way of rectifying this unwanted consequence would be to distinguish real from merely apparent singular terms (that is, terms that function grammatically, but not semantically, like singular terms), thus refining the crude theory of reference, and then to re-apply our criterion of ontological commitment to the real singular terms. Tampering with the conceptual system in natural language and thought is guided throughout by the same criterion of ontological commitment (we have not here rejected the original, reference-based criterion in favour of another), and at each stage we can evaluate the implicit commitments of the theory we have. The goal of tampering with the original theory is to arrive at a theory of the world that we can take to be a canonical statement, an ontologically perspicuous statement of the theory. Then, when we apply our criterion, what we get are our serious ontological commitments: what we think really exists.

In other words, if we start with a crude theory of reference, which says that a true sentence entails the existence of entities that its contained singular terms appear to refer to, we end up with the view that there are sakes, because it is true that Jones died for the sake of his country. So a refinement of the crude theory is necessary. According to this, a true sentence entails the existence of the entities that are referred to by all the singular terms that are really in it, where the 'really' is cashed out by a serious theory. This theory is only partly semantic. We don't banish sakes merely because we can produce a semantic theory of English that does not have expressions that name them, or because we can replace expressions that contain the noun 'sake' with expressions that don't. We banish them because our metaphysical scruples will not tolerate them, for reasons developed more fully below.

If there is only one theory to serve as the object of our metaphysical reasonings, then this process of moving from one description to another, canonical one will yield our best theory of what we think really exists. But if there is more than one such theory, then even after this process is complete, it may not be that only one theory will emerge as 'the best' theory of the world. At this stage, metaphysics may be incapable of fixing on a unique theory of what we think there really is. Further, it is possible for different people to arrive at very different final theories via the process. Consider, for example, the different ways that Meinong and Russell deal with singular terms which apparently lack reference: whereas Russell attempts to show that they are not really singular terms at all, Meinong takes them to be genuinely referential, and expands his ontology accordingly.[17] Both, however, use a reference-based criterion of ontological commitment, which places the weight of ontological commitment on the singular terms, specifically, the names, in sentences of the language fragment. As this example indicates, the nature of the tampering is important, so there should be some constraints on what counts as acceptable, even if this issue is poorly understood and little discussed.

One such constraint, and a crucial one at that, is common sense. Metaphysical thinking, being meta-theoretical, does not take place in a vacuum: it takes place against the background of ongoing theoretical practices, such as science. Just as those practices must be reconciled with our commonsensical beliefs about the world, so too must metaphysics. When we theorize about the nature of reality, we do so against the background of beliefs such as the belief that there is a mind-independent reality, a world with various kinds of objects and phenomena in it, such as trees, persons, lions, and earthquakes, which relate to one another causally and in other ways. One way of constraining the process by which a metaphysical theory is arrived at is to test it against the dictates of common sense. Commonsensical beliefs are the springboard of much of our theorizing; they are what motivate it, and they are, in the end, what such theorizing attempts to explain. But they aren't sacrosanct: like most other beliefs, they may be false. The dictates of common sense may also be defeasible, or capable of being overridden, for other reasons. One is that it might not be possible to vindicate all of our commonsensical beliefs, since there may be inconsistencies between them. This is why metaphysics, if a defence of common sense, is also a refinement of it.

Nevertheless, common sense provides one, albeit defeasible, constraint on the kind and extent of tampering that is acceptable. Another emerges from doing ontology itself. Suppose, for example, that we have before us two possible paraphrases of the English sentence, 'Sally was born at midnight'. One says that the sentence speaks of two entities, Sally and her birth, and both entities must exist in order for the sentence to be true. The other says that the sentence speaks of only one entity, Sally, and that that entity is the only one that must exist in order for the sentence to be true. Which one is right?

Doing semantics will not by itself yield an answer to this question. Nor will appealing to common sense alone. We know that some of our talk is talk of events: we speak of earthquakes and avalanches, and we even use singular terms that apparently refer to events (e.g., 'The Big Bang'). We also know that much of our talk is talk of substances, typically effected by means of singular terms. We could generate an argument from semantical considerations to favour one over the other of these paraphrases, the event-positing one, and, if this consideration wins, then there are events, since 'Sally was born at midnight' entails 'there are events'. But this alone would not be decisive in favour of that paraphrase. Why? Because one wants to know whether, in addition to things that undergo change, such as substances, there really are changes. In order to know that, we really need to know what kinds of things events might be; what they are like, and how they might relate to such items as substances: in what ways they might be like, and in what crucial respects different. We need, in other words, a metaphysical theory of events. And, although the paraphrase requires us to suppose that there are such things, it cannot by itself make it true that there are such things. If there are, then the paraphrase is correct. If not, then although it may be well motivated semantically, the semantics is wrong.

So, when we engage in metaphysical thinking, we do not just do semantics for sentences of natural language, for two reasons. The first is that, in arriving at a best theory of the world, we may need to tamper with those natural language sentences. In particular, we may take theories as they are naturally expressed and paraphrase away certain prima facie commitments. As I stated earlier, this introduces a serious degree of freedom between determining the apparent ontological commitments in natural language (where every sentences' semantic properties must be accounted for) and the final account that we take to be ontologically committing (where only some of these sentences will be of interest). The freedom extends beyond choosing one over another paraphrase of a natural language sentence such as 'Sally was born at midnight', where the question of what the real semantic structure of such a sentence is (one which speaks only of substances, or one which speaks of substances and events) arises. This might require doing more than semantics, but here we are still attempting to account for the real semantic structure of such a sentence. The freedom involved in doing metaphysics extends further because paraphrase is not limited to giving the real semantic structure of natural language sentences (which may not be apparent on the surface). One might paraphrase in such a way that no essential appeal to certain entities implicitly appealed to in the natural language 'correlate' is made, and this marks a real departure from semantics for natural language.[18]

This first reason leads directly to the second, which is that doing ontology is largely independent of doing semantics, even when we have applied a criterion of ontological commitment and have a canonical statement of the theory expressed by a given language. The criterion can discern what semantic values are the real ontological commitments of the criterion (say, the semantic values of names, viz. their referents), but not what their natures are, nor how they are related to one another. For example, a criterion of ontological commitment can perhaps tell us whether a best theory of the world will contain reference to numbers and reference to sets, or to material things and persons; but it cannot tell us whether numbers are (nothing but) sets, or whether persons are (nothing but) material things, and so it cannot tell us whether this best theory is ontologically committed to both numbers and sets or persons as well as material things. This second point in particular brings out clearly that arriving at an adequate criterion of ontological commitment is only part of what is involved in doing metaphysics. The rest – which is what doing 'real' metaphysics is – is trying to arrive at our best theory of what kinds of things there are, and what their natures are. And by 'best' is meant, 'true'.

We have attempted to develop an account of the nature and function of metaphysics that is both consistent with, and builds upon, foundations suggested by Susan Haack in her work. There is much that remains to be said, but we shall confine ourselves here to a final – suggestive – remark. Haack favours a dynamic view of concepts, according to which they evolve over time and contain remnants of earlier metaphysical and scientific theories. Her purpose in doing this, apparently, is to undermine the distinction between descriptive and revisionary metaphysics. However, it is doubtful that the distinction between a static and a dynamic view of concepts alone can do this. The reason is that it seems to be orthogonal to the distinction between descriptive and revisionary metaphysics. Strawson's distinction between how we apparently think and how we really think is compatible with a view of concepts according to which they are dynamic rather than static: on this view, descriptive metaphysics describes the actual concepts we employ to think about the world. That such concepts contain remainders of past theories (even restricting these to common-sense ones, as Strawson does) doesn't threaten the enterprise. What threatens the enterprise is the thought that describing how we really think, and (perhaps) what the history of the concepts we now use is not what 'real' metaphysics claims to be doing. What is missing in descriptive metaphysics, even if it describes our concepts as they evolve, is an account of why they evolve. In the case of certain, fundamental concepts, such evolution is motivated by the aim to come by our best theory of the world. Finding better concepts – or concepts which better 'fit' the world as it is – is part of that aim. So revisionary metaphysics – recommending conceptual change – is necessarily part of 'real' metaphysics.

Notes

1   The word 'metaphysics' is Greek in origin, whose two root terms, *meta* and *physika*, mean, respectively, 'after' and 'nature'. The term was created by the Greeks as a name for works written by Aristotle that subsequently became known as his Metaphysics. (Aristotle himself evidently did not use this term, but rather preferred the term 'first philosophy'.) The title records the fact that the books on first philosophy were written by Aristotle after he wrote the *Physics*, or the books on nature. Aristotle thought that the books on first philosophy concern things 'prior and better known in themselves' and should be studied after the books on nature, which concern

things 'prior and better known to us' (for this distinction see *Posterior Analytics* 71b32; *Prior Analytics* 68b35–7; *Physics* A.1, 184a6–20; *Metaphysics* Z.3, 1029b3–12; and *Topics* Z.4, 141b2–142a12). He also characterized first philosophy as the study of 'being qua being' (or the study of the being of things, this study being conducted from or under the aspect of being), in contrast with the study of 'being qua known' (or the study of the being of things, from or under some other aspect by which they are known to us). For more on this, see the discussion of Aristotle on pp. 8–11. The title 'metaphysics' has subsequently become associated with the idea that its subject matter is further away or remote from sense experience.

2 The logical rules are ones such as the law of non-contradiction, Leibniz's Law (or the combined Principles of the Indiscernibility of Identicals and the Identity of Indiscernibles), and rules of inference such as *modus ponens* and *modus tollens*, rules of transitivity, and so on. For more on some of these, see chapter 2.

3 For further discussion of these features, see Walsh (1967), van Inwagen (1993, 1998a, 1998b), and Loux (2002).

4 Indeterminacy in that there could be two or more such theories that are equally compatible with all possible evidence for their truth, and that there is therefore no 'fact of the matter' about which, if any, is the correct one. This characterization has its roots in the work of W. V. O. Quine, who advanced the thesis of the indeterminacy of translation. See Quine (1960 and 1970); and for discussion of the thesis, see Hookway (1988), McCulloch (1999), and Soames (1999).

5 There is a question as to what kind of necessity the propositions of metaphysics have, since they do not appear to have the kind of necessity that, say, conceptually true propositions are thought to have. Specifically, the propositions of metaphysics do not seem to be ones whose negations are contradictions, as are conceptually true propositions like 'A square is a four-sided figure' and 'Anything red is coloured'. Still, they are thought to be ones that must be true if they are true at all. Some believe that they must be true if the world is to be possible (this is possibly Aristotle's view); others (like Kant) believe that they must be true if the world is to be experienceable or thinkable.

6 If all knowledge, including metaphysical knowledge, is mediated by sensory organs and internal structures that shape and inform all of our experience, then, as Kant argued, we have no way of telling whether the world as it is in itself is the way it appears to us to be. But it doesn't follow from this alone, nor should it be taken as a consequence of this criticism of Aristotle, that the world might be utterly different from the way it appears, so that what we know is not what things are in themselves. For, just as we have no way of telling that the world as it is in itself is the way it appears to us to be, we have no way of telling that the world as it is in itself is not the way it appears to us to be. What things are in themselves may not be inaccessible to us, just inaccessible without the mediation by sensory organs and internal structures that shape our experience.

7　One way to understand Kant's view here is to see him as distinguishing between the structure of perception and thought, on the one hand, and the content of perception and thought, on the other. Experience provides us with the content of perception and thought, but not its structure. Nevertheless, all experience and thought is structured, so the structure of each is something that is applicable to it but not derived from it (it is a priori).

8　Examples of contemporary metaphysicians who endorse this general approach are Collingwood (1940), Strawson (1959), Körner (1974), and Putnam (1981 and 1987), although, as Loux (2002) points out, Strawson's work is broadly Aristotelian despite his neo-Kantian language. This will be a matter for discussion in the final section of this chapter (pp. 14–30). The approach taken in this book is broadly Aristotelian in just this way.

9　This falls short of the claim, which Kant did not endorse, that there can be no world of things in themselves. Many interpret Kant as maintaining that there is a world of things in themselves, as well as the world of things that we experience. The problem, as he saw it, was that we can have no knowledge of things in themselves. There are truths about God, causation, and so on, but we can have no access to them. This is because, in order to know a truth, one must be able to think, or understand it, and in the case of things in themselves, the conditions on understanding cannot be met; we cannot sense, and so cannot understand, facts about them.

10　To reject the conception of metaphysics as the study of being qua being is not thereby to reject the view that there is a mind-independent reality to be known and studied by the sciences and by metaphysics. For it is open to a Kantian to hold that although all knowledge is shaped or informed by the human conceptual apparatus, whether reality conforms to those concepts is not up to humans. What there is and what its nature is like cannot be established by the mere existence of certain fundamental concepts.

11　The Logical Positivist, verificationist program was initiated and made popular by a group of philosophers and scientists, among them A. J. Ayer, Moritz Schlick, Rudolph Carnap, Otto Neurath, and Frederick Waissmann, in the 1920s and 1930s, and originated in discussions of a group known as the Vienna Circle. The roots of the philosophical position taken by its members stem from the doctrines of the seventeenth-century empiricists, notably those of Hume. Maintaining the Humean position that all knowledge is ultimately derived from 'impression' and 'introspection', the Logical Positivists embarked on what they considered to be a more thoroughgoing empiricism, according to which propositions that are neither empirically *verifiable* (in being capable of establishment as true) nor *analytic* (in being logical or conceptual truths) were deemed literally meaningless. In other words, the program of the Logical Positivists was to adopt an empiricist principle of significance and adapt it by applying it, not, as Hume did, to *ideas*, but directly to propositions or statements, as a test of meaningfulness. Any proposition or statement that failed the test for empirical significance and yet was also non-analytic was to be judged meaningless on the grounds that it purported to provide information about a reality that one could never in principle experience.

Implicit in the Logical Positivist attack on metaphysics is the view that all meaningful empirical statements or propositions are a posteriori, and that all meaningful a priori statements or propositions are analytic, i.e., they are 'true by virtue of meaning alone, and independently of fact', or are purely *conceptual* truths. In this they fully endorsed the Humean position that all propositions fall into two categories, those expressing 'relations of ideas' and those expressing 'matters of fact'. Since metaphysical propositions fail to fall squarely into either of these two categories, and these two categories exhaust the list of meaningful propositions, metaphysical propositions are literally meaningless.

12 It is doubtful, however, that Carnap would consider the appeal to a metalanguage as a way of making sense of an external theoretical question, since he would view any question couched in such a language to be one raised after the adoption of an interpreted language fragment.

13 It is possible that Carnap would claim that his view is not that we can admit that two is a number but deny that there are numbers. Rather, the view is that we can admit that two is a number whilst remaining agnostic about whether there are numbers, since the latter is a framework question.

14 The global thesis is that the same conceptual scheme is associated with all languages.

15 For a conception of metaphysics that is similar to this, see Lowe (1998).

16 Note that this is not to say that the identity and individuation conditions of theories can be given in this way: the same theory can be expressed by different sets of sentences.

17 See Russell (1905), Russell and Whitehead (1910), and Meinong (1904).

18 Consider, for example, Field (1980), who 'reinterprets' physics so that it makes no essential appeal to mathematical entities. In doing so, he probably doesn't see himself as doing the semantics of the statements of physical theory.

Suggestions for Further Reading

Historical

Ayer, A. J. (1990): *Language, Truth, and Logic*. London: Penguin. First published by Victor Gollancz (1936).

Barnes, J. (ed.) (1984): *The Complete Works of Aristotle*. Princeton, NJ: Princeton University Press.

Beck, L. W. (transl.) (1950): *Prolegomena to Any Future Metaphysics*. Indianapolis: Bobbs-Merrill.

Carnap, R. (1950): 'Empiricism, Semantics, and Ontology'. In *Revue Internationale de Philosophie* 4, 20–40. Revised and reprinted in Carnap, R. *Meaning and Necessity*. 2nd edn. Chicago: University of Chicago Press, 1956.

Guyer, P. (ed.) (1992): *The Cambridge Companion to Kant*. Cambridge: Cambridge University Press.

Guyer, P. and Wood, A. (transl. and eds) (1998): *The Cambridge Edition of the Works of Immanuel Kant: The Critique of Pure Reason*. Cambridge: Cambridge University Press.

Irwin, T. (1988): *Aristotle's First Principles*. Oxford: Oxford University Press.

McKeon, R. (ed.) (1941): *The Basic Works of Aristotle*. New York: Random House.

Meinong, A. (1904): 'The Theory of Objects'. In Chisholm, R. (ed.), 1960, pp. 76–117.

Russell, B. (1905): 'On Denoting'. In *Mind*, 479–93. Reprinted in Marsh, R. (ed.), 1956, pp. 39–56.

General

Aune, B. (1986): *Metaphysics: The Elements*. Oxford: Blackwell, chapters 1 and 2.

Benardete, J. (1989): *Metaphysics: The Logical Approach*. Oxford: Oxford University Press, Introduction and chapter 1.

Cohen, S. M. (2003): 'Aristotle's Metaphysics'. In Zalta, E. (ed.), *The Stanford Encyclopedia of Philosophy (*Winter 2003 edn*)*. URL = <http://plato.stanford.edu/archives/win2003/entries/aristotle-metaphysics/>.

Edwards, P. (ed.) 1967: *Encyclopedia of Philosophy*. New York: Macmillan Publishing Company.

Haack, S. (1976): 'Some Preliminaries to Ontology'. In *Journal of Philosophical Logic* 5, 457–74.

Haack, S. (1979): 'Descriptive and Revisionary Metaphysics'. In *Philosophical Studies* 35, 361–71. Reprinted in Laurence and Macdonald (eds) (1998), pp. 22–31.

Körner, S. (1974): *Categorial Frameworks*. Oxford: Blackwell.

Laurence, S. and Macdonald, C. (eds) (1998): *Readings in the Foundations of Contemporary Metaphysics*. Oxford: Blackwell, essays in Part One.

Lombard, L. B. (1986): *Events: A Metaphysical Study*. London: Routledge & Kegan Paul, chapters 1 and 2.

Lowe, E. J. (1998): *The Possibility of Metaphysics*. Oxford: Oxford University Press, chapter 1.

Loux, M. (2002): *Metaphysics: A Contemporary Introduction*. 2nd edn. London: Routledge, Introduction.

Quine, W. V. O. (1964a): 'On What There Is'. In Quine 1964f, pp. 1–19.

Quine, W. V. O. (1964b): 'Logic and the Reification of Universals'. In Quine 1964f, pp. 102–29.

Quine, W. V. O. (1964f): *From a Logical Point of View*. 2nd edn. Cambridge, Mass.: Harvard University Press.

Strawson, P. F. (1959): *Individuals: An Essay in Descriptive Metaphysics*. London: Methuen.

van Inwagen, P. (1998a): 'The Nature of Metaphysics'. In Laurence and Macdonald (eds) 1998, pp. 12–21.

van Inwagen, P. (1998b): 'Introduction: What is Metaphysics?'. In van Inwagen and Zimmerman (eds) 1998, pp. 1–13.

van Inwagen, P. (1993): *Metaphysics*. Oxford: Oxford University Press. Introduction.

van Inwagen, P. and Zimmerman, D. (eds) (1998): *Metaphysics: The Big Questions*. Oxford: Blackwell.

Walsh, W. H. (1967): 'Metaphysics, Nature of'. In Edwards (ed.) 1967, pp. 300–7.

2

Some Tools
of Metaphysics

In the previous chapter, we specified a conception of metaphysics as the study of the fundamental kinds of objects or entities that there are. We saw that doing metaphysics involves working out not just the apparent ontological commitments of our ordinary talk and thought, but also the real commitments embodied in such talk and thought – what we really think there is. All of this is by way of furthering the aim of arriving at our best theory of the world; of what, fundamentally, there really is.

There are tools that metaphysicians can use to help carry out this enterprise. This chapter is about some of the most important of these tools: criteria of ontological commitment, and principles and criteria of identity. It describes them, and attempts to explain what work they can do and why they are important to metaphysical theorizing. A good deal of what is contained in this chapter may be difficult for those without a fair amount of philosophical training to grasp. However, because the material in it and in the previous chapter informs the methodology and the discussions in later chapters, it is important to attempt an initial reading. Readers may wish to return to this chapter, or sections of it, as the need arises while reading later chapters, and/or after finishing the book.

Criteria of Ontological Commitment: Two Examples

We have noted that when metaphysicians theorize about the nature of reality, they do so against the background of beliefs such as the belief that there is a mind-independent reality, a world with various kinds of objects or entities and phenomena in it. These beliefs form part of a common-sense theory of the world that is embodied in ordinary thought and talk. But not all of such thought and talk is taken to be ontologically committing. So, when we, as metaphysicians, examine our ordinary everyday thought and talk, we do so, in part, in order to determine what are the serious ontological commitments embodied in it. A criterion of ontological commitment is a tool that can help us to work out what our serious ontological commitments are.

A criterion of ontological commitment is a principle for determining what objects must exist in order for a theory to be true. Below we shall consider two candidates for such a principle. The first is found in the work of P. F. Strawson and is based on the grammatical subject-predicate distinction. The second is found in the work of W. V. O. Quine and is based on the predicate calculus, the language of first-order quantification theory (which we shall describe in more detail below). These provide a good basis for discussion because both are refinements of the natural but very crude reference-based criterion suggested at the end of chapter 1. Despite this, we shall see that Quine's criterion is preferable to Strawson's because it enables us to distinguish more easily the apparent semantic structure of our talk from its real semantic structure, thereby enabling us to distinguish more easily our apparent ontological comments from our real commitments.

Strawson's Criterion

If, as seems natural, we assume that theories are expressed in languages, then one way to begin the search for an adequate criterion of ontological commitment – one that specifies the real commitments of such theories – would be to identify certain features of the languages in which those theories are expressed as ones that seem to be ontologically committing. We have already seen one way in which this process can lead to the formulation of a criterion. This identifies all of the apparent singular terms in English – including such terms as 'the sake' and 'Pegasus' – and then takes them all to be ontologically committing. The result is unacceptable because the theory of reference on which it is based is too crude to capture the ontological commitments implicit in English. However, a more sophisticated version of this kind of criterion, based on a refinement of that theory of reference, might well be adequate.

This thought has fuelled many proposals for criteria of ontological commitment. Specifically, it has informed the work of P. F. Strawson (1959, 1974a) and W. V. O. Quine (1960, 1964a, 1964b); and it has been used by many others as a starting point in discussions of ontological commitment (cf. Benardete 1989; Campbell 1976; Mackie 1993; Russell 1905; Simons 1997; van Inwagen 1998a, b, 2003). These thinkers generally accept that in natural languages (such as English) in which the grammatical subject-predicate distinction exists, subject terms, and specifically singular terms such as proper names, are paradigmatically the linguistic means by which objects or entities of many kinds are introduced into discourse.[1] Thus, they are the paradigmatic means by which the ontological commitments of the theories expressed in such languages are made.

Subject terms in natural languages are considered to be ontologically committing because they typically function semantically to pick out or refer to individual objects or entities (or classes of them). However, if they are to serve as a basis for a satisfactory criterion of ontological commitment, they need to be individuated, or distinguished, grammatically and semantically, from other types of terms or expressions in a language. How might this be done for a language such as English?

Strawson shows us one way. It is his view that the theory embodied in English is to be discovered from certain structural features of language, and, in particular, from the grammatical subject-predicate distinction. This distinction is assumed to exist in all natural languages, and serves as a guide not only to the ontological commitments of a theory but also to the levels of such commitment. So, for example, he argues that concrete particulars such as material bodies are not only the very paradigms of items introduced by subject terms, but they also form the most fundamental ontological category of objects.

Before proceeding, we need to mark some distinctions. An object or entity is a particular if it is wholly and completely in only one place at a given time. Thus, for example, an individual apple is a particular. This contrasts with a universal, such as, perhaps, the property, red, which can be wholly and completely in many places at a given time. This pair of contrasts differs from another, which will be the focus of later chapters of this book, namely, the pair, concrete/abstract. An object or entity is concrete if and only if its presence in a given place at a given time prohibits any other object or entity of the same kind's being in that place at that time. Thus, for example, an individual apple is a concrete thing: no two apples can be in exactly the same place at the same time. This contrasts with an object's or entity's being abstract, that is, its being such that many of them can be in the same place at the same time. An event such as an object's continuously changing shape might occur at exactly the same time and in the same place as another event, such as that object's continuously changing colour.

Now, the Strawsonian claim is that particulars have ontological priority over other items such as universals because they play the fundamental role of being objects of reference for subject terms.[2] Moreover, all other objects admissible into the ontology associated with English are dependent, for their admission, on the admission of particulars. In order for particulars to be admitted into this ontology, given the sort of criterion that Strawson is using, it is necessary both that the language have subject terms and that particulars be identifiable by means of them.

This idea of 'identifying' is characterized in terms of three conditions.

1 First, a speaker needs to make identifying reference to a particular, and she does this if she uses a subject term (e.g., a name), whose standard function is to enable the hearer to identify that particular.

2 Second, a hearer needs to identify the particular to which the speaker makes identifying reference; and she does this if either she can sensibly discriminate it (via demonstrative identification) or she knows an individuating fact about the particular that relates it, either directly or indirectly, to some other particular which she can demonstratively identify.

3 Third, the speaker must succeed in identifying a particular; and she does this if she makes an identifying reference to it that enables the hearer to identify it.

As these conditions make clear, Strawson's criterion of ontological commitment is only partly determined by the grammatical subject-predicate distinction. One needs subject terms in order to identify items; but the mere presence of subject terms in a language is not sufficient for the theory embodied in that language to be ontologically committed. Such terms must be used by speakers to identify items, notably particulars, and identifiability requires the presence of at least two parties, a speaker and a hearer, and the successful cooperation of the two. It is this last condition that makes Strawson's particulars public rather than private objects.

On this refinement of the referential criterion discussed in chapter 1, not every subject term has ontological significance just by virtue of being a subject term. Still, subject terms need to be distinguishable from others if they are to be the bearers of ontological commitment. So, how are subject terms distinguished from others in a language?

Strawson grounds the semantical subject-predicate distinction in certain purely grammatical asymmetries that exist in English between subject terms and predicates. Specifically, he notes that, whereas subject terms can only take subject position in English sentences, predicates can take both subject and predicate position; and that predicate terms in English are 'restricted by' subject terms, whereas subject terms are not restricted by other subject terms (Strawson 1976, pp. 4–5). By this he means that, in all forms of sentences that involve the subject-predicate combination, predicates are restricted by a fixed number of subject terms, e.g., either the form has just one place for a subject term (as in monadic, or one-place predicates such as 'is red'), or just two places for two subject terms (as in two-place predicates such as 'is larger than'), and so on. Subject terms, however, are not restricted by other subject terms in this way: the same subject terms may occur together with any number of others in different subject-predicate forms of sentence (e.g., 'Sarah and John are human', 'Sarah, John, and Susan are human').

Strawson argues that particulars are more fundamental ontologically than objects of any other kind, such as properties, because it would be impossible for us to identify objects of other categories unless we could identify particulars, but not vice versa.[3] Since the identification of particulars cannot take place without subject terms, and, in particular, without demonstrative terms, the grammatical subject-predicate distinction is a necessary condition on the admission of objects into one's ontology.

But this requirement on ontological commitment seems far too strong, even as applied to known natural languages. For instance, it has been argued that the grammatical considerations to which Strawson appeals cannot be applied to Chinese (Mei 1961). Specifically, critics have pointed out that, in Chinese, verbs are not inflected for number, person, and tense (unlike English, where verbs are so inflected, as in '(she) speaks', '(they) speak' '(they) spoke', etc.), and thus, that its subject terms are not restricted by predicate terms. Critics have also pointed out that, in Chinese, subject terms can occur both in subject position and in predicate position, and this has ramifications for the view that subject terms can only appear in subject position whereas predicate terms can occur in both subject and predicate position.

Other critics have pointed out that these grammatical distinctions cannot be applied to certain American Indian languages such as the Hopi and Nookta either (Burtt 1963). Indeed, according to Whorf (1956), whose work is cited in support of the claim, these American Indian languages work with no grammatical subject-predicate distinction *at all*. In the light of this evidence, it is difficult to see how the grammatical subject-predicate distinction could be even a necessary condition on ontological commitment. If it were, and if the claims regarding natural languages such as Chinese, Hopi, and Nookta, are correct, we would be forced to conclude that speakers of these languages are not ontologically committed to particulars. But this is wildly implausible.

Nor is the problem here just that Strawson seems to have placed a constraint on ontological commitment based on grammatical considerations that are too 'local' to English. If that were so, then one might suppose that he is right to base a criterion of ontological commitment on the grammatical subject-predicate distinction, but that some more general way of drawing it that takes into account languages such as Chinese is required. This would vindicate the claims on behalf of the grammatical subject-predicate distinction, but not the specific ones concerning the appropriate grammatical considerations upon which to base this distinction.

However, the points concerning the Hopi and Nookta languages make it difficult to pursue this line. For, if Whorf is correct, such languages work with no subject-predicate distinction at all. The conclusion seems unavoidable that, for the view under discussion, such languages do not express theories with ontological commitments. And in fact this conclusion is unavoidable in Strawson's framework. Why?

Strawson is not prepared when doing metaphysics to tamper with sentences of natural language in a way that departs radically from paraphrases that purport to give the real semantics of natural language sentences (Strawson 1976). He is deeply suspicious of the distinction between surface and 'deep' semantic structure, in the first place.[4] And, as we have seen, he doesn't view metaphysics as a 'revisionary' project, and so as a project that might countenance the sort of paraphrase that simply proposes replacing certain sentences, with their prima facie ontological commitments, with others which have no such commitments.

It is perhaps this attitude towards metaphysics itself, more than any other aspect of Strawson's position, which poses problems for his criterion of ontological commitment. If he did not hold this view, then the inapplicability of the (English) grammatical subject-predicate distinction to sentences of other natural languages would not itself constitute a reason for thinking that such languages do not express theories with ontological commitments. We would be free to formulate a canonical statement of the theories expressed by such languages that might allow us either to discern subject terms in them (in their 'deep structure'), or simply to paraphrase sentences that lack them in terms of sentences that have them. Strawson's attitude towards metaphysics, however, blocks this.

This suggests that it is the view of metaphysics, rather than the criterion of ontological commitment, that is the problem here, and that the way to remedy it would be to reject that view rather than to reject the criterion. Once we recognize that a language may have semantic devices that are not mirrored in its syntax, we must then recognize a difference between surface and deep structure. So, something must give, and the easiest thing to relinquish is the aversion to deep structure. This disturbs the important aspects of the view at least. Further, the conception of metaphysics outlined in chapter 1 is not only consistent with, but actively encourages, this way of remedying the problem. So why not adopt that more liberal conception, exercise the freedom that paraphrase allows, and endorse Strawson's version of a reference-based criterion of ontological commitment?

The reason is that, even with the more liberal conception in place, it isn't clear why a language must have subject terms in order to express a theory with ontological commitments. What is worrying about a criterion of ontological commitment that imposes a grammatical constraint like this is that it seems to rule out the very possibility of there being a language in which there is no grammatical subject-predicate distinction but which expresses ontological commitments. But why should we accept this? Who knows whether there could be such a language, even if Whorf is wrong in thinking that the Hopi and Nookta are examples of one?

A criterion of ontological commitment aims to specify conditions that are necessary and sufficient for a theory to be ontologically committed. It may be a fact that in most natural languages, subject terms are paradigmatically the linguistic means by which ontological commitments are expressed. But this may be no more than an interesting fact about what happens to be the case. And even if it is not, it may be no more than a psychologically necessary fact about how human beings can think and speak about the world in natural language. However, in order to justify couching a criterion of ontological commitment in terms of a grammatical subject-predicate distinction, one would need to justify the stronger claim, that a language in which there were no such terms could not express ontological commitments. But we have no clear reason to accept this stronger claim. Our best theory of the world may be capable of expression in a language in which there are no subject terms, even if the language from which a canonical statement of this theory is derived is one in which there are subject terms, and even if it is not psychologically possible for human beings to think and speak about the world just in terms of this canonical language. And this is enough to cast doubt on the adequacy of Strawson's criterion irrespective of his stance on metaphysics.

Quine's Criterion

According to Quine, the grammatical subject-predicate distinction has no ontological significance whatever; at most it has pragmatic value. Quine does not question the ontological priority of particulars over other candidates in any ontological framework, and, within that framework, the priority of individuals such as material objects over others. On these matters he is in complete agreement with Strawson. As he puts the point,

'In a contest for sheer systematic utility to science, the notion of a physical object still leads the field' (Quine 1960, p. 238).[5] What he disagrees with, fundamentally, is whether the ontological commitments of a theory are and must be carried by the subject terms of the language in which the theory is expressed, and for three reasons.

The first concerns a problem associated with non-referring singular terms, known as Plato's Beard. The second concerns the dispensability of all subject terms, specifically, of names and singular terms such as 'the cat', in natural language. The third has to do with the existence, in domains of objects associated with theories, of nameless objects.

The problem that non-referring singular terms poses for a subject-term-based criterion of ontological commitment is this. The criterion suggests that the use of a name, or other singular term, presupposes the existence of a bearer. But if this is so, how can one significantly deny or dispute the existence of an entity using a singular term without contradiction?[6] How, for example, can I significantly and consistently assert that Pegasus does not exist? Since we clearly do significantly (and, in at least some cases, truly) deny the existence of entities using subject terms without contradicting ourselves, not all subject terms refer, and sensible talk of what does not exist does not require us to suppose that apparently non-referring terms really do refer.[7] This is one reason for thinking that a criterion of ontological commitment should be found that makes no essential use of subject terms.

Quine also believes that names and singular terms generally can be dispensed with altogether, using the apparatus of first-order quantification theory, in favour of bound variables of quantification and predicates. We can explain what this means as follows. When we quantify over an object or objects, we talk about or specify them in general terms without naming them. When I say 'All the objects in this room are green', I do not name the objects in this room, but I nevertheless identify them for the purposes of saying something about them by using the term 'all'. This is a universal quantifier, because it talks about every object within the domain of discourse (here, the domain consists of the objects in this room). Again, when I say 'Something in this room is green', I say something that is true if and only if there is at least one thing in the room that is green. But I do not name that thing, and I do not identify any particular object. It does not matter for the truth of what I say exactly which object is green, only that there is some object in the room and that object is green. 'Something', and related terms like 'some', and 'at least one', are known as existential quantifiers, because they imply the existence of an object, even if they do not name that object.[8]

Now, the second objection to Strawson's criterion is that subject terms are replaceable by bound variables and predicates. So theories do not need to be expressed by languages containing singular terms, according to Quine. There is a simple procedure for eliminating them from languages in which they are present, and it is possible that there should be languages that are both ontologically committed and contain no singular terms. This is another reason for preferring a criterion of ontological commitment that places no particular weight on the presence in a language of subject terms.[9]

Finally, Quine believes that in any domain of objects associated with a theory, such as the domain of numbers, there may be nameless objects. This is not simply a point about there existing objects that just happen not to have names, since, so long as there are only a finite number of them, we can in principle provide them all with names. Quine has in mind domains like the domain of real numbers, which contain an infinity so large that there are, in principle, not enough names to go around. It is impossible to name all such numbers, yet we may and often do wish to and do express truths concerning this infinity. How do we do this? We do it by quantifying over, rather than by naming, the real numbers.

The idea is that, in order to determine the ontological commitments of a theory, one must first transform or regiment it into a more perspicuous notation, one in which its commitments are clear. (This presumes, of course, that natural language is not the most perspicuous notation by which to determine a theory's ontological commitments.) Quine's favoured one is the formal language of first-order quantification theory, or the predicate calculus. In this language, there are at least two types of sentence.

One type of sentence combines the formal analogue of a name, signified by lower-case letters from the beginning of the English alphabet, such as 'a', 'b', and 'c', with the formal analogue of a predicate, signified by upper-case letters of the alphabet, such as 'F', 'G' 'W', and so on. Thus, a natural language sentence like 'Socrates is wise' might be formalized in the predicate calculus as 'Ws'; and here we have the formal equivalent of a subject-predicate sentence whose subject term is a name.

However, there is another type of sentence in this language, which is the formal equivalent of a natural language sentence that speaks of objects, but in an indefinite way, examples of which were cited a few paragraphs back. This type of sentence combines, not the formal equivalent of a name, but rather, combines a variable with the formal analogue of a predicate. A variable functions like a pronoun such as 'it'. Such a term ranges over objects in a domain or universe – objects that are said to be its values – and may be attached to the quantifiers 'all' (the universal quantifier) and 'some' (the existential quantifier). When it is, the objects that the term ranges over are said to be its values, and the formulation of the formal analogue of a sentence such as 'Something is wise' or 'There is something such that it is wise' is made possible. Variables (which the lower-case letters from the end of the English alphabet such as '*x*', '*y*', and '*z*' signify) are variables because they can be associated with any single, or many, or all objects within a given domain. Unlike names and singular terms generally, they need not refer to any specific object in order to do their semantic work. Until they are attached to the quantifiers, they do not express any determinate proposition that could be evaluated for truth or falsity, since it is indeterminate how many objects are required to satisfy the predicates associated with them in order to make sentences containing them true. Thus, for example, the (open) sentence '*x* is wise' has no truth conditions. But once the variable, '*x*', is attached to a quantifier, the quantifier is said to bind it, and the result is a sentence that is capable of being true or false: 'Everything is such that it is wise', or 'There is something such that it is wise'. The former, universally quantified, sentence is true if and only if every object within the domain associated with the sentence is wise, and the latter, existentially quantified, sentence is true if and only if at least (but possibly more than) one object within that domain is wise.

Quantified sentences, and in particular the existentially quantified sentences of the predicate calculus, wear their ontological commitments, as it were, on their sleeves. So they provide a second way of determining what the ontological commitments of a theory are that is broadly speaking reference-based but which does not (or does not appear to) require the use of subject terms. Precisely stated, the criterion of ontological commitment can be put thus:

> A theory is committed to just those entities that are required as values of its bound variables when the theory is expressed in primitive notation on any interpretation that renders its theorems and axioms true.[10]

It is Quine's view that the ontological commitments of a theory are ultimately carried by the existentially bound variables of sentences of the language expressing it, hence the dictum, 'To be is to be the value of a variable'.[11]

The existentially quantified sentences of the language of the predicate calculus make precise the ontological commitments of the theory couched in its terms for two reasons. We have already seen one: the predicate calculus provides an unambiguous way of identifying precisely where the burden of ontological commitment lies in the sentences of a theory. The burden lies in the existentially quantified variables.

But there is a second reason. The predicate calculus makes the onto-logical commitments of the theory clear because the language of the predicate calculus is extensional. A language is extensional when the truth-values of its complex expressions (e.g., sentences) are a function of only the references (and extensions) of its parts. An extensional context is one in which substitution of terms that refer to the same object(s) or entity/entities preserves the truth-value of the original (in that it guarantees that the original and the result of substituting another term that refers to the same object(s) have the same truth-value).[12] Here is an example of a context that is extensional:

Mark Twain was the author of *Huckleberry Finn*.
Mark Twain is identical with Samuel Clemens.
Therefore, Samuel Clemens was the author of *Huckleberry Finn*.

It is extensional because the result of substituting one of the terms that refers to Mark Twain ('Samuel Clemens') for another term that refers to the same man ('Mark Twain') preserves the truth-value of the original sentence ('Mark Twain was the author of *Huckleberry Finn*').

Why is it important for a context to be extensional? It is important because, when we want to determine what there really is, what exists, we want to locate those expressions in the language expressing our theory of the world that connect with that world. A context that is not extensional is one in which that connection is broken, either in that its terms do not connect at all with objects in the world, or in that the referential function of its terms is interfered with in such a way that that connection is obscured by some additional function that they serve. Con-sider the following example of a context that is not extensional:

1 John believes that Mark Twain was the author of *Huckleberry Finn*.
2 Mark Twain is identical with Samuel Clemens.
3 Therefore, John believes that Samuel Clemens was the author of *Huckleberry Finn*.

Both (1) and (2) could be true, but (3) false (perhaps because John does not know that (2) is true). Substituting terms that refer to the same thing (Mark Twain) here fails to preserve the truth-value of the original.

Any context that is non-extensional is one whose ontological com-mitments are unclear. If we cannot tell what the ontological commitments of the sentential contexts of a language are, then we cannot tell, by examining that language, what the ontological commitments of the theory expressed in it are. So we want a criterion of ontological commitment to be formulated in an extensional language consisting of sentential contexts that are extensional.

As we have seen, Quine's view is that the question of what there is can and should be put in the form of a question concerning the truth of a theory, which in turn is to be answered by determining whether, when stated canonically (or in its most perspicuous form), the existentially quantified sentences of the language expressing it (specifically, those expressing the axioms and theorems, or basic laws or principles) are true. If the language of the predicate calculus is extensional, then it can make explicit what objects are required for its sentences to be true.[13]

However, extensional languages have problems of their own when it comes to the issue of ontological commitment. In particular, the extensionality of the language of the predicate calculus is the source of two major criticisms of Quine's criterion of ontological commitment. Both of these concern the question of how to express the ontological commitments of a false theory that is false *because* nothing satisfies it in the language of the predicate calculus, whose existentially bound variables are understood as ranging over objects in domains.[14]

The first criticism is this. Suppose that we have a theory, T, expressed in this language, to which we wish to apply Quine's criterion. The criterion tells us that we must ask what sorts of objects are required to exist, or to be in the universe or domain of objects associated with T, in order to make T true. A natural way of expressing this is to say:

For any theory T, T is committed to objects of kind K (for any K) if and only if any universe that satisfies T, or makes T true, contains Ks.

That is to say, any theory T is committed to the existence of objects of any kind K if and only if it meets this condition: if any universe satisfies T, then it contains Ks. But this is disastrous. For that condition is itself in the form of a conditional: it is in the form, 'if p then q', where 'p' and 'q' are *propositional* variables, variables that range over propositions expressed by sentences. And in the language of the predicate calculus, such a conditional is true (i) when 'p' is true and 'q' is true, (ii) when 'p' is false and 'q' is true, and (iii) when 'p' is false and 'q' is false. But then the condition on a theory's being ontologically committed to objects of any kind is *satisfied* in the case of a false theory that is false because nothing satisfies it, no matter what the Ks are. For if T is false, then no universe satisfies it. Accordingly, that part of the condition that replaces the antecedent, '*p*', in the conditional, 'if *p* then *q*', namely, any universe satisfies *T*, is false. But then the condition on *T*'s being ontologically committed itself, that which replaces the entire conditional, 'if *p* then *q*', is satisfied trivially, no matter what *K*s are. For we know that that conditional will be true when its antecedent ('*p*') is false, irrespective of the truth of its consequent ('*q*'). So phlogiston theory, in being false because nothing satisfies it, is committed to objects of any kind – not just phlogiston, but Pegasus, unicorns, the present King of France, and so on.

The problem, paradoxically, is this. Because all false theories that are false because nothing satisfies them are in the same position with regard to there being nothing that satisfies them, a criterion formulated in extensional terms seems incapable of distinguishing between them with regard to their commitments precisely because they are committed to things that don't exist. Given that the criterion of ontological commitment applies to and is itself formulated in an extensional language whose bound variables are taken to range over domains of objects, its application to false theories that are false because nothing satisfies them issues in those theories being committed to objects of any kind because nothing satisfies the existentially quantified sentences of the languages expressing them. Different commitments of theories can only be discerned in these extensional languages by a criterion formulated in the same terms when there are different domains of objects associated with those theories. When there are no such domains, then there is no difference that the criterion can discern.

It might be tempting to think that we can patch up the criterion here by tacking on an existence condition (i.e., by requiring that some universes do satisfy the theory). The result would look something like this:

For any theory *T*, *T* is committed to objects of kind *K* (for any *K*) if and only if any universe that satisfies *T* contains *K*s, and there is some universe that satisfies *T*.

The condition that now needs to be met is that in the form of a conjunction: it must both be true that if any universe satisfies *T*, then it contains *K*s (as above), and be true that there is some universe that satisfies *T*.

However, this leads to the equally unacceptable result that false theories that are false because nothing satisfies them are committed to nothing. Why? Because in the case of a false theory, no universe satisfies it, and so no universe satisfies the existence condition. Since a conjunction (expressed by a sentence of the form '*p* and *q*') is only true if both of its conjuncts are true, and is false otherwise, this means that the entire conjunction expressing the condition on a theory T's being ontologically committed is false when the existence condition is not met, as it is not in the case of a false theory that is false because nothing satisfies it. So false theories of this kind can never meet the condition on ontological commitment: in being false because nothing satisfies them, they fail to be ontologically committed!

Thus, theories that are false because nothing satisfies them appear, on extensional versions of Quine's criterion of ontological commitment, to be committed to everything or to nothing. But this seems wrong. We want to be able to say that such theories are false precisely because they are committed to items that do not exist. So neither of the above two ways of formulating Quine's criterion is acceptable.

There is a second problem with the criterion, which again concerns expressing the commitments of a false theory and which again arises because the language of the predicate calculus is extensional. One of the points of the criterion, and one that Quine himself emphasizes, is that it can be used as a guide in discussions of theories whose ontological commitments we do not ourselves accept. That is to say, the criterion is a meta-theoretical principle that applies to theories. So we metaphysicians ought to be able to use it to specify the ontological commitments of theories without thereby being committed to the entities to which those theories are committed. However, it is difficult to avoid commitment to the entities of a theory T in the process of applying the criterion. Suppose, for example, that T is committed to unicorns. Then the criterion invites formulating the commitments of T as follows:

Something is a unicorn and T is committed to it.[15]

Why does it invite this formulation? Because if a theory's commitments are best made explicit by means of its bound variables in an extensional language, then any statement of that theory's commitments would seem also to best make explicit those commitments by means of bound variables in an extensional language. But now it appears that in order for the criterion of ontological commitment itself to be true, i.e., to truly express the commitments of the theories to which it applies, its bound variables evidently must be taken to range over the same items as the theory T to which it applies. Given this, how can we use the criterion to state the commitments of a false theory without thereby committing ourselves to the existence of every object to which the theory is committed? How can we truly state in the language of the predicate calculus that T is ontologically committed to unicorns without committing ourselves to unicorns?

Here is one way. All of the criticisms of extensional formulations of Quine's criterion assume that, in order to make explicit the commitments of a theory T, the bound variables of the criterion expressing the commitments must be taken to refer to or quantify over precisely the same entities over which the bound variables of T quantify. However, Quine's criterion is a *meta-theoretical* or *meta-metaphysical* principle; one that applies to, but is not itself a part of, other theories (in this case those expressed in natural languages such as English). There seems to be no a priori reason to think that the domain of objects with which the criterion deals is identical with, or even overlaps with, that over which the bound variables of those lower-level theories range, any more than there is reason to think that, in saying 'Margaret' is a seven-letter word', we are referring to Margaret. Often we use the word 'Margaret' to refer to a particular person, as we do when we say things like 'Margaret was once Prime Minister'; but sometimes we want to refer to the word itself, not the person. Quotation marks enable us to do so: they are meta-linguistic devices that enable us to talk about words themselves, rather than the things those words refer to. So we can use language to talk about the extra-linguistic world, and we can also use quotation marks and other meta-linguistic devices to talk about language itself.

It seems clear that the domain with which extensional formulations of Quine's criterion deals is theories, and theories are articulated and expressed in languages. So the prime candidates for entities over which the bound variables of the criterion range are linguistic items and the theories expressed in them. Quantifying over such items does not entail quantifying over any extra-linguistic objects in the world to which those linguistic items might refer and to which the theory expressed by them might apply, any more than referring to the word 'Margaret' entails referring to Margaret.

In short, the most promising way of avoiding the kinds of objections that have just been voiced against Quine's criterion is to resort to what is known as semantic ascent. To do this is to construe the domain associated with the criterion as consisting of languages formalized in the predicate calculus and the theories expressed by them, not what the bound variables of sentences of those languages are taken to range over, or what the extensions are of the terms of the theories that those languages express. How might we express Quine's criterion along these lines, and how might we express the commitments of a theory by means of it? The criterion, now construed as quantifying over languages and the theories they express, might be formulated as follows:

For any theory *T*, *T* is ontologically committed if and only if, when stated canonically, those quantified sentences that express its axioms and theorems are assigned the truth-value, true.

This formulation of the criterion no longer talks, even in general terms, about potential satisfiers of bound variables. If it did, it would once again be saddled with the problem of quantifying over objects that, in the case of theories that are false because nothing satisfies them, do not exist. So there is a loss in specificity between the formulation with which we began this section and the present formulation. However, it is not a loss that should be grounds for concern, since that very specificity was the source of the two main problems with the original.

Does this version capture Quine's intuition, that the ontological commitments of a theory are to be determined by the bound variables of that theory when formulated canonically – perspicuously – in the language of the predicate calculus? Well, it captures what was important about that intuition, namely that when we want to know what are the ontological commitments of a theory, the place to look is to the quantified sentences of the language expressing it. It does not state in explicit terms why, but nor does Quine's dictum 'to be is to be the valuable of a variable'. This dictum and its precise formulation make no explicit appeal to sorts or kinds of objects that might serve as potential satisfiers of bound variables. So, while there may be a loss in specificity between the formulation of the criterion with which this section began and the present one, that specificity is not part of either Quine's dictum itself or its precise formulation.

How do we use the criterion to state the commitments of a theory without thereby quantifying over every object to which that theory is committed? Instead of using quantified sentences that range or purport to range over the same objects that the quantified sentences of the theory range or purport to range over – instead, that is, of speaking of the objects that are required to serve as values of bound variables – we speak of those quantified sentences and the propositions themselves, and the theory's commitment to their truth. The result is something like this:

'Something is Pegasus' is assigned the truth-value, true, in *T*.[16]

Here, in the meta-theory, we use the criterion to mention, not to use, sentences of the theory, and instead of speaking of the objects that are required to make such sentences true, we speak of the assignment of truth to such sentences. Again, there is a loss of specificity, but there is also gain, in that we can now express the commitments of theories that are false because nothing satisfies them.

It is important to see, though, what we have avoided by means of the strategy of semantic ascent. We have avoided quantifying over entities that do not exist. We have not avoided a non-extensional formulation of the criterion of ontological commitment. If 'Something is Pegasus' is assigned the truth-value, true, in T, it follows that 'according to T, Pegasus exists' is true. Since, then, Pegasus does not exist, the context created by 'according to T, ___' is non-extensional. The only way that we could avoid this conclusion would be by maintaining that the onto-logical commitments of a theory cannot be stated, in claims of the form 'According to T, there are Ks' or in claims of the form 'T is committed to Ks', but only shown (by displaying the existentially quantified sentences it holds true). And someone might object that we cannot take seriously a criterion of ontological commitment if we cannot use it to formulate claims of these forms. So perhaps we might as well just admit that 'T is committed to ___' is a non-extensional context. After all, what it means is not much more or less than 'People who believe T, by that very fact, believe that there are ___', and as we have just seen above, this is a well-known non-extensional context.

Admitting this should not blind us to the fact that the strategy of semantic ascent avoids what seems to be the main source of objections to Quine's criterion, namely, that it must, in order to express the com-mitments of theories that are false because nothing satisfies them, quan-tify over items that do not exist. Moreover, it does so without trivializing the criterion. After all, the criterion, and the use we can make of it, iden-tifies those parts of theories that carry the burden of ontological com-mitment, and it tells us why these parts are important: because the sentences expressing them are existentially quantified sentences. The criterion can also be used to state more precisely, by helping to identify more precisely, an individual theory's ontological commitments, by telling us what to look for in that individual theory. Different theories' commitments can then be identified by identifying the different quanti-fied sentences to which those theories assign the value, true. Further, and crucially, if we understand these sentences, then we know what terms need to refer or to have extensions in order for those sentences to be true. This is necessary for knowing what theory is expressed by a lan-guage. And to know this is effectively to know what sorts of things need to be supposed to exist in order for those sentences to be true. Is it rea-sonable to expect more from a criterion of ontological commitment? Not if we need, as we do, to express the commitments both of true theories and of theories that are false because nothing satisfies them.

However, there is one final objection to Quine's criterion that many will think is the most serious one of all, and that is that it trades on the subject-predicate distinction and so actually presupposes something like Strawson's criterion. This is because, in the predicate calculus, the prime candidates for places in a sentence that can 'yield' to a quantifier – ones that can be replaced by variables that can then be attached to quantifiers – are places where names or other singular terms occur. Places other than subject position may also yield to the quantifiers, as when second-order quantification, quantification over properties, occurs. However, this does not occur instead of, but rather, in addition to, quantification into subject position. But then it looks as though the predicate calculus can only be applied to languages in which the grammatical subject-predicate distinction exists (Strawson 1974a). And this makes it look as if Quine's criterion is superfluous; it can do no more than one couched in terms of the grammatical subject-predicate distinction. Further, it makes the additional controversial assumption, which Strawson's does not, that the ontological commitments of a theory can only be made perspicuous when translated into a formal language.

It is true that, if the natural language to which Quine's criterion of ontological commitment is to be applied already employs a subject-predicate distinction, the 'translation' of that language into the language of the predicate calculus will (in the first instance at least) take the subject terms of that natural language to occupy positions that are accessible to quantification. So, in these cases at least, the question of whether Quine's criterion is any improvement on one couched in terms of the grammatical subject-predicate distinction might seem to be a legitimate one.

But it is not. Why not? Because in determining even the prima facie ontological commitments of a theory there is no guarantee that there will be a neat match between sentences of subject-predicate form in natural language and the quantified ones when that language is put in canonical form. Earlier in this section (pp. 43–4) we saw that some sentences apparently of subject-predicate form may not survive as quantified sentences (if, say, we distinguish the merely grammatical from the real singular terms); and this of course is consistent with Strawson's criterion. However, we also saw that some sentences may go into canonical form as sentences which involve quantification over objects for which the original sentences had no subject terms (say, sentences about infinite domains so large that their members cannot in principle be named). And this is not consistent with Strawson's criterion. If, as has been argued, the metaphysician's task is not simply to do semantics for natural language, then the freedom that departure from that task allows secures a role for criterion that is not simply the role played by Strawson's.

Quine's criterion is a more liberal one than Strawson's, then, even as applied to natural languages. However, there is a more important difference between the two criteria. This emerges when one considers the question of whether there could be a language in which there were no subject terms, but which expressed a theory with ontological commitments. Such a language might, for example, be the formal language of the predicate calculus purged of its individual constants. In a language like this, ontological commitments could be made and captured by a criterion of ontological commitment like Quine's, whereas they could not be made and so could not be captured by means of a criterion of ontological commitment which requires, as Strawson's does, the presence in the language of subject terms. Since there seems to be no a priori reason to suppose that such a language could not exist, Quine's criterion is arguably the better one.

Suppose, however, that grounds could be given for thinking that such a language was not possible. (Remember that this could not just mean: a natural language such as this is not possible. For the issue here is not about natural language.) Then would it follow that Quine's criterion is no improvement on one that, like Strawson's, employs a grammatical subject-predicate distinction? This depends partly on whether Quine's appeal to the formal language of the predicate calculus to make perspicuous the ontological commitments of a theory is legitimate. Earlier (p. 41), we noted that Strawson thinks that the appeal to such a language to settle issues concerning reference and meaning is misplaced (Strawson 1976). His claim is that if, on the one hand, formal languages uncover, or make explicit, the semantic structure of sentences in natural language – the structure they actually have in natural language – then they are superfluous. They can tell us nothing that we cannot know without appeal to such languages. If, on the other hand, they are not superfluous – if they really do make claims on behalf of the semantic structure of sentences in natural language that go beyond what is discoverable in their natural language 'equivalents' – then there is a real question why we should accept the claim that they are indeed equivalent. Why should we believe that the formal counterpart of a natural language sentence 'really' captures its semantic structure?

Let us suppose for the moment that Strawson is correct in assuming that the metaphysician's task is to do semantics for natural language sentences. Still, a response can be made to his challenge. If the formal 'counterparts' of sentences in natural language really are equivalent to them – if they have the same truth conditions, if they express the same truths – then they will not express anything essentially different from what is expressed by their natural language counterparts. If they did, then they would not be equivalent to them after all. However, the regimentation of natural language sentences into formal language ones is a matter of thinking reflectively on unreflective use in an attempt to make explicit the presumptions of that use. In the process of effecting a more perspicuous formulation of the semantic structure of such sentences, reflection on use may help us to see that certain, or many, sentences of natural language have a structure that is in fact very different from what, superficially, they appear to have. This is not to say that the formal equivalent is not, after all, an equivalent. It is rather to say that the semantic structure of natural language sentences is not always what it might seem, unreflectively, to be; and the process of attempting to put such sentences into formal notation can help us to see this. Could we do this by reflecting on the structure of sentences of natural language, without appeal to a formal language? Well, perhaps we could; after all, the appeal of a formal language in this context is that it makes perspicuous what may be only implicit in natural language, and it is arguable that although it is useful to have the resources of a formal language to do this, it is not necessary. However, if appeal to a formal language does help us to see more clearly what structure natural language sentences have, then it is justified even if not necessary. And this appears to be all that can reasonably be expected from Quine's criterion – or any criterion – of ontological commitment, on the assumption that the aim is to do semantics for natural language sentences.

However, the metaphysician's aim is not just to do semantics for natural language sentences; and so, on Quine's behalf, we should complete this response by pointing out that, in determining the ontological commitments of a theory expressed in natural language, there is a considerable amount of freedom awarded to the metaphysician. Certainly she is constrained by apparent semantic structure of natural language sentences, since she must pay attention to the way people appear to talk and think. But this is not the only, nor even the most important, constraint, since her ultimate aim is to find a best theory of the world. Along the way she must determine the actual (and not just the prima facie) ontological commitments of the theories expressed in natural language; and she will have a considerable amount of freedom in determining those commitments. The paraphrases she comes up with in formulating canonical statements of those theories may not meet Strawson's standards of 'equivalent', however loose. But this just shows that the aim is not simply to do semantics for natural language sentences; not that Quine's enterprise, construed as an attempt to do this, is bankrupt.

So there is a role for Quine's criterion to play that does not simply imitate Strawson's. Further, it is a role that can be better played by that criterion than by Strawson's, given the aims of metaphysics.

'No Entity without Identity':
Identity Conditions for Objects

We have justified the need for a criterion of ontological commitment, and defended the choice of one criterion over another. However, discerning the ontological commitments of a theory, and adjudicating between rival ontologies, cannot be accomplished by means of a criterion of ontological commitment alone. Why not? Consider Quine's criterion. It says that a theory is ontologically committed if and only if it assigns the truth-value, true, to just those quantified sentences that express its axioms and theorems. In appealing to the quantified sentences of the theory, the criterion appeals to sentences whose bound variables are understood as ranging over objects or entities that can be taken as their values. But Quine's criterion does not itself tell us *what* objects those theories are committed to. It only tells us which parts of the theory carry ontological weight and why.

In order to be able to use the criterion to determine what are the specific commitments of individual theories, then, we need to know what those theories offer up as candidates for objects or kinds of objects that might serve as values of the bound variables of the quantified sentences expressing it. This raises the issue of identity conditions for objects, since quantification over objects is only possible when there is at least one clear satisfier of a quantified sentence. An existentially quantified sentence is true on the condition that at least *one* object in a given domain satisfies it; and a universally quantified sentence is true on the condition that *every* object within a given domain satisfies it, or makes it true. Both types of sentence require that we make sense of the idea of a single satisfier, since we cannot make sense of the idea of more than one satisfier without it. But then quantification requires that we understand the idea of numerical identity for objects. And any theory couched in quantificational terms will presume this idea.

It is the identity conditions for objects that tell us what makes objects the numerically unique things that they are. What they do is to tell us, for any object of a kind, the conditions under which it is a single object of the kind it is. When we do metaphysics, we need at least to presume that there are identity conditions for the things that the theories take their quantified sentences to quantify over. But we also need to suppose that the theories themselves take there to be identity conditions for the things that they presume their quantified sentences to quantify over. Otherwise, it would be hard to see why such sentences would be assigned the truth-value, true, in those theories.

When doing metaphysics we need to know still more than this. We need to know what are the identity conditions for objects. Why? One reason is that we need to know not only what the theory *apparently* takes there to be, but also what the theory *really* takes there to be. Here the question arises of whether certain candidates for objects can be given a place in a theory's actual ontology, and answering this requires addressing the question of whether those candidates have satisfactory identity conditions.

Suppose, for example, that a theory apparently takes there to be such things as properties: in addition to particular red things, such as red apples, it apparently takes there to be redness, a general characteristic, or property, that may be had by many red things. Now, this commitment may only be apparent. One reason for thinking that it might be is that properties are problematic entities: they seem to be wholly present in the things that have them, and so to be completely in many places at once. This is problematic because we normally suppose (a) that the numerical identity of a thing in the spatio-temporal world is fixed or determined by where it is at any given time, and (b) that a single thing cannot be in two places at the same time. Properties like redness, in being wholly and completely in many places at the same time, seem to provide us with an example of an object that has either no clear identity conditions or contradictory ones.[17] Quine captures this problem, and the relation it bears to the issue of ontological commitment, nicely when he says:

> The lack of a proper identity concept for attributes [properties] is a lack that philosophers feel compelled to supply; for, what sense is there in saying that there are attributes when there is no sense in saying when there is one and when two? (Quine 1969a, p. 19)

This is one place where, in doing metaphysics, we may be forced to ask specific questions about identity conditions for objects, to which we will need to give answers.

Another reason why we need to know the identity conditions for objects when doing metaphysics has to do with the metaphysician's aim of finding a best theory of the world. Attempting to find such a theory will involve weighing one ontology against another, and trying to adjudicate between them. In order to do this, we will need to know what the identity conditions are for the objects in them. If we don't know that, we won't know whether ontologies differ, or if they do, in what ways.

Suppose, for example, that one theory, expressed canonically, quantifies over numbers, and another theory, expressed canonically, quantifies over sets. Do we need to adjudicate between them? That depends on whether the identity conditions for numbers are the same as those for sets. If they are, then there is no real decision to make here: we can keep both numbers and sets, since, in having the same identity conditions, they are not different things! Quine again puts the point, and its connection with the question of ontological commitment, nicely:

> how are we to adjudicate among rival ontologies? Certainly the answer is not provided by the semantical formula 'To be is to be the value of a variable'; this formula serves, rather, conversely, in testing the conformity of a given remark or doctrine to a prior ontological standard. (Quine 1964a, p. 15)

This prior ontological standard just is the requirement that there be identity conditions for objects that are taken to be values of bound variables in the relevant quantified sentences. The importance to ontology of such conditions is captured by Quine's slogan 'no entity without identity'. What it means is this: no theory can be committed to objects of any sort or kind unless it possesses conditions necessary and sufficient

(i)   to distinguish, or individuate, objects of that kind from objects not of that kind,

and

(ii) to distinguish or individuate objects within that kind from one another.

It may be easy to see the relevance of (ii) but not of (i). Suppose that my theory includes sets. So, if what has been argued above is correct, my theory needs to be able to say when I have one and when I have two sets. Otherwise, we cannot make sense of, say, the claim that there is at most one empty set. And the axiom of extensionality for sets, which says that sets are identical if and only if they have the same members, in giving us the identity conditions for sets, does this. But it is not obvious why I need, in addition, a principle that tells me how sets are different from cats, if indeed they are. Whether sets are distinct from cats or are to be numbered among them (or vice versa) seems irrelevant to the issue of whether there are sets. But it is not, for reasons given at the outset of the next section.

Individuation Conditions, Identity Conditions, and Metaphysical Kinds

We can usefully label the conditions associated with (i) above 'individuation conditions', and the conditions associated with (ii) above 'identity conditions'.[18] Clearly, (i) tells us that any object that falls into a kind or sort must have associated with it conditions necessary and sufficient to mark it off, or individuate it, as an object of that kind, from objects not of that kind. These conditions determine what it is to be a kind. So, suppose metaphysics were to be interested in giving individuation conditions for, say, things that fall into the kind, *material substances* (such as individual apples, trees, and animals). Then one thing that it would be concerned to provide is conditions that all and only objects that fall within that kind satisfy. However, while sufficing to mark off material substances from things not of that kind, say, events, or properties, individuation conditions will not suffice to mark off or individuate one material substance from another. As we have seen, this is why we need (ii). An object must have associated with it identity conditions; conditions necessary and sufficient to individuate it, within that kind, from every other object of that kind (and so from every other object).[19]

Some theories may be committed to the existence of objects or entities of many different kinds, as is the theory expressed in English. Others may be committed to the existence of objects or entities of only one kind. In both cases, however, there is a need for condition (i). Why? Because in metaphysics we are interested in the most basic, or fundamental kinds that there are, into which objects or entities fall. We want to know what makes them of the kind or kinds that they are because this is germane to their natures, and to their capacities to behave in certain ways. This is as true for ontologies where there are only objects of one kind as it is for ontologies where there are objects of many kinds. So, for example, even if there were only material substances in a given ontology, we would want to know that the objects that fall into this kind are all material substances and in what this consists. This is because certain characteristics, such as, perhaps, being composed of matter, taking up space and enduring through time, and being capable of undergoing and surviving change, are either due to or are constitutive of (that is, part of what is involved in) being of that kind.

It is, perhaps, also worth pointing out that even if there were only one kind of object, it still might be *possible* for there to be more than one kind of object. And metaphysics, as we have seen, is supposed to produce truths that are necessary, or about what must be the case rather than about what merely happens to be the case. So, it is important to say how material substances differ from events, even if there were no, but there could be, events.

What relation, if any, is there between an object's individuation conditions and its identity conditions? One view, and the view we shall take, is this. An object's individuation conditions specify *determinable* properties, properties such as having spatio-temporal position, or being a particular, or having colour, or having shape, whose possession by an object ensures that it is an object of the metaphysical kind it is. For example, the individuation conditions for material substances may specify being spatio-temporal plus being of a substance kind. Any material substance, to be a material substance, must satisfy these conditions. An object's identity conditions specify *determinate forms* of the determinable properties that figure in its individuation conditions. Consider a particular cat, an example of a material substance. Its identity conditions might be given by specifying the determinate form of substance kind into which it falls, namely, the *cat* kind, plus the specific spatio-temporal position that that cat occupies. Being of that kind and occupying just that spatio-temporal position makes this particular cat the unique individual cat that it is, and so the unique material substance it is.

As this makes clear, kinds themselves are important, not just to the individuation conditions, but also to the identity conditions of objects. We know that objects can be of more than one kind. For example, a cat is of the *cat* kind, of the *animal* kind, and of the *material substance* kind. But some of these kinds may be more important to the individuation conditions of a cat. Being of the *cat* kind, for example, ensures that an object is also of the *animal* kind and of the *material substance* kind, but not *vice versa*. So being of the *cat* kind is evidently more important to the individuation conditions of cats. But is the *cat* kind itself metaphysically important? How, in general, do we work out which kinds are the metaphysically important ones?

When we do metaphysics we are not concerned with the individuation conditions of each and every ontological category that there may be, irrespective of how broad or how specific it is. We are not, in fact, concerned as metaphysicians with the individuation conditions of cats. What we are concerned with are individuation conditions that mark out the basic or fundamental metaphysical kinds into which things fall.[20] For these purposes, some kinds, like the *cat* kind, are too specific. Others are too general. Consider, for example, the kind, *material substance*. Objects that fall into this kind are also particulars (in being wholly and completely in a single place at any given time), and so fall into the kind, *particular*. But it is more metaphysically fundamental to them that they are material substances. For if they are material substances, then they are particulars; but (merely) in being particulars they are not necessarily material substances. Persons, perhaps, are also particulars, but they may not be material substances, for they may not be material things. Then there is also the possibility that there might be abstract particulars as well as concrete ones; particulars that are such that more than one of them might be wholly and completely in the same place at the same time (events might be an example). Because material substances, persons, and events, may not have a single set of characteristics in common, in virtue of which they can be individuated as particulars from things that are not particulars, the kind, *particular*, is too general for metaphysical purposes.

Why is being a broader or more general kind undesirable in certain cases for metaphysical purposes, but not in others? Consider the very specific kind, *cat*. That kind is a sub-kind within the broader kind, *animal*, which is itself a sub-kind within the still broader kind, *material substance*. Why is it that metaphysicians consider the broader kind, *material substance*, to be more metaphysically important than the more specific, *cat*, kind?

The reason is that the more specific sub-kinds form a homogeneous group: they exhibit commonalties that make them all material substances. The sub-kinds may exclude one another, but they exhibit a natural unity that is captured by the features that mark them off as material substances. For example, the specific causal powers that cats may have, which are associated with their being of the kind, *cat*, such as the capacity to hiss, are realizations of more general causal powers that they have in being animals, such as the capacity to make vocal sounds, which in turn are realizations of still more general causal powers that they have in being material substances, such as the capacity to enter into causal transactions with other material substances. The kind, *material substance*, is a metaphysically important kind because its features or characteristics are realized in specific ways by all of the objects of the different sub-kinds that comprise it. Material substances are the sort of things that have spatio-temporal position, effect change in one another (and so enter into causal transactions), have shape, colour, and size, are (relatively) impenetrable, and so on.

So, in being a broader kind, the kind, *material substance*, is more metaphysically important than the kinds that comprise it. But is it important relative to the broader kinds into which it falls? No. Consider the much broader kind, *particular*, into which material substances fall. It is too broad a category to be metaphysically interesting because it contains within it other, very heterogeneous kinds that have nothing in common with one another other than that they are particulars. Being a particular, while serving to group the kinds that are particulars, tells us nothing specific about what the natures are of the kinds that are particulars. Because it fails to do this, it tells us nothing specific about the capacities that objects that fall into these different kinds have to behave causally and/or in other ways. But these capacities are metaphysically interesting and important.

There is another reason why the kind, *particular*, is too broad. To know what kind an object falls within is to know something about its capacities to behave causally and in other ways. But to be a particular is simply to be an individual, a single thing. It is not even to be a concrete, or spatio-temporal thing, since, as we have noted, there may be abstract as well as concrete particulars. This tells us nothing about the causal capacities of the things that fall within the kind, *particular*. So it is not a metaphysically interesting or important kind in a theory in which there are particulars of many kinds.

Suppose that someone were to say that we do know something metaphysically interesting and important when we know that something is a particular. We know that it is a single individual, incapable of being in more than one place at any given time. This contrasts with being a property, for example, which is capable of being in many places at the same time.

It is true that we know this much. But to know this is simply to know what the concept of a particular is. That this knowledge falls short of being metaphysically interesting and important emerges when we see that things as different as concrete objects (such as material substances) and abstract objects (such as, perhaps, events) can fall into its extension. To know this fact is to know something metaphysically interesting and important. But we do not come to know it just by grasping the concept of a particular.

Is the kind, *particular*, metaphysically interesting or important in an ontology where there are only particulars, but no particulars of more specific kinds? In one way it is even less interesting and important than in a more varied ontology, where there are both particulars and things of other kinds, say, properties. Why? Because in the latter case, in knowing that the kind, *particular*, contrasts with the kind, *property*, we have some information about what it is to be a particular. Still, it is possible that we might possess this information in the absence of other, non-particular, kinds. Do we know anything metaphysically interesting and important? We know nothing about the properties that individuals comprising that kind have, other than that they are individuals. We do not know whether these properties exclude one another, nor if they do, why. Since we know none of these things, we do not know what capacities these individuals have to behave towards or relate to one another. If metaphysics *can* provide us with this additional knowledge, a metaphysics that did not provide it would be lacking in important respects.

Principles and Criteria of Identity

Every object has associated with it conditions without which the kind to which it belongs (and hence it) would not exist, as well as conditions without which it (although not perhaps others of its kind) would fail to exist.[21] These conditions are often taken by those working in the area of ontology to be expressed by principles and/or criteria of identity (Lombard 1986; Lowe 1989a, 1989b, 1998; Wiggins 2001). It is to these, and the role they play in discussions of ontology, that we now turn.

The most fundamental principle governing identity is known as Leibniz's Law. Unfortunately, in the form in which Leibniz himself expressed it, it covers three distinct versions of the principle, all of which can legitimately be traced to remarks made by Leibniz and all of which have been referred to by the same name (Cartwright 1971). We can distinguish them by giving them separate names.

First, there is the Principle of the Identity of Indiscernibles. This principle expresses a relation between objects and their properties. Crudely stated, it says that objects that are indiscernible with respect to their properties are identical. It follows from their being indiscernible with regard to their properties that they are identical. We can state this principle slightly more precisely as follows:

> For any objects x and y, if every property of x is a property of y, and vice versa, then x is identical with y.[22]

This principle is associated with a certain theory of substances held by Leibniz, Hume, and, at one stage in his philosophical career, Ayer, known as the bundle theory. According to this theory, substances are identical with their properties.[23] Two substances cannot differ solely in number; if they differ, the difference must be discernible qualitatively, as a difference in property. Conversely, objects that are indiscernible are identical.

Second, there is the Principle of the Indiscernibility of Identicals. This principle also expresses a relation between objects and their properties. Crudely put, it says that objects that are identical are indiscernible with regard to their properties. It follows from their being identical that they are indiscernible with respect to their properties. We can also state this principle slightly more precisely thus:

> For any objects x and y, if x is identical with y, then every property of x is a property of y and vice versa.[24]

Since two things can never be identical, perhaps a better informal rendering of the principle is: a thing cannot be discernible from itself (no thing can have a property that it itself lacks). This brings out the obvious truth of the principle, and why it is often thought to be *the* principle of identity in the sense of defining the concept of identity. The reason is that this principle, and only this one, can discriminate between numerically different but exactly similar things, and so distinguish genuine identity from 'mere' indiscernibility relations.[25] It is associated with the theory of substances held by Bergmann and his followers, and by Locke, known as the bare substratum theory.[26] According to it, substances are bare, characterless entities, completely other than their properties.

Often these two principles are combined in one statement, under the general name of 'Leibniz's Law'. This says that objects are identical if and only if they are indiscernible with regard to all of their properties. More precisely, it states that

> For any objects, x and y, x is identical with y if and only if every property of x is a property of y and vice versa.[27]

As we shall see, the two principles embodied in this one have important implications for the question of identity conditions for entities such as material substances, persons, and events. The differences between the Principle of the Identity of Indiscernibles and the Principle of the Indiscernibility of Identicals are important to the discussion to follow, however.

Finally, there is the Substitution Principle. Roughly speaking, this principle states that, if and only if two sentences contain co-referring terms (i.e., terms referring to the same object), those terms can be exchanged for one another without altering the truth-value of the resulting sentences. Precisely stated, it says that

> For all expressions 'a' and 'b', '$a = b$' expresses a true proposition if and only if, for all sentences S and S', if S' is like S except in containing an occurrence of 'b' where S contains an occurrence of 'a', then if S expresses a true proposition, then S' does also.[28]

Some view this third principle as a sort of linguistic version of the Leibniz's Law (Cartwright 1971). One can see why this might be. Suppose that the function of a name is solely to pick out or to refer to an object, and the function of a predicate is solely to determine a property. Then the linguistic version of Leibniz's Law could be seen to be encapsulated in the statement that two names, 'a' and 'b', are names of the same object (i.e., 'a = b' expresses a true proposition) if and only if every predicate true of the object named by 'a' is true of the object named by 'b'. (It is something like this thought that lies behind the view that the Substitution Principle embodies the very idea of singular reference, or of what it is for something to be a name.)

The twin Principles of the Identity of Indiscernibles and the Indiscernibility of Identicals express something fundamental about identity, namely that an object's identity – its being a single thing with a nature – is essentially bound up with its properties. The Identity of Indiscernibles makes this point explicit by stating that an object's singularity and uniqueness is determined solely by its properties. Many who believe that the bundle theory is true are committed to its truth, although, as we shall see in chapter 3, the principle, at least in its non-trivial form, is at best controversial and arguably false. The Indiscernibility of Identicals makes the point explicit by stating that an object's singularity and uniqueness guarantees that anything identical with it is indiscernibile with regard to its properties (i.e., by stating that identity guarantees indiscernibility with respect to properties).

Now, whether we assume either that the universe contains objects of only one sort of kind, or that it contains objects of more than one kind, Leibniz's Law would suffice to specify the identity conditions of those objects. For the law says nothing about sort- or kind-specific properties. It simply states that objects are identical if and only if they share all the same properties, *whatever* those properties might be. If, then, the universe contained only sets (whose only members were sets), identical sets would both satisfy the Axiom of Extensionality (that sets are identical if and only if they have the same members) and Leibniz's Law (that things are identical if and only if they have the same properties). And if it contained objects of more than one kind, say, both sets and material substances, Leibniz's Law would still give necessary and sufficient conditions for identity, for it is true (and must be true) of any set and any material substance that it is self-identical if and only if it has no property that it lacks.

However, in neither a single-kind universe nor a multi-kind universe does Leibniz's Law tell us what it is for something to belong to the kind

it belongs to. It is not that the law isn't true of the objects in those ontologies. After all, if what has been said above is correct, Leibniz's Law
embodies the very idea of what it is for an object to be self-identical. It
is that it does not distinguish between those properties that do, and those
that do not, determine objects to be of distinct and fundamental metaphysical kinds. It does not tell us what it is to belong to kind K, so it
cannot tell us what it is to belong to kind K (say, the kind, *set*) *as opposed
to* kind K' (say, the kind, *material substance*). Of course, Leibniz's Law
is not designed to do that; so it is no criticism of that principle that it
doesn't. Still, because it does not, it cannot suffice for the purpose of
settling issues of the sort that arise with regard to theories expressed
in English and in other natural languages, and which will arise in the
ensuing discussion in this book.

Such theories suppose there to be objects of more than one fundamental metaphysical kind. So objects in their ontologies can fail to be
identical, and thus fail to satisfy Leibniz's Law, for two quite different
reasons. One is that they are both of the same metaphysical kind and
simply happen not to share the same determinate form of the determinable properties that constitute their individuation conditions. These
two cats, for example, may fail to be identical because, although both
fall into the kind, *material substances*, by falling into the same sub-
category of that kind (*cat*), and both occupy spatio-temporal positions,
the determinate positions that they occupy are not the same. Another
reason why objects can fail to be identical, in an ontology where there
are objects of more than one fundamental metaphysical kind, however,
is that they fail to be of the same metaphysical kind, and so fail to have
the same kind-making properties. Here they are not identical because the
metaphysical kinds into which they fall exclude one another. A material
substance, for example, could not be an event, or a number, or a
property if the kind, *material substance*, constitutes a fundamental
metaphysical kind.

We want to be able to distinguish these two reasons for being non-
identical: they mark metaphysically important differences. It is not that
Leibniz's Law takes no notice of the fact that, say set S has a property
that cat C does not have; of course it does. It just does not notice that
some properties of sets (and cats) are relevant to the Aristotelian 'what
it is' – question (their membership properties as applied to sets) and
others are not (for example, the property of being liked by me). Thus,
although a correct application of Leibniz's Law to S and C will show
they are distinct, it will not explain why this is of metaphysical interest.
Identity conditions must for this purpose be sort- or kind-specific. This
being so, they must specify properties whose possession in some deter-

minate form by any object of the relevant kind suffices to ensure that it is a single object of that kind. Some people give the name 'criterion of identity' to statements of identity conditions that meet this requirement, to distinguish such statements from the more general principles of identity such as Leibniz's Law.

This requirement in fact covers two conditions. The first of these is sometimes referred to as the condition that a criterion of identity be stronger than Leibniz's Law; and the second is commonly referred to as the condition that a criterion of identity be minimal. The first emphasizes a feature of a criterion of identity that is crucial to it in any ontology where there are objects of more than one kind, namely, that at least one of the properties specified by it should be unique to objects of the kind to which it applies. The general idea behind this condition is that, although it may be true that identical things must share all properties, not all things are capable of having the same sorts of properties.

Why does it matter that we capture this idea? It matters because we may need to justify claims to the effect that objects of a given kind exist. Criteria of identity can be seen to serve this vital function. For example, an event could not share all properties with a substance if events and substances are of metaphysically distinct kinds: there must be some property that events and only events have which determines them to be of that, rather than of some other kind. A criterion of identity, in specifying that property, can help to justify the claim that events form a fundamental metaphysical kind.

The minimality condition emphasizes something else, namely, that the properties specified by a criterion of identity should be only those upon which the identity conditions of objects of the kind to which it applies depend. Such properties should therefore be only a proper sub-set (i.e, set within the set) of all those properties able to be possessed by them. The general idea behind this condition is that many of the properties of objects of any kind are such that they are, even if unique to them as objects of that kind, ones without which they might nevertheless exist and so ones upon which their identity conditions do not depend. That is to say, they are non-essential properties. Many of the so-called relational properties of physical objects and events, such as being Caesar's widow, or being a shooting (of Lincoln), as well as ones that are not obviously so, such as wearing bifocals, being round, or being momentous (as applied to events), are intuitively properties of this kind.

It is important not to confuse these two conditions. At least some properties essential to objects of one kind may also be essential to objects of another kind and so will fail to be unique to either. Events and material substances, for instance, seem equally to be essentially spatio-temporal inasmuch as both are non-repeatable dated particulars (that is, they don't recur; they don't have temporal gaps between the times that they are wholly present). Conversely, certain properties might be unique to objects of a kind without being in any intuitive sense essential to them, as the above examples (e.g., being Caesar's widow, or wearing bifocals indicate. However, the joint satisfaction of the two conditions by a criterion of identity should guarantee that any objects that satisfy the conditions specified by it in some determinate form are thereby guaranteed to be alike with regard to all other properties. For any object that satisfies those conditions satisfies the antecedent of the Principle of the Indiscernibility of Identicals (that objects are identical), and so satisfies its consequent (that those objects are indiscernible with regard to all of their properties).

This suggests that an acceptable criterion of identity for objects of any kind must specify a property or properties, at least one of which is both essential and unique to objects of the kind for which it serves as a criterion. To this end, it must at least state that objects of a given kind are identical if and only if they are the same with regard to their kind-determining properties, where these properties are essential to all members of the relevant kind, or are kind-determining essences. Following Lombard (1986), we can characterize a kind-determining essence as a property, P, which:

(1) it is possible for a thing to have,
(2) is one without which that thing could not exist,[29]

and

(3) is capable of figuring in a minimal criterion of identity for the things that have it.

The point of (2) is to rule out as kind-determining essences properties, like being Socrates, that can be had essentially by individuals that fall into kinds such as the kind, *human being*, but which are not had essentially (because not had at all) by other members of the kind. A real, or kind essence is a property that every object that falls into the kind has essentially. Being of a substance-kind may serve this purpose for material substances, for example.

In effect, this means that any acceptable criterion of identity must specify properties necessary and sufficient (i) to individuate objects of a kind from objects of any other kind, and (ii) to guarantee the numerical identity of any object within that kind, in guaranteeing that whatever satisfies it is a single thing. (These are our original conditions (i) and (ii), set out on p. 58). It must rule out the possibility that any two objects of the same kind should satisfy the conditions specified by the criterion of identity for objects of that kind in the same determinate form. Why? Because the identity relation is a reflexive relation, which can only hold between a thing and itself. It is not only reflexive; it is necessarily reflexive: it cannot just happen to be the case that a thing bears the relation of identity to itself and to no other. So a criterion of identity cannot allow that two things might satisfy the conditions necessary and sufficient for identity. If, for instance, events are identical if and only if they share all the same causes and effects, then it cannot be possible that two events share precisely the same causal history.[30]

So, a criterion of identity should take the following form:

> Necessarily, for any objects x and y, if x is of kind K and y is of kind K, then x is identical with y if and only if x and y are the same with regard to F.[31]

where K stands for some kind, such as the kind, *substance*, or the kind, *event*, and the F is a kind-determining property or properties, indiscernibility with respect to which, in some determinate form, is both necessary and sufficient for x to be the same object as y. The presence of the modal operator, 'necessarily', is simply to signal that a criterion of identity has the status of a necessary truth: that if it is true, this does not just happen to be so. It could not be false because the conditions mark what it is to be a single object of that kind; they specify properties that are both unique and essential to that object's being the unique thing it is.[32] Nothing could fail to satisfy those conditions in some determinate form without failing to be an object of that kind altogether.

Here is an example of such a criterion of identity for events: Necessarily, events are identical if and only if they occupy exactly the same spatio-temporal position. Here the kind K is the kind, *event*, and the properties that are taken to be the kind-determining ones are positional (i.e., spatio-temporal) ones. The condition on event identity is that anything that satisfies it not only has positional properties but has them in some determinate form. Any event that is self-identical cannot be discernible with regard to the spatio-temporal position it has (no event can have the determinate spatio-temporal position that it itself lacks).

Any criterion of identity that is both stronger than Leibniz's Law and minimal will also be both epistemologically useful and informative. It will be useful at least to the extent that it specifies properties of objects of a kind such that, if those objects are discernible with respect to these in some determinate form, then they are guaranteed to be distinct. An acceptable criterion can therefore be used to answer at least some questions of identity and distinctness regarding objects of a given kind. For instance, it can be used to individuate objects of that kind from one another. For example, if two events do not share the same spatio-temporal position, then they are distinct.

It will also be informative to the extent that it says something about the nature of objects of a given kind: about what it is to be an object of that kind, as opposed to an object of another kind. So it can tell us what kinds of properties of things are relevant to answering questions of identity, when those things fall into metaphysical kinds. In doing so, it can help us to see that the reason why Leibniz's Law fails to be satisfied when the objects in question are of distinct metaphysical kinds, say, one is a substance and the other is an event, differs from the reason why it fails to be satisfied when the objects in question are of the same kind. Since criteria of identity are kind-specific, it could not be that objects of distinct metaphysical kinds might be identical. And so it could not be that the antecedent of Leibniz's Law is satisfied in such a case. Nor could it be that the consequent is satisfied; since x and y cannot have all properties in common (x, but not y, will lack the property of being an event, for example). And that is why Leibniz's Law must come out true.

Notes

1   Strawson in fact argues for a view that is stronger than this, and stronger in two ways. First, he claims that singular terms or names function are paradigmatically the means by which particulars – individual things such as physical objects – are introduced into discourse. Second, he claims that, since particulars are basic or fundamental to our ontology, and no collection of predicates, however large, can ensure uniqueness of reference, i.e., ensure that one and only one object satisfies them, a natural language without singular terms is impossible. We discuss the second claim later in this section.

2   Note that although Strawson holds this view, it is part of his metaphysics, and has nothing to do with founding a criterion of ontological commitment. For, suppose that he is wrong, and in fact an ontology of universals is the correct one. It could still be that our commitment to universals is effected by the use of singular terms in subject-predicate discourse. In fact, this is one motivation for thinking that there are universals. So the criterion of ontological commitment that says that our ontological commitments are revealed by our use of singular terms in subject-predicate discourse is – and should be – completely neutral as to the ontology that that criterion may reveal us to be committed to.

3   But, again, this claim about ontological priority is part of Strawson's meta-
    physics and is not what founds the criterion of ontological commitment. See
    note 2.

4   This may seem inconsistent with the view, noted in chapter 1, that 'The
    structure [which the metaphysician] seeks does not readily display itself on
    the surface of language, but lies submerged. He must abandon his only sure
    guide when the guide cannot take him as far as he wishes to go' (Strawson
    1959, pp. 9f.). But recall that the distinction of interest for Strawson is
    between how we appear to think, on the one hand, and how we really think,
    on the other. This might be captured by paraphrases of natural language
    sentences that do not depart radically from their surface structure in per-
    mitting, say, paraphrases that lead to different ontological commitments, in
    contrast to the paraphrases that revisionary metaphysics might permit.

5   This is Quine's metaphysical view. It does – and should – not have anything
    to do with founding a criterion of ontological commitment for reasons given
    in note 2 above.

6   Quine puts the problem in the form of a question: 'Nonbeing must in some
    sense be, otherwise what is it that there is not?' (1964a, pp. 1–2).

7   Russell in fact had something like this in mind when he developed his Theory
    of Descriptions (1905). He maintained that a true name (e.g., a term such
    as 'Margaret Thatcher'), which purports to uniquely identify a single object,
    guarantees the existence of its bearer. The existence of apparently non-
    denoting singular terms, such as 'Pegasus' and 'The Present King of France'
    posed a problem for this view. The problem was a version of the problem
    of Plato's Beard: if, in order to significantly deny the existence of such enti-
    ties using these terms, their bearers must exist, we must in such cases be
    both asserting that they exist and asserting (or presupposing) that they do
    not exist. Russell's solution was to contextually analyse, i.e., analyse in the
    context of the sentence, the apparent name by means of a set of transfor-
    mation rules, or contextual definitions, in such a way as to yield a sentence
    that no longer contains a name. Rather, it contains a bound variable of
    quantification (a bound variable being a variable – a sort of pronoun –
    attached to a quantifier – a term such as 'some', 'no', 'every') and a con-
    junction of predicates that either are satisfied or not by an object. Thus, for
    example, 'Pegasus is a winged horse' gets paraphrased in context, or con-
    textually defined, as 'Something is such that it is Pegasus' (or 'Something is
    such that it pegasizes'), and is winged and is a horse and no more than one
    thing is such that it is Pegasus and is winged and is a horse. (The idea behind
    the second conjunct is to make explicit that names purport to uniquely iden-
    tify the objects that they refer to or pick out.)

    One virtue of this analysis is that the troublesome name is contextually
    rephrased in such a way that the result is a sentence that is either true or
    false, and no difficulty arises over significantly – indeed, truly – denying the
    existence of entities using non-denoting singular terms.

8   The existential quantifier is formalized as '($\exists$ ...)', which, when it is
    attached to a variable, such as 'x', is said to bind that variable. When such

a quantifier is attached to an open sentence, such as 'x is red', the result is an existentially quantified sentence, '$(\exists x)(x$ is red)', which is true if and only if there is at least one thing in the domain of discourse that is red. The universal quantifier is formalized as '$(\ldots)$' or '$(\forall \ldots)$', which again, when it is attached to a variable, is said to bind it. When this quantifier is attached to an open sentence, such as 'x is red', the result is a universally quantified sentence, '$(\forall x)(x$ is red)', which is true if and only everything in the domain of discourse is such that it is red.

9　But Quine might be wrong here. 'Socrates is wise' and 'The unique socratizer is wise' express different propositions, or, to put it differently, if one eschews talk of propositions, the sentences behave differently in modal contexts, contexts in which there is talk of possibility or necessity. Socrates could not have failed to be Socrates. But the unique socratizer could have failed to be Socrates, unless 'the unique socratizer' means 'the one and only thing that is identical with Socrates'. But then it seems that we have re-introduced the genuine singular term. Quine would not be impressed with this argument since he rejects *de re* modalities, true statements about what might or must be the case which do not depend on how the case is described. But Quine might be wrong about whether there are such modalities; and metaphysicians in general do not reject them. Still, there are other arguments for Quine's criterion that do not depend on this point; for one, see the final paragraphs of this section (pp. 54–6).

10　Not all theories are axiomatized. So perhaps this version of the criterion is too narrow. It might be weakened by adding, after 'theorems and axioms', something like 'or basic laws or principles'. Quine actually formulates his criterion as follows:

> We are convicted of a particular ontological presupposition if, and only if, the alleged presuppositum has to be reckoned among the entities over which our variables range in order to render one of our affirmations true (Quine 1964a, p. 13)

and

> An entity is assumed by a theory if and only if it must be counted among the values of the variables in order that the statements affirmed in the theory be true. (1964b, p. 103)

Note that both versions involve the use of *modal* terms (such as 'must'), which create contexts that are non-extensional (see the discussion in the text and note 12 for an explanation of this term). Quine eschews modal talk because it creates contexts that are non-extensional for reasons discussed later on in the present section. But it will become apparent from the discussion in the text that non-extensional formulations of the criterion are unavoidable. It should be noted that some (van Inwagen 2003) take exception to the claim that Quine has *any* criterion of ontological commitment, claiming that at most he has a strategy or a technique that can be applied in ontological debates.

11 For someone who rejects this way of determining what it is to be an object, along with the Strawsonian, reference-based one, see Lowe (1998).

12 More precisely, a context '...x...' is extensional if and only if any expression in it obeys what is known as the principle of extensionality. This principle can be formulated precisely as follows:

> Given any sentential contexts '...x...' and '...y...', if '...x...' differs from '...y...' only in that the former contains one or more occurrences of 'x' where the latter contains 'y', and if 'x = y' is true, then 'x' and 'y' are intersubstitutable *salva veritate* (without change in truth-value).

13 In Quine's case the quantifiers in the language of the predicate calculus are understood objectually; they are understood as ranging over objects that can either satisfy or fail to satisfy sentences in which those quantifiers appear. If there are no objects in the domain associated with a theory, then there will be no objects for the existentially bound variables to range over, and the theory will be false.

An alternative, and less standard reading of the quantifiers, is to interpret them substitutionally. Here, instead of reading a quantified sentence like 'Something is wise' as 'There is some object such that it is wise', which is true if and only if there is or exists at least one wise object, we read that sentence as 'There is some true substitution instance of 'x' in "x is wise"', where a substitution instance is one in which a singular term, usually a name, replaces the variable, 'x'. This is called 'substitutional quantification' because names are substituted for bound variables. Many who prefer the substitutional reading of the quantifiers over the objectual reading do so because a theory expressed in this language has no commitments to the existence of any objects in any universe. One reason why Quine prefers the more standard, objectual reading of the quantifiers is that the substitutional reading is problematic in domains where there is a non-denumerable infinity of objects, where it is in principle impossible to provide all objects in the domain with names. Here, finding an equivalent sentence, substitutionally interpreted, of a sentence expressing a truth about all of the objects in that domain, is problematic, since there will not be enough names to go round. Substitutional interpretation of the quantifiers is also problematic from the point of view of determining whether the theory, expressed canonically, is true. For the question arises, how do we determine whether there is a true substitution instance of a given existentially quantified sentence? It looks as though, in order to answer this question, we need to distinguish names from other, non-referring expressions, and, further, to distinguish the apparent from the real names (i.e., those names that have only the grammatical form of a name from those that have both the form and the semantic function of referring). But how do we do this without talking of domains of objects associated with those names? For more on the advantages vs. the disadvantages of substitutional interpretations of the quantifiers over objectual readings, see Haack (1978).

14 This account of the problems with Quine's criterion draws on Campbell's (1976).

15 Put formally, $(\exists x)(x$ is a unicorn $\&\ T$ is committed to $x)$.

16 Or, perhaps, 'Something is such that it pegasizes', if the name 'Pegasus' in predicate position in the original is objectionable. (However, for problems associated with this, see note 9.) Put formally, '$(\exists x)(x$ is Pegasus)' is assigned the truth-value, true, in T.

17 But this might be unfair. Properties, not being particulars, are not the sorts of things that can be wholly and completely in only one place at a given time. We shall return to this point in chapter 6.

18 This parallels Quinton's (1973) distinction between what he calls 'the problem of individuation' and 'the problem of identity'. See also Lowe (1998, 2003) and Wiggins (2001).

19 We presume here and throughout the remainder of this book the Aristotelian view that every item falls into some kind or other. For recent defences of this view, see Lowe (1998), Wiggins (2001), and Loux (2002).

20 For an excellent discussion of metaphysical kinds in metaphysics that is similar to this, see Lawrence Lombard (1986, chapter II).

21 Even this is not quite right and requires qualification, since not every kind into which an object may fall is essential to it, in the sense that that object could not fail to be of that kind without also failing to exist. The kind, *cat*, for example, may be essential to my cat's being the thing it is, but the kind, *domesticated animal*, may not. It is the most basic ontological categories of object that are of concern to the metaphysician; those into which any object must fall in order for there to be objects at all. Of course, this assumes what has already been made explicit in note 19, namely (the Aristotelian view) that all objects fall into some sort or kind.

22 Put formally, the principle is this: $(x)(y)((Fx \leftrightarrow Fy) \rightarrow x = y)$.

23 The Principle of the Identity of Indiscernibles is, however, detachable from the bundle theory of substances, and it is true or false independently of that theory. This is important since the principle is of interest regardless of one's interest in the bundle theory. After all, the principle, with no restrictions on what is to count as a property, is trivially true: let one such property be the property of being identical with Socrates, a property that only Socrates can have. Just how to restrict it is an interesting enterprise in itself. Thanks here to Larry Lombard.

24 Put formally, the principle is: $(x)(y)(x = y \rightarrow (Fx \leftrightarrow Fy))$.

25 See, for example, Wiggins (2001).

26 See Locke (1975, Book II, section xxxIII.6), where he discusses substance as a *substratum*. This assumes a traditional interpretation of Locke's views. See also Bergmann (1964, 1967). Note again that the principle is detachable from the theory of substances associated with it and is true or false independently of it.

27   Put formally: $(x)(y)(x = y \leftrightarrow (Fx \leftrightarrow Fy))$.

28   This is an adaptation of Cartwright's (1971) formulation. He notes that it is the conjunction of two claims. These are (adapted): (1) For all expressions 'a' and 'b', '$a = b$' expresses a true proposition if substitution of 'b' for 'a' is truth preserving, and (2) For all expressions 'a' and 'b', '$a = b$' expresses a true proposition only if substitution of 'b' for 'a' is truth preserving; and he points out that it is (2) that is often referred to as 'The Principle of Substitutivity' (p. 120). Quine formulates this as follows: 'given a true statement of identity, one of its two terms may be substituted for the other in any true statement and the result will be true'. (Quine 1964c, p. 139).

29   That is, is such that it is necessarily true that if some entity has P, then it is necessary that if that entity exists, then it has P, where the sense of 'necessarily' in use is that employed in a Kripke-type semantics for quantified S5 in which the Barcan formula fails.

30   Note that this is not to say that an event might not have had a causal history other than the one it in fact has. This is an issue concerning, not kind essences of events, properties that determine them to be of the kind, event, but rather an issue concerning individual essences of events, properties that some events can have while other events lack them altogether.

31   Put formally: $\Box(x)(y)(K(x) \ \& \ K(y) \rightarrow (x = y \leftrightarrow (Fx \leftrightarrow y)))$.

32   Why then is that operator missing from statements of the two Principles of the Identity of Indiscernibles and the Indiscernibility of Identicals, and from Leibniz's Law? Probably because these principles are assumed to have the status of necessary truths, if truths at all. For example, one common argument to the conclusion that the Principle of the Identity of Indiscernibles is false is that it is not necessarily true. See Loux 1978.

Suggested Further Reading

Burtt, E. A. (1963): 'Descriptive Metaphysics'. In *Mind* 72, 18–39.

Campbell, K. (1976): *Metaphysics: An Introduction*. Encino, Calif.: Dickenson. chapters 8–12.

Cartwright, R. (1971): 'Identity and Substitutivity'. In M. Munitz 1971, pp. 119–33.

Hookway, C. (1988): *Quine: Language, Experience and Reality*. Cambridge: Polity, chapters 1 and 5.

Lombard, L. B. (1986): *Events: A Metaphysical Study*. London: Routledge & Kegan Paul, chapters 1 and 2.

Loux, M. (2002): *Metaphysics: A Contemporary Introduction*. 2nd edn. London: Routledge, Introduction.

Lowe, E. J. (1989a): *Kinds of Being: A Study of Individuation, Identity and the Logic of Sortal Terms*. Oxford: Blackwell, chapter 2.

Lowe, E. J. (1989b): 'What is a Criterion of Identity?'. In *Philosophical Quarterly* 39, 1–21.

Lowe, E. J. (1998): *The Possibility of Metaphysics*. Oxford: Oxford University Press, chapter 2.

Mei, Tsu-Lin (1961): 'Subject and Predicate: A Grammatical Preliminary'. In *Philosophical Review* 70, 153–75.

Munitz, M. (ed.) (1971): *Identity and Individuation*. New York: New York University Press.

Quine, W. V. O. (1964a): 'On What There Is'. In Quine 1964f, pp. 1–19.

Quine, W. V. O. (1964f): *From a Logical Point of View*. 2nd edn. Cambridge, Mass.: Harvard University Press.

Quine, W. V. O. (1969a): 'Speaking of Objects'. In Quine 1969b, pp. 1–25.

Quine, W. V. O. (1969b): *Ontological Relativity and Other Essays*. New York: Columbia University Press.

Quinton, A. (1973): *The Nature of Things*. London: Routledge & Kegan Paul, Introduction and chapter 1.

Strawson, P. F. (1974a): *Subject and Predicate in Logic and Grammar*. London: Methuen, chapter 1.

Strawson, P. F. (1974b): *Freedom and Resentment and Other Essays*. London: Methuen.

Strawson, P. F. (1976): 'On Understanding the Structure of One's Language'. In Strawson 1974b. Reprinted in Evans and McDowell (eds) 1976, pp. 189–98.

van Inwagen, P. (2003): 'Existence, Ontological Commitment, and Fictional Entities'. In van Inwagen and Zimmerman (eds) 2003, pp. 131–57.

van Inwagen, P. and Zimmerman, D. (eds) (2003): *The Oxford Handbook to Metaphysics*. Oxford: Oxford University Press.

Whorf, B. J. (1956): *Language, Thought & Reality*. Cambridge, Mass.: MIT Press.

Wiggins, D. (2001): *Sameness and Substance*. New edn. Cambridge: Cambridge University Press, chapters 2 and 3.

Part II
Particulars

3

Material Substances

Up to now we have been concerned with meta-theoretical questions about the nature of metaphysics and the principles by means of which metaphysical discussions can proceed. In this and the next part of the book we will make use of the conception of metaphysics and the principles and criteria of identity outlined in the last two chapters to do some metaphysics. More precisely, we will use Quine's criterion of ontological commitment and principles and criteria of identity as tools to aid us in discussing metaphysical issues concerning our own ontology, the ontology expressed in English. In this part we will consider various categories of particulars, beginning with that of material substances, and then turning to those of persons and events, respectively. We'll consider the possible motivations for thinking that there are particulars of these kinds, various theories of their nature, and what relations these kinds might bear to one another. In the next part, we will consider whether there are universals, and if so, what these might be like and how they might relate to particulars.

Our Ontological Commitment to Material Substances

In our everyday thought and talk about the world, we commonly refer to individual material things such as human beings, apples, cats, and trees. We also employ sentences that involve quantification over them, such as 'There are cats', 'Some cats are larger than others', 'There is a tree over there', and so on. These individuals, and others like them, are favoured both in our discourse and epistemically; they are the things we most easily know because they are the things we see, touch, smell, and hear. No doubt they are favoured in discourse because of this special epistemic position they occupy in our knowledge of the world.

Material things fall into the ontological category of substances, and we believe both that these things exist, and that they have a nature.[1] We think of material substances as taking up space, being capable of movement and other sorts of change, and, because of this, persisting through time. We also think of them as contingent entities, as things that might have failed to exist, and as *continuants* – things that continue to exist, or persist, wholly and completely from one time to another throughout the changes that they undergo, so that they survive change while remaining the very same things. In short, we take material substances to be individual things that *endure* rather than *perdure*, in that they take up space and persist through time, as opposed to taking up, or lasting through, time (as, perhaps, events do) (Lowe 1998; Haslinger 2003; Elder 2004).[2] Their properties characterize them in ways that mark them off from things of other kinds, such as events (like explosions and snowfalls), and other objects (like numbers), and the determinate forms that these properties take in individual substances seem to make them the unique individuals that they are. We think, for instance, that the particular spatio-temporal positions that individual substances occupy are unique to them, and so help to mark them off, or distinguish them, from one another.

Paradigmatic examples of material substances are apples, trees, human beings, and tigers, which are all natural kinds of things, kinds in nature. However, we also commonly recognize other things as substances, such as tables, chairs, cars and clocks. These are members of artefactual kinds, since they are artefacts. On the rough conception of substances described above, these too count as substances. But are they? If we want to say that they are (or that they are not!), we need a theory that can tell us what it is for a substance to be a material substance, which we can then use to show that artefactual kinds either are or are not kinds of material substances.

What we need, in fact, is a metaphysical theory of substances, one that will tell us what, fundamentally, a material substance is. Such an account will tell us, amongst other things, how a substance is related to its properties, and whether it could exist without some, most, or even all of them. It will also tell us what properties are essential and unique to substances, i.e., which properties are ones whose possession, in some determinate form, makes them the unique individual things that they are. As we saw in chapter 2, a theory of entities belonging to a given kind will, by telling us what is unique and essential to being a member of that kind, entail a criterion of identity for entities of that kind. And this will help to justify the claim that entities of a given metaphysical kind – in this case, substances – exist.[3]

In this chapter, we will be looking at three theories of substances: the bundle theory, the bare substratum theory, and the essentialist theory, respectively, and evaluate their prospects as satisfactory theories of material substances. We shall see that the first two of these theories suffer from crippling objections. In the light of these, we will settle on and defend the third, the essentialist theory.

All three of the theories to be considered have a particularly interesting connection with the two principles of identity discussed in chapter 2, namely, the Principle of the Identity of Indiscernibles and the Principle of the Indiscernibility of Identicals. The importance of these principles, and the extent to which they are simply principles of identity, so fundamental to the concept of an object in general that they are perhaps better viewed as definitions, will emerge in the discussion of the inadequacies of the first two of the three theories just mentioned, the bundle theory and the bare substratum theory.

All three theories under discussion presume, rather than argue for, the view that there are material substances. What we will be doing in the remaining sections of this chapter is deploying the meta-theoretical principles that concern identity and essence, and not those that concern existence, from chapter 2. That is, what we will be doing is 'hypothetical metaphysics' – determining what substances would be like if there were any. But there is a connection between this and the matter of existence, given the foregoing paragraphs. Justifying the claim that there are material substances involves arriving at an adequate criterion of identity for them. An adequate theory of substances will entail a criterion of identity for them. In doing so, it will help to justify the claim that substances exist.

The Bundle Theory and the Principle of the Identity of Indiscernibles

The bundle theory of substances trades on the intuition, noted above, that there is an intimate relationship between a substance and its properties. Individual substances are the things they are because of the specific forms their properties take in them. Hence, for example, we think that this apple is different from that dog because, although both are relatively solid, are capable of change, and persist through time and occupy space, they have different chemical and molecular constitutions, different shapes and sizes, are capable of quite different kinds of change, and occupy different spatio-temporal positions.

The bundle theory exploits this intuition and the thought, associated with it, that our understanding or grip on what substances are is so firmly connected with their associated properties that we have no real conception of what substances could be that is independent of those properties. According to the theory, so intimate is this relationship between substances and their associated properties that they are nothing 'over and above' their properties. That is to say, a substance is determined and exhausted by the properties with which it is typically associated and which it possesses. Further, the sense in which a substance possesses or has properties is that it is *constituted* by them. Thus, for example, this apple is entirely and exhaustively constituted by its properties of being red, being round, being solid, having a determinate spatio-temporal position, and so on.[4]

This makes the bundle theory a reductive theory, and a surprising one from the point of view of common sense. Our ordinary unreflective talk and thought suggests that substances are one thing, their properties another. We tend to suppose on the basis of it that although substances possess properties they are distinct from them. They are, so to speak, things characterized, rather than things that characterize. But if the bundle theory is true, this unreflective view is false. For, according to the theory, there are not two sorts of things here: a substance, on the one hand, and the properties it bears or possesses, on the other. The nature, existence conditions, and identity conditions of a substance are all to be given in terms of the properties that constitute it. Moreover, there is no further element that constitutes it that is *not* a property. It is in this sense that the theory reduces substances to their properties.[5] The bundle theory has had staunch supporters in the history of philosophy in the rationalist thought of Leibniz (1998), the British empiricist works of Berkeley (1996) and Hume (1967), and, more recently, in the work of A. J. Ayer (1953).

Since substances are nothing but the bundles, collections, or bunches of properties that constitute them, substances are identical with the bundles, collections, or bunches of properties that constitute them.[6] Anything that had all and only the properties possessed by a given substance would be that very substance. So the bundle theory requires unconditional commitment to the truth of the Principle of the Identity of Indiscernibles: that things that are alike with respect to all of their properties are identical.[7] It follows, then, that substances are distinct only if they differ (are unlike) with respect to at best a single property, that is, if one of them has a feature that the other lacks.

Further, the bundle theory, if true, is necessarily true. Since, according to it, there is nothing more to a substance than its properties – a substance just is identical with the totality of properties that constitute it – it is impossible for there to be two substances – two bundles – with exactly the same constituent properties. This being so, the bundle theory requires commitment, not just to the truth, but also to the necessary truth of the Principle of the Identity of Indiscernibles. For, a necessary truth – a truth that cannot be otherwise, that could not fail to be true – cannot entail a contingent one, one that could be otherwise, or could fail to be true. Not only is it the case, then, that, necessarily, if the bundle theory is true, then the Principle of the Identity of Indiscernibles is true. It is also the case that, if the bundle theory is true, then the Principle of the Identity of Indiscernibles is necessarily true. So, it cannot just happen to be that things that are indiscernible with regard to their properties are identical. It must be *impossible* for there to be two numerically distinct but indiscernible (indiscernible with respect to properties) substances.

One can be committed to the necessary truth of the Principle of the Identity of Indiscernibles because one is committed to the necessary truth of the bundle theory, or one can be committed to the necessary truth of the bundle theory because one is committed to the necessary truth of the Principle of the Identity of Indiscernibles. Historically speaking, both of these alternatives have been pursued. The second alternative is evident in the work of Leibniz (1998), the first in the work of Hume (1967), and Ayer (1953).

Leibniz was committed to the necessary truth of the bundle theory because he was committed to the necessary truth of the Principle of the Identity of Indiscernibles. He believed that the view that substances are other than their properties was logically incoherent.[8] This view, which he (and others) attributed to the British Empiricist Locke, is motivated by the assumption that properties cannot exist 'unsupported', or on their own, an assumption that has commonly thought to have been made by many philosophers, amongst them Aristotle and Descartes.[9] This assumption grounds the distinction between substances, on the one hand, and their attributes, or properties, on the other, by motivating commitment to the existence of substances as entities in which properties can inhere, or in which properties can exist, although they are, in themselves, property-less.

Leibniz, however, rejected the assumption, and with it the distinction between substance and property. As he saw it, to distinguish between a substance and its properties in order to provide a thing or entity in which properties can inhere leads necessarily to the absurd conclusion that the substance itself must be a truly characterless non-entity. That is, it is nothing rather than something. Since the distinction between substances and their properties leads, not to the conclusion that there are two sorts of thing, but rather, to the conclusion that there is only one sort of thing, the other being a non-entity, there must be no further element or component to a substance than the properties that constitute it. Given the necessary truth of the Principle of the Identity of Indiscernibles, there cannot be two substances with exactly the same properties.

Hume was committed to the necessary truth of the Principle of the Identity of Indiscernibles for rather different reasons. Being a strict empiricist, he was committed to the view that we can be justified in thinking that something exists only if it can be a possible object of sensory experience.[10] If this view is correct, it rules out the possibility of a property-less substance, one completely devoid of properties such as shape, size, and colour, since nothing that answers to this description could ever in principle be the object of sensory experience. It is an 'intellectual fiction', something whose existence could not be justified on empiricist grounds.

In short, commitment to the view that only what can be an object of possible sensory experience can exist eliminates the possibility of distinguishing between substance and attribute, leaving only one alternative, namely the bundle view. Since there can be no more to the numerical identity of a substance than the totality of properties that constitutes it, there cannot be two such totalities with exactly the same properties. Empiricists who are committed to the necessary truth of the bundle theory are thus committed to the necessary truth of the Principle of the Identity of Indiscernibles.

So, the bundle theory of substances can be motivated either by broadly logical grounds or by broadly empiricist grounds. Both of these grounds are intuitively very strong, especially those deriving from broadly empiricist considerations.[11] Nevertheless, the bundle theory suffers from serious objections. Let us see how serious they are.

Problems with the Bundle Theory

The bundle theory is intuitively very appealing. As mentioned earlier, we think of substances in terms of the properties that we suppose them to have: that they take up space and persist through time, that they are capable of movement, that they change, and that they persist through change, where change involves the acquisition or loss of a property over time. Further, we tend to identify and distinguish between individual substances by means of their properties. It is hard to believe that they are not intimately connected with, if not completely and exhaustively determined by, their properties. Despite all this, however, the theory suffers from a number of objections, some of which are devastating. We consider these in order of severity, beginning with the least serious.

Objection One: The Contingency of Substances

The first and arguably least serious objection to the bundle theory is that it cannot account for the contingency of substance. The objection is that substances are contingent things or entities, in that, although they exist, it is possible that they should have failed to exist. Properties, in contrast, are necessary things or entities; if they exist at all they cannot but exist. It is not possible that they could have failed to exist. Since substances might have failed to exist, but properties could not have failed to exist, substances cannot be identical with their associated properties.[12]

Put like this, the objection seems to commit a fallacy of composition – a mistake in logical reasoning that is based on the erroneous assumption that every property of the things that constitute a thing is a property of the thing as well. A substance is a single thing. Thus it is not identical with its properties, taken collectively, since a single thing cannot be identical with many things, and these properties are many things. A substance is, rather, wholly *constituted* by its properties. Suppose, then, that it is true that properties are necessary entities. Still, it does not follow that the bundle theory is committed to the view that substances are necessary entities. In order for that to be so, it would have to be true that every property of the things that constitute a thing is a property of the thing as well. But this is false: every large object is constituted by small parts, for example, and every red object is constituted by colourless parts. So it does not follow that because the constituents of substances are necessary things, substances themselves are necessary things.

However, it is not clear that all versions of the bundle theory commit this fallacy.[13] It depends how one understands the 'bundle' metaphor. Suppose, for example, that one takes the bundle theory to be stating that substances are identical with bundles of properties in the sense that they are identical with sets of properties. Then it is plausible to suppose that these sets are necessary things, even if is doubtful that *all* sets are necessary things. It may be doubtful whether a set that has contingent things as members, say the set of all apples, is a necessary thing (since if there were no apples there would not be the set of all apples). But similar doubts cannot arise for sets, all and only of whose members are necessary things. Or suppose that the bundle theory is understood as saying that substances are identical with bundles of properties in the sense that they are identical with conjunctions of properties, properties formed by conjoining or combining all of the properties that they have or possess. Thus, for example, if substance S has properties, D, E, F, and G, the bundle theory says that S is identical with the property formed by conjoining properties, D, E, F, and G, the 'conjunctive' property,

$D\&E\&F\&G$. Then (given that properties are necessary things), it is guaranteed that S, and substances in general, are necessary things. One might think that 'conjunctive' properties are strange kinds of things, and perhaps they are. But if substances can have properties such as being red and being round, why can't they have such properties as being red *and* round? And if these aren't really properties, why aren't they? Our intuitions aren't really firm enough to decide the matter one way or the other, and so not strong enough to dismiss this possibility out of hand.

So there do seem to be ways of understanding the 'bundle' metaphor that allow this objection to be voiced without committing the fallacy of composition, and the objection does need to be addressed. Moreover, it needs to be addressed in a way that preserves the strong intuition that individual substances – this dog, that tree, that person – though they do happen to exist, might not have done so. Indeed, we think that there might not have been *any* dogs, *any* people, or *any* trees. The reason may be that we know – or think we know – that they actually come into and go out of existence, and since what is actual is possible it is possible that they should fail to exist. To say that it is possible that they should fail to exist is just to say that they are not necessary existents.

What kinds of things *are* necessary existents? And why is it not possible for a necessary thing or entity to fail to exist? Paradigmatic examples of necessary things are items like sets (whose only members are sets, or other necessary things), numbers, and, as it happens, properties. One way of making sense of talk about necessary things is in terms of talk about necessary truths and a kind of heuristic, viz. talk of possible worlds. Certain truths, such as '3 is prime', or '*Red* is a property', seem to be ones that are, if true at all, necessarily true. A necessary truth is one that *could not* be false. It is true not only in this, the actual, world, but in every possible world. A possible world is a kind of complex state of affairs, one that could have obtained, even if it does not obtain in the actual world.[14] Thus, Lycan says,

> There are complex situations or states of affairs that are unreal, such as Napoleon's having won at Waterloo or my being President of the United States. Indeed, there are whole non-existent universes – imaginary alternatives to the actual world we inhabit. Such universes are called 'possible worlds'. (Of course our own world, the real one, is a possible world too, but it is no *merely* possible world, because it is actual.)
>
> Philosophers speak seriously of 'other' possible worlds for any number of reasons: by positing non-actual worlds, we may give illuminating semantics for modal logics, identifying *possibility* with truth at some possible world and *necessity* with truth at every world. (Lycan 1998, p. 84)

Necessary truths, are, if true, true in all possible worlds. One way of explaining how they could be true in all possible worlds is this. '3 is prime' and 'Red is a property' are true in all possible worlds because the number, 3, and the property, red, exist, if they exist at all, in all possible worlds. So too do the properties, being prime, and being a property. Further, if the number 3 exists at all, it must be prime; it could not fail to be prime without failing to exist altogether. Similarly for red and being a property. So, if 3, and red, are necessary existents, then, since they cannot exist without being prime and being a property, respectively, '3 is prime' and 'Red is a property', if true at all, are true in all possible worlds.

Put precisely, then, the objection is this. If, as the bundle theory states, substances are simply 'bundles' of properties, in the sense of being identical with things (bundles) that are wholly constituted by those properties, then whatever properties are truly attributable to the one must be truly attributable to the other. That is to say, substances and the bundles of properties with which they are said to be identical must have exactly the same properties. For, as the Principle of the Indiscernibility of Identicals tells us, it is necessarily true that if things are identical, then they share all properties. But we know that substances do not have the property of being a necessary being, whereas bundles of properties do have the property of being a necessary being. So each property that constitutes the bundle of properties that makes a substance a substance has the property of being a necessary being.[15] Further, since substances are wholly constituted by properties, any bundle or collection of properties must itself have the property of being a necessary being. This is because something that is wholly constituted by necessary beings must itself be a necessary being. So, since bundles of properties have the property of being necessary beings, and substances lack this property, the bundle theory is false.

The bundle theorist can respond to this objection in one or the other of two ways. The first is to deny that a bundle of necessary beings is itself a necessary being. An obvious way of going about this would be to deny that 'bundle' is to be interpreted as meaning either 'set' or 'conjunction' – or anything else that would allow us to infer, from the fact that each of the properties that constitute the bundle with which a substance is identical is a necessary thing, that the bundle itself is a necessary thing without thereby committing the fallacy of composition. Then one might respond to the objection as follows. Suppose that we think that substance S is constituted entirely by the properties D, E and F. Of course, these latter properties exist necessarily. But this does not mean that S exists necessarily, since it is not sufficient for the existence of any substance that the properties in its bundle exist. Those properties must bear some relation to each other in order for them to constitute an object. Specifically, they must be co-exemplified. Roughly speaking, properties are co-exemplified when they are exemplified in the same place.[16]

However, this response looks like it will lead to an infinite regress in the account, for it now seems that substance S is constituted not just by D, E, and F, but also by the relation of co-exemplification. That is, the bundle that is S contains D, E, F, and the relation of co-exemplification. But surely D, and E, and F, and the relation of co-exemplification all exist necessarily (if properties do). And so it would appear that the existence of S is necessary.

It doesn't help to reply that the substance S exists only if all the properties in its bundle are co-exemplified, and that is a contingent matter. Thus, the bundle that is S contains D, E, F, the relation of co-exemplification (that relate D, E, and F), and *another* relation that contingently relates D, E, F, and the relation of co-exemplification. But again, surely, D, and E, and F, and the relation of co-exemplification that relates D, E, and F, *and* the relation that contingently relates D, E, F, and the relation of co-exemplification, all exist necessarily (if properties do). And so it would appear that the existence of S is necessary. And so on, and so on, into infinity. Since the attempt to avoid the objection leads at each stage to the postulation of another property (a relation), whose existence is necessary, the original objection can be repeated, and this just shows that the original attempt to avoid the objection fails.

However, there is a second, more decisive response to the objection, and that is to claim that it fails to appreciate the sense of the term 'property' in which it might be true to say that substances are identical with bundles of their properties. Although bundle theorists are indeed committed to the claim that substances are identical with bundles of their properties, there is more than one way to understand that claim because of this ambiguity in the term, 'property'.

On one way of understanding it, the properties that constitute substances are understood to be abstract universal things. They are abstract in the sense that many of them can be in the same place at the same time (as when, for example, the properties of being red and being round are both in the same place as the red round ball currently sitting on my desk), and universal in that they can be exemplified in many places at the same time, as when, for example, both the red ball and the red cup on my desk exemplify one and the same property, red. These entities, such as red and round, are different from the things that exemplify or instantiate them, things like red, round apples. When we say such things as 'the property, green, is not the property, red, although both are colour properties', we are talking about properties as abstract universal things.

Whether the property, red, or the property, round, exists, is a necessary matter. It either exists necessarily, or it does not exist at all. However, whether the property, red, is exemplified or instantiated in this world, say, in this apple, is a contingent matter.[17] The property, red, could have failed to have been instantiated in or exemplified by this apple, in which case this apple would have failed to be red. That is to say, it would have failed to instantiate or exemplify the property, red. What this amounts to is that this apple could have failed to *be* (amongst other things) an instantiation or exemplification of the property, red. What it suggests is not that individual substances, such as apples, are literally constituted by abstract entities such as the property, red. Rather, it suggests that they are constituted by the particular instantiations of, or instances of those properties – what we might call 'particularized properties', or tropes, such as redness-in-place-*p*-at-time-*t*.[18]

This provides us with a second way of understanding the claim that substances are bundles of properties. Individual substances, such as apples and trees, are identical with bundles of properties, where these are construed as tropes (Martin 1980, Simons 1994, Bacon 1995, Heil 2003). Tropes are abstract entities, at least in the sense that more than one can be in the same place at the same time (e.g., tropes of redness and roundness). They're not universals, however; they have unique (i.e., particular) locations. And they are contingent things or entities. Since it is a contingent matter whether any trope of a given property exists, it is also a contingent matter whether any particular substance exists.

There is a further sense in which substances are contingently existing things, on the trope view. It is a contingent matter whether the tropes that constitute the bundle with which a given substance is identical enter into a *compresence* (or 'occurring together'), or *collocation*, or *consubstantiation* relation. That is to say, it is also a contingent matter whether any contingently existing instances of properties form a bundle.[19]

This would be so even if one were to hold, as Aristotle did, that there could be no uninstantiated properties (Aristotle, *Metaphysics* Book IV, in Barnes (ed.) 1984). That is, it would still be true that substances are contingently existing beings even if it were true that a necessary condition on the existence of a property is that it have at least one instance in the spatio-temporal world. In this case it would be true that there must be at least one instantiation or exemplification of every property that there is. But this would not make substances themselves necessary beings, for two reasons.

First, that there must be at least one instantiation of a property in order for it to exist does not show that any particular instance of it must exist. This is true even for properties that happen to have only one instantiation. For even in this case, the particular instance that happens to exist need not have existed. All that is required is that some instance or other exists.

To think otherwise is to confuse two quite different claims. One is that a property exists only if, necessarily, there is some instance of that property. The other is that a property exists only if there is some instance of it such that, necessarily, it exists. The former says that there must be some instance of a given property if that property itself is to exist. The latter says, of some particular instance of a property, that that instance must exist if the property itself is to exist. It is the truth of the former claim, not the truth of the latter one, which is required by the claim that there can be no uninstantiated properties. But this truth does not suffice to show that at least some substances are necessary existents.

The second reason why the requirement that there be no uninstantiated properties is compatible with substances being contingent entities has already been mentioned. In order for a substance to be a substance, it is not enough that each of the particularized properties, or tropes, that constitute the bundles with which they are identical exists or is instantiated. These tropes must also enter into a compresence relation, and as we have seen, that is a contingent matter. For, in order for there to be a substance, S, there must be tropes D, E, and F. But that is not enough, since E might be a trope belonging to substance $S1$, and F might be a trope belonging to substance $S2$. The tropes that constitute S must be compresent. That is, a trope of the relation of compresence must also belong to the bundle that is S (if there is to be S at all). But since, as just noted, the existence of the tropes themselves is not sufficient to guarantee the existence of a single substance that instantiates them, the fact that they are compresent – the fact that a trope of compresence 'lives amongst them' – is a contingent matter. So substances themselves are contingently existing things.

For present purposes, we will remain agnostic on whether the trope view of substances and/or of particulars in general is correct. However, in chapter 6 we shall see that there is good reason to reject the view known as Trope Nominalism – the view that *all* that there is are tropes and classes or sets of them, and that this puts pressure on the trope conception of particulars. Those who are persuaded by the arguments given there should opt for strategies suggested in this chapter of attempting to meet objections to the bundle theory that do not depend on the trope conception.

Objection Two: Substances are Intrinsic Unities

We think of a substance as a single thing that possesses a natural unity, a unity that is intrinsic to it at least in the sense that it lies within it. Collocations or collections are not thought of in this way. We think of them as groups, as having no intrinsic unity of their own. If the bundle theory is true, however, then substances are nothing more than mere collocations or collections of properties. Thus, they have no intrinsic unity. This forms the second objection to the bundle theory: substances have a kind of unity that mere collocations of properties do not have, namely an intrinsic unity. So substances cannot be collocations – bundles – of properties.

This objection to the bundle theory is very like the first in its method and strategy. The claim is that the application of the Principle of the Indiscernibility of Identicals shows that collocations of properties lack a feature possessed by substances, namely, the property of having intrinsic unity. Since this is so, the bundle theory is false.

What does it mean to say that an entity has intrinsic unity? Suppose that an entity is a complex thing, say, that it has parts or constituents, as a human being has limbs and a heart, and constituents such as molecules.[20] Then we could say that it has intrinsic unity only if nothing further is required for that thing to be a single thing than that those parts exist and are related to one another in a particular way. But what particular way? A group of individual human beings could satisfy this condition as it stands, but we would not wish to say that this group is a single substance. So there must be a further requirement on the nature of the particular relation. Let us say that it is that the relations that the constituents or parts bear to one another are due to the natures of the constituents themselves and not to any relations that these bear to entities other than those constituents. The relations 'flow', as it were, from the natures of the constituents themselves and are not imposed 'from the outside'.[21] One way of putting this would be to say that the constituents are intrinsically related.

Here is an example of the kind of contrast that seems to be at issue. Consider two 'bundles': one is constituted by the properties of being red, and being round, and other properties of the red apple in my hand; the other, consisting of me, the chair I am now sitting on, and the red apple in my hand, is constituted by properties of me, properties of my chair, and properties of the red apple. We do not think that there is a substance whose parts are me, my chair, and the red apple. But there surely is the collection all of whose members are properties of those things. We do, however, think that there is a substance whose properties, amongst others, are those of being red and being round, namely, the red apple. One way to mark this difference within the constraints imposed by the bundle theory is to say that the relations that the constituents or parts of the apple bear to one another are due to the natures of the constituents themselves, whereas the relations that the constituents or parts of me, the chair on which I am sitting, and the red apple in my hand are not.

This seems to be roughly what is at issue in the second objection to the bundle theory (although we shall see that it needs further refinement). Given it, the argument is that collocations of properties have whatever unity they have in virtue of relations their constituents bear to things other than themselves, whereas substances have their unity in virtue of relations that their constituents bear to each other because of the nature of the constituents themselves. That is to say, the constituents are intrinsically related. But now just what does it mean to say that properties are intrinsically related? Here is one sense in which properties might be intrinsically related that is relevant here: the instantiation of one necessitates, or guarantees, the instantiation of the other.

The objection poses a problem for the bundle theorist because it demonstrates that the properties that constitute bundles or collocations are not, just by virtue of that fact alone, intrinsically related to one another, and it looks like that is what is needed in order to make sense of the idea that substances are natural unities. However, without further explanation, this seems to present no more than a challenge to the bundle theorist. That theorist will respond by insisting that certain properties, viz. the ones that constitute substances, *are* intrinsically related, since that is what is required for them to be substances.

But can this view be defended? The clearest cases where properties might be said to be intrinsically related – where the instantiation of one necessitates the instantiation of the other – are ones where the properties are either necessarily connected, as are the properties of being red and being coloured, or are related by some other dependency relation. In the former case, the instantiation of the one property necessitates the instantiation of the other (but not vice versa) simply because it is logically impossible for the one property to be instantiated while the other is not. A thing cannot be red without being coloured, so if the property, being red, is instantiated, the property, being coloured, must also be instantiated. Similarly for the properties of being triangular and having shape, being three inches long and having length, and so on.

In other sorts of cases, the instantiation of the one property necessitates or guarantees the instantiation of the other property, not as a matter of logical necessity, but rather as a matter of some other, weaker kind of necessity (perhaps, for example, physical necessity, where this necessita-

tion is due to physical law). The relation between, say, the chemical properties of salt, such as that of being constituted by NaCl, and its other
qualities, such as that of being soluble, or between the physical properties of human beings, such as that of having C-fibre stimulation, and
their mental properties, such as that of having pain, may be examples of
this weaker-than-logical dependency relation.

However, it is clear that the bundle theorist cannot rely on the first,
logical, sense of necessitation in defence of the claim that the constituents
of substances are intrinsically related, since most of the determinate
properties of substances, such as those of being round and being red, or
being green and being square, are not logically or conceptually related
in the required sense. Nor are the determinable properties of which these
are determinates, such as those of having shape and being coloured. Even
the weaker dependency relation mentioned above seems too strong a
dependency relation to be what is at issue in the bundle theorist's claim
that the properties constitutive of substances are intrinsically related, for
even this is a necessitation relation: the instantiation of the one property
must ensure the instantiation of the other. Translated into talk of
instances of properties that are constitutive of bundles, this amounts to
the claim that the instances of properties that constitute bundles *must*
co-exist or be co-instantiated. But here we run into more or less the same
problem that dogged the stronger claim: in no sense of 'must' does it
seem that an instantiation of the property, being red, must co-exist with
an instantiation of the property, being round, or an instantiation of the
property, being green, must co-exist with an instantiation of the property, being square. Nor does it seem true, for the determinables of which
these are determinates, that an instantiation of the property, being
coloured must co-exist with an instantiation of the property, having
shape.

We've been considering the question of whether the bundle theory can
account for the natural unity of substances as a question concerning
whether the properties constituting the bundles with which substances
are identical are intrinsically related. And we've been considering this
latter question as one concerning whether the relations between the properties constituting the bundles are due to the natures of the properties
themselves, or 'flow from within' the bundles rather than being due to
a relation to something outside them. But is this objection about the unity
of substances at least partly dispelled, if every bundle *includes* the property (universal or trope, depending on one's favourite version of the
theory) of being co-exemplified?

Earlier in this section it was pointed out that the sense of 'intrinsic'
involved in the objection might need some refinement, and this is where

that need is apparent. If we include the property of being co-exemplified as one of the components or constituents of a given bundle, and if, as seems plausible, co-instantiation is a property – specifically, a relation – that binds the remaining properties of that bundle together, it looks as though we can satisfy the requirement that the relations between the properties that constitute the bundle are intrinsic, or 'flow from within' it, and in so doing, account for the natural unity of substances.

This doesn't really solve the problem that the bundle theory has accounting for the natural unity of substances, though. What it does show, paradoxically, is that it is not sufficient for substances to be natural unities that the relations that the properties that constitute the bundles associated with them bear to one another 'flow from within' those bundles, rather than from something outside the bundles. We can now see that this isn't sufficient, since the property of being co-exemplified can both be included as one of the properties in the bundles and can, it seems, unify those properties or bind them together, *without the resultant bundle possessing the required intrinsic unity*.

Earlier we saw that, for a relation to be intrinsic, it isn't sufficient that it 'flow from within' the bundles rather than from outside them. A further requirement must be in place from the start, namely, that the relation should flow from the *natures* of the properties in the bundles themselves (whether these are understood as abstract universals or as tropes). And now the problem is clear. The property of being co-exemplified, even if it is a constituent of any bundle with which a substance is identical, is a relation that holds, when it holds, between the remaining properties in the bundle, when that bundle exists. But, as the foregoing discussion has shown, when this relation holds, it cannot be guaranteed to do so because of the natures of those properties themselves, and in most cases – the importantly relevant ones – it does not. Although, as we have seen, it may be plausible to say that when the properties of being red and being coloured are co-exemplified and so bear this relation to one another, they do so because of the natures of the properties themselves, it is *not* plausible to say that when the properties of being red and being round, or of being green and being square are co-exemplified and so bear the relation of co-exemplification to one another, it is because of the natures of the properties themselves. Nor is it plausible to say this of the determinable properties of having shape and being coloured. So, simply being another constituent property in a bundle, even if that property is a property that relates other properties in that bundle, will not satisfy the requirement that the relations that hold between the constituents of a bundle must be intrinsic.

So, in the end, it looks like the bundle theorist does have a real problem attempting to counter the objection that substances have a real unity, whereas mere collocations of properties do not. This objection is related to another, which is that the only way of distinguishing those properties that constitute a substance and those that do not (i.e., mere collocations of properties) is by assuming that certain properties are substance-involving and others are not. Consider again that collocation of properties that are properties of me, the chair upon which I am sitting, and the red apple in my hand. Clearly this is not a substance. But why? The answer, according to this objection, will be that certain properties 'go together' naturally and others do not. But how do we determine which properties 'go together', and what work is this phrase really doing in helping us to understand the difference between 'mere' collocations of properties and substances? It seems that any attempt to answer this question will inevitably invoke a distinction between properties that are, and properties that are not, substance-involving, in the sense that those substances that have them are, by virtue of that fact, substances. But then we seem to be appealing to a prior notion of substance to help distinguish the properties that are constitutive of substances rather than the other way around. However, given that the bundle theory is, as stated earlier, a reductive theory, this is unacceptable because it is circular.

So, this second objection concerning the unity of substance, poses a real problem for the bundle theory. (We shall see that, in a rather different way, it also poses a real problem for the bare substratum theory. For this reason it is not counted here as one of the decisive objections to the bundle theory.)

Objection Three: All True Subject-predicate Statements about Substances are Logical Truths

Statements like 'Felix the cat is a feline animal', 'John is a biological organism', and 'That elm tree is deciduous' are informative to us. They do not seem to us to be obvious truths, in the way that statements like 'John is John', or 'John, the bachelor next door, is unmarried' are. We can be surprised to find that they are true. Even knowing that it is John I am talking about, and even knowing that he is a human being, I can be surprised to learn that he is a biological organism. Even knowing that it is that elm tree that I am talking about, I can be surprised to learn that it is a deciduous tree. The third objection to the bundle theory trades on this intuition. According to it, the bundle theory makes all true statements ascribing properties to substances uninformative by making them logical truths, and so like statements such as 'John is John' or 'That unmarried male is unmarried'. However, we take the vast majority of true statements attributing properties to substances to be informative. Since the bundle theory has the consequence that what are informative truths are uninformative ones, the bundle theory is false.

The objection here is that if substances are literally identical with the sum totality of their properties, any true statement ascribing a property to a substance can tell us no more than what we know when we know what substance it is that is being ascribed that property. So, for example, if it is true that Felix the cat is a feline animal, then that cat has the property of being a feline animal. But then, according to the bundle theory, the property of being a feline animal is literally a constituent of that cat. So, if I know what I am talking about when I use the word 'Felix' to refer to that cat, then I know that 'Felix the cat is a feline animal' is true, since what it expresses is, amongst other things, that 'The feline animal is a feline animal'. I could only fail to know this by failing to know what I am referring to when I use the word 'Felix'. That is, I could fail to know it only by failing to know what it is I am talking about. This goes against the very strong intuition we have that, in knowing what substance is being referred to or described in a true statement ascribing a property to it, one does not thereby know that the statement is true. And this is just to say that *true* statements ascribing properties to substances are informative. Therefore the bundle theory is false.

This objection puts a lot of pressure on the idea of 'knowing what I am referring to', and it is pressure that it is uncertain the objection can bear. The objection seems stronger than it might be, because the examples above are cases of the attribution to things of properties that might be essential to them: how could I not know that Felix the cat is a feline animal and still know that I am speaking of that cat? But what about the claim that Felix has forty teeth? If the bundle theory is true, then the property of having forty teeth is a constituent of the bundle that is Felix. Should we think that if I didn't know that Felix has forty teeth, then I wouldn't really know that I was speaking of Felix when I utter a truth such as 'Felix is in the bedroom'?

The answer to this seems clearly to be no. The most obvious and appropriate rejoinder for the bundle theorist to make to the objection, then, is simply to insist that we do know what we are talking about when we refer to a substance and correctly ascribe a property to it, even when we do not know all of its properties. The objection assumes that an individual can only really know what she is talking about when she uses a term to refer to a substance if she knows what all of the properties of that substance are. But this is clearly an unreasonable demand to place on speakers, as the above example about Felix illustrates. Substances possess innumerably many properties, the vast majority of which are unknown by speakers when they refer to them and correctly ascribe properties to them. Normally, all that they need to know is some sub-set of all of the properties of a given substance in order to know what substance they are talking about. That is, it is sufficient for them to know what substance they are talking about that they have incomplete knowl-edge of its properties, and so of it. They may not even know enough of the properties of that substance to be able to identify it uniquely, to dis-tinguish it from all other substances of the same kind.

Still, there are residual problems here that need to be addressed, and at least one of these is a serious blow to the theory. The fact is that, according to the bundle theory, true subject-predicate statements about substances *are* logical truths. And this is the source of two separate prob-lems. The first concerns the uninformative nature of logical truths, and the second concerns the fact that such truths are necessary ones.

According to the first problem, all logical truths are uninformative. But, as just pointed out, speakers find many true subject-predicate statements about substances informative. Even if these speakers know what they are talking about when they refer to substances and correctly attribute properties to them, then, they can be surprised to find that some of these truths are true. So, how can speakers find such truths informa-tive when these truths are *not* informative? That is to say, how can speak-ers find these truths informative when they carry no new information about the substances they are about?

One response is to admit that such truths are logical ones but to deny that all logical truths are uninformative. There are two ways of going about this, both of which depend on a certain understanding of the rela-tion between a truth's being a logical one and a truth's being uninfor-mative. A logical truth is a statement whose truth is due solely to the rules of logic. That is, it is one that remains true under every consistent interpretation of its non-logical expressions. So, for example, the state-ment, 'All bachelors are bachelors' counts as a logical truth, since on any consistent interpretation of the non-logical expression, 'bachelors', it will come out true. What is an interpretation? An interpretation is a deter-mination of a reference for an expression, where this is understood as determining what that expression is to be taken as referring to (as, e.g., in naming). So, for example, an interpretation of 'Felix' fixes as its ref-erence that cat.

To know what substance is being referred to by an expression is to know how that expression is to be interpreted. However, as noted above, it seems that one can know this without knowing all of the properties of a substance. One way in which to hold this consistently with commitment to the claim that all true statements ascribing properties to substances are logically true and so uninformative is by claiming that not all logical truths are themselves obvious. Some are obvious, whereas others are not. And some are less obvious than others.[22]

'Bachelors are bachelors' is obvious, since one can grasp its truth without knowing what 'bachelors' refers to. One can know this without knowing any of the constituent properties of bachelors. This is particularly interesting, since it shows that I can understand a logical truth, and understand that it is a logical truth, without either knowing what its non-logical constituent expressions refer to (and so, without knowing how it is to be interpreted) or, for this reason, knowing what the constituents of what it does refer to are. Paradoxically, it seems, it is obvious precisely because grasping its truth doesn't require knowing how it is to be interpreted!

'Bachelors are unmarried males' is less obvious. One might fail to know this, and so be surprised to learn that bachelors are unmarried males, yet know what one was talking about with one's use of the word 'bachelor'. Think of a child who knows that her uncle is a bachelor but not that he has the property of being an unmarried male. When she refers to him as a bachelor, she knows whom she is talking about. She might also know what she is talking about when she refers to bachelors in general, since she may know that bachelors don't have wives. What she may not know is that wives are married women. One might object that she doesn't know what bachelors are if she doesn't know that wives are married women. But to require her to have this knowledge in order to know what she is talking about when she refers to bachelors seems to be an unreasonable demand. Since this process can be repeated endlessly, to require this would effectively be to require that one must know the constituents of an indefinite number of substances in order to know what one is talking about when one talks about one particular substance.

'Felix is black' is the least obvious of all, since one cannot grasp this truth without knowing what 'Felix' refers to, and knowing this is compatible with ignorance of many of Felix's constituent properties, specifically, that one of them is being black.

So, the defender of the bundle theory could say that although the theory is committed to the view that all truths of a certain kind are logical truths, it is not thereby committed to the claim that all are equally obvious truths. Whether a truth is obvious or not depends on one's current state of knowledge, on what other propositions one knows at that time. Since none of us are perfect knowers, truths – ones that are generally accepted by articulate adults – that are firmly within the domain of the so-called logical ones may be obvious to some of these adults and not so obvious to others. If this is so, even for the domain of what is generally recognized to be the logical truths, then what makes for a truth's being logical or non-logical cannot be firmly associated with how obvious it is. This opens up space within which to defend the claim that, however unobvious truths that ascribe properties to substances may be, it does not follow that they are not logical truths.[23]

This response to the objection may fail to convince. If it does, however, there is another one to hand. Earlier, when considering the objection to the bundle theory concerning the contingency of substances, we noted that one response to the objection is to say that there is more than one way of understanding the term 'properties' in the claim that substances are bundles of properties. The way that is relevant to the bundle theorist construes substances as identical, not with properties understood as abstract universal things or entities, but with particularized instances of properties, or tropes, which, being tropes, have particular spatio-temporal locations. Tropes are contingent entities, as are the bundles that they constitute.

The distinction between properties as abstract entities and properties as tropes may also help to defuse the objection at hand. For, the objection states that true statements attributing a property to a substance must be uninformative because the properties that are attributed to a substance in such statements are constituents of that substance. But if the sense in which a property is a constituent of a substance is not the sense in which a property is attributed to a substance, this is false. For example, when I say 'This apple is red', I attribute a property to this apple; but it does not follow from this that the property I refer to by 'red' is the property that is a constituent of the apple. Why? Because it may be that what is referred to with 'red' is a property construed as an abstract universal, whereas what is a constituent of the bundle referred to by 'this apple' is an instance of that abstract entity. Indeed, a natural interpretation of the statement I utter when I say 'This apple is red' is 'This apple is an instance of the property, being red', which is in turn plausibly read as 'This apple contains a trope of the property, being red'. But if this is so, then the objection to the bundle theory, that it makes all statements attributing properties to substances uninformative, confuses properties as abstract universals with properties as tropes. And in doing so, it wrongly supposes that, in knowing the constituents of substances, one thereby knows that the properties attributed to them are literally parts of them.

How does this help to defuse the objection? If, in order to know what I am talking about when I talk about a substance, I need to know its constituents, and if those constituents are what are referred to when I attribute properties to that substance, then it may be hard to see how I can find true statements attributing a property to a substance informative. But if the constituents of a substance are not what are referred to when I proceed to attribute properties to that substance, then I can be surprised to find that a constituent of a substance is an instance of the property that I attribute to it. For, in a statement of the form, '*a* is *F*', where '*a*' refers to a substance, '*F*' expresses a universal, *F*-ness, or the property, being *F*. But '*a*' refers to something that is constituted by tropes, one of which, if the statement is true, is an *F*-ness trope. Thus, it can be informative to be told that a thing, one of whose constituents is an *F*-ness trope, is an instance of the universal, *F*-ness, since a trope is one thing, a universal, another. The distinction between properties as abstract universal entities and properties as tropes opens up conceptual space within which to argue that one can both know one thing and be surprised to learn another. And so it can come as a surprise to learn that this apple is an instance of the property, being red. So it can come as a surprise to learn that this apple is red.

What both of these responses attempt to accomplish is to explain how true subject-predicate statements about substances that are, in being logical truths, uninformative, could nevertheless be such that we can be surprised to discover that they are true. They do not attempt to address a second feature of logical truths, namely, that they are necessary rather than contingent truths. Even if the responses succeed, then, they do not answer a second objection that arises with regard to true subject-predicate statements about substances.

According to this objection, we think that many, if not all, of these claims are contingently true if true. For example, we think that the claim that Felix has forty teeth is contingent truth; that, even if it is true, it could have been false. Similarly, we think that the claim that this apple is red, even if understood along the lines above, as the claim that this apple contains a trope of the property, being red, is contingently true if true at all. But if the bundle theory is true, and all true subject-predicate statements about substances are logical truths, then the truths expressed by sentences like 'Felix has forty teeth' and 'This apple is red' are not contingent truths at all.[24] Even on the trope construal of the bundle theory, every trope necessarily belongs to its type; so a redness-trope must be a redness-trope, so the redness of this apple (this redness-trope) could not but be a trope of the universal property, redness.

Now, if we were to restrict ourselves to the kinds of examples given at the beginning of this section, ones like 'Felix is a feline animal' or 'This elm tree is a deciduous tree', we might be tempted to suppose that at least some of these truths are necessarily true, just because the examples are cases of the attribution to substances of properties that might be essential to them. In many other cases, though, the properties correctly attributed to substances in such statements simply are not plausibly viewed as essential to them. This is not only true of ones that correctly attribute relational properties to them, as, for example, when I truly say that Felix is my favourite cat. In cases like these, it seems clear that the property truly attributed to the substance is not essential to it. But it is also true of cases where the property attributed is non-relational in the sense described in chapter 2: it does not presuppose the existence of another substance. When I truly state that this apple is red, it seems equally clear that the property truly attributed to this apple is not essential to it.

This objection is not decisive against the bundle theory; in fact, it is open to the bundle theorist to respond that it begs the question against the theory, since, if the theory is true, all of the properties of a substance are essential to it. So the objection can only work to show that the theory is false by assuming that it is false. Still, the intuition that not all true subject-predicate statements about substances are necessary truths is a powerful one – so powerful that the bundle theorist owes us an explanation of why, if it is false, it seems so obviously true.

One avenue that is promising is to distinguish between necessary truths that are knowable a priori and necessary truths that are knowable only a posteriori (for more on this, see chapter 1). A truth that is necessary and knowable a priori is such that it not only could not be false, but we can know independently of sense experience that it could not be false. An example might be that expressed by 'Bachelors are unmarried males', or, perhaps the mathematical truth expressed by '2 + 2 = 4'. A truth that is necessary and knowable only a posteriori is such that it could not be false, but we cannot know independently of sense experience that it could not be false. An example might be the truth expressed by 'Water is H$_2$O', or 'Heat is molecular motion'.[25]

The bundle theorist might defend the claim that all true subject-predicate statements about substances are, despite appearances, necessarily true, by appealing to this distinction between necessary truths that are knowable a priori and necessary truths that are knowable only a posteriori and maintaining that the ones that appear to be only contingently true appear so because they are not knowable a priori. Like the claims that water is H$_2$O and that heat is molecular motion, the claims that this apple is red and the claim that Felix has forty teeth are, if knowable, only knowable a posteriori. Still, these claims are, if true, necessarily true; they could not be false.

This defence is interesting and important, for two reasons. The first is that it helps to defuse the objection just discussed, that logical truths are necessary truths but not all true subject-predicate statements about substances are necessary truths. Second, it also helps to defuse the objection, discussed earlier in this section, that logical truths are uninformative but many true subject-predicate statements about substances are informative. The way it does this is by suggesting that at least some of the essential properties of substances are not ones that we can know a priori that those substances have. So, if it succeeds, it has the potential to deal with both sources of the objection that the bundle theory is committed to the (false) view that all true subject-predicate statements about substances are uninformative. It will not get the bundle theorist out of the woods entirely, since it is typically assumed that logical truths are not only necessary but knowable a priori, and if that is right, the strategy will not show that logical truths can be informative in the required way. For the sake of this discussion, let us assume that logical truths *can be* informative. This really doesn't help the bundle theorist, as the essence of the objection is to the idea that, if the bundle theory is true, true subject-predicate statements about substances are *necessary* truths. The main difficulty is that it simply does not appear to be a necessary truth that, say, Felix the cat has forty teeth. It not only does not appear to be necessary and a priori knowable, but it does not appear to be necessary and a posteriori knowable. Bundle theorists who pursue this avenue will therefore need to engage in a lot of hard work in order to dispel the conviction that such truths are, despite appearances, necessary.[26]

Objection Four: Substances Persist Through and Survive Change

One of the notable features of substances is that they persist through time, i.e., that they are continuants, and so are capable of persisting through change, where this involves change in properties. According to the fourth objection, however, the bundle theory has the consequence that substances cannot survive change. The theory says that a substance is identical with a bundle of properties. But the objection is that, whereas a substance can change with respect to its properties (i.e., it can have some at one time and lack them at another), a bundle cannot do so, since a given bundle essentially has the members it actually has. Thus, in order for a substance, construed as a bundle, to change, the substance would have to be identical with bundle a at time t_1, and identical with bundle b at time t_2. And that is impossible; it is impossible for any thing to be identical with one thing at one time and another thing at another time. The reason is that if $a = b$ at any time t, then $a = b$ at all times.[27] (Notice that this objection too trades on the Principle of the Indiscernibility of Identicals. The claim is that, whereas substances have the property of surviving change, bundles of properties do not. Therefore substances are not identical with bundles of properties.)

The objection assumes, correctly, that at any time, t, substances are identical with all the properties that constitute them at that time. Suppose that a round, red apple at time t_1 is identical with the bundle of properties consisting of being red, being round, weighing 25 grams, being at place p, and so on, at time t_1, and that it changes colour, to being brown, between time t_1 and a later time, say t_2. The apple at time t_2 would now be identical with a different bundle of properties, consisting of being brown, being round, weighing 25 grams, being at place p, and so on, at time t_2. Since, the objection continues, the bundle of properties at time t_1 differs from the bundle of properties at time t_2 (one has the constituent of being red, the other has the constituent of being brown), they cannot be identical substances, by the Principle of the Indiscernibility of Identicals, for that principle requires that, if things are identical, they have all the same properties. Distinct properties therefore ensure distinctness of things that have them. So, since the red, round apple at time t_1 differs in its constituent properties from the round, brown apple at time t_2, they are distinct substances. And, since any change involves a change in properties, the bundle theory has the consequence that substances cannot survive change.

There is a superficially plausible response to this, one that supposes that identity statements regarding substances, or any other continuant (e.g., persons) are to be understood as implicitly relativized to times (Loux 1978). Thus construed, the question of whether bundle a is identical with bundle b is not to be understood as the question of whether a at time t_1 is identical with b at time t_2 (i.e., as a question of identity across times), but rather, is to be understood as the question of whether, at time t_1, a is identical with b, at time t_2, a is identical with b, at t_3, a is identical with b, and so on, for all times at which a and b exist. So, the principle that the bundle theorist is appealing to here is this:

> For any substance, a, and any substance, b, and any time, t, if every property that is a constituent of a is a constituent of b, then $a = b$.[28]

Understood in this way, there is no real problem concerning change, according to the response, since both at time t_1 and at time t_2, a, which, according to the bundle theory, is composed of a particular bundle of properties, and b, which is also composed of a particular bundle of properties, will not be undergoing any change. The loss/acquisition of properties that causes problems for the bundle theorist occurs between time t_1 and time t_2, but not at either time t_1 or time t_2. That is to say, change *takes* time. Thus, at both times t_1 and t_2, it is possible for a and b to be composed of exactly the same properties.

But this is not really a satisfactory response to the fourth objection. This objection is based on the doubt as to whether the bundle theory can account for the fact that the substance a is, at both time t_1 *and* at time t_2, the very same substance, despite the fact that the bundles of properties with which a is identical at these two times differ. It is only when one compares the two bundles at *different* times that the question arises of whether change (and survival of change) has occurred. So the response, in failing to address this doubt, really fails to come to terms with the objection at all. In failing to appreciate that the question of change itself involves comparisons of properties of a substance across distinct times, it simply does not address the question of survival of change.

A bundle theorist might grant that a bundle must contain the properties it contains, and hence cannot change, but then insist that substances are things that persist, not by *enduring*, by lasting through change and surviving it, but rather by *perduring*, that is, by having temporal parts, each of which is identical with some bundle. (For more on perdurantism see note 2 of the present chapter and references therein.) Thus, it might be argued, at each time the whole of a substance does not exist, but some part of it does – that bundle of properties that exists at that time. A substance is not itself a bundle of properties, then, but a sum or sequence of bundles of properties, a bundle of bundles of properties.

On this view, substances are not things that persist through time and survive change, but are things that take up time and so and have temporal parts, in something like the way that an event does. Substances, on this view, are not wholly and completely in the places that they occupy at any given time, any more than an event like an avalanche or an explosion is. According to the suggestion, we are to understand the phenomenon of change as follows: substance a changes if and only if it is composed of temporal parts at least two of which are qualitatively different.

But there are two serious problems with this. First, and most obviously, it doesn't account for change. It simulates change, but does not give a real account of it. So it doesn't account for the belief that substances do undergo and survive change. Second, and relatedly, the account it does offer treats substances as event-like. But we do not think that substances are anything like events. We do think that substances undergo changes but are not themselves changes; that things happen to them but they are not themselves happenings. If the suggestion is correct, though, we are fundamentally mistaken in thinking this, and we must reject our ordinary conception of substances as false. However, the suggestion provides no motivation, independently of the bundle theory's need to account for the phenomenon of survival through change, for rejecting our ordinary conception of substances as enduring things.

Is there another way to handle this fourth objection that does take into account the fact that change takes time? One possibility, similar to the suggestion just mentioned, would be to treat the properties that are constituents of substances as themselves tensed, or as being 'temporally indexed', i.e., relativized with respect to the times at which they are such constituents, as might be the case if we construe them as tropes.[29] Consider once again our red apple. The bundle theorist says that this apple is identical with the bundle of properties that constitute it throughout its existence. And the objection is that there will be properties in that bundle that are incompatible with one another, those with respect to which the bundle changes. In the example of our red apple, the relevant incompatibility is between the properties of being red and being brown. The suggestion is that, if one treats *all* of the properties that constitute the bundle, including those with respect to which the bundle changes, as being indexed with respect to the times, say, being red-at-t_1 and being brown-at-t_2, then substances can be viewed as being identical with the bundle of properties that contains all the time-indexed properties it ever has and all the properties that the substance has at all times at which it exists. On the one hand, this does seem to accommodate the fact that substances undergo change; one can see whether there is loss or acquisition of a property at a later time that was had or lacked at a previous time just by looking at the list of time-indexed properties that constitute a substance. For example, at time t_1, our apple is identical with the bundle consisting of the properties, being red-at-t_1, being spherical-at-t_1, weighing 25-grams-at-t_1, and *also* being brown-at-t_2, being spherical-at-t_2, and so on. On the other hand, we can make sense of the claim that it is one and the same substance that undergoes change, since the suggestion is that each substance is identical timelessly with these temporally indexed properties. Our apple, which is red-at-t_1 and brown-at-t_2, is the same apple throughout these two times, since at both times it has as constituents the properties, being red-at-t_1, and being brown-at-t_2.

This may look to be a more promising strategy for dealing with the objection than the one immediately preceding it. Unfortunately, however, it is not. This revised bundle theory – the theory that the bundle that is a substance contains time-indexed properties – doesn't really show how it is possible for a substance, construed as a bundle, to survive change. After all, there is no property in any such bundle that the bundle first has and then lacks. But given that change involves change of properties, from one time to another, this strategy actually amounts to a denial of change. Further, it too requires us to conceive of substances as 'spread out' through time, as things that take up time rather than endure through it. So it looks like the bundle theory cannot account for the fact that substances undergo change and survive it.

Objection Five: The Principle of the Identity of Indiscernibles is False

The final objection to the bundle theory is the most serious one of those so far considered. Early on in our discussion of the theory, we noted that it is committed to the necessary truth of the Principle of the Identity of Indiscernibles, the principle which says that, for any objects x and y, if x and y share all the same properties, then x is identical with y. If the principle is necessarily true, there could not exist two substances with exactly the same properties. The problem is, however, that there do not seem to be any compelling reasons for thinking that this principle (in the non-trivial version to which the bundle theory is committed) is necessarily true. And if it is not necessarily true, the bundle theory is false.

Let us distinguish two versions of the principle, a stronger version and a weaker one. We can do this by distinguishing between two sorts of properties or attributes of substances, 'pure' ones, and 'impure' ones.[30] A pure property is one whose possession by a substance does not require the existence of any other contingent substance.[31] Intuitively speaking, pure properties are non-relational properties of substances. Examples are those of being round and being red. In contrast with this, an impure property is one whose possession by a substance does require the existence of another contingent substance. Again, intuitively speaking, impure properties are relational properties of substances.[32] Examples of such properties are those of being south of Detroit, being higher than Mount Snowdon, and being an admirer of Mandela.

Given this distinction, we can formulate two versions of the Principle of the Identity of Indiscernibles. According to the first, weaker version of the principle, the range of properties that is relevant to the question of identity is all properties, pure and impure, of substances. It states that

(I) For any objects x and y, if x and y share all the same pure and impure properties, then x is identical with y.

According to the second, stronger version of the principle, the range of properties that is relevant is only the pure properties of substances. It states that

(P) For any objects x and y, if x and y share all the same pure properties, then x is identical with y.

The objection to the bundle theory is that, in its weaker form (I), the principle is trivially necessarily true but leads to vicious circularity, and so the bundle theorist cannot appeal to it, and in its stronger form (P), the principle is not necessarily true. Consider the weaker form first. If we allow all of the properties of a substance to count as relevant, then the principle (I) comes out as trivially necessarily true. It does so because it permits impure properties like that of being identical with Socrates, so any objects that are alike with respect to that property are automatically identical and automatically identical with Socrates. But, though trivially necessarily true, (I) cannot be appealed to by the bundle theorist, since that theorist is trying to give a reductive account of substances, and (I) comes out as necessarily true only by re-introducing substances into the account. So, the bundle theorist must employ and be committed to the truth of a restricted version of the principle (one which allows only pure properties to count).

So, consider the stronger version (P) of the principle, which restricts the question of identity to the pure properties of substances. As stated above, these are properties whose possession by a substance does not require the existence of any other contingent substance. But it is simply unclear why it is impossible for there to be two substances with exactly the same pure properties. It certainly does not seem impossible that there should be two red, round substances, or two red, round substances weighing 25 grams, or two red, round substances weighing 25 grams with a circumference of 6 inches, and so on, for all of the other pure properties that a substance might possess. Think of a factory production line, whose output is thousands of little red balls, all of which have just these properties. So, in its stronger form, the Principle of the Identity of Indiscernibles seems clearly not to be necessarily true (Black 1952).[33]

But what about positional properties – spatial and temporal, or spatio-temporal, ones? Could there really be two red, round substances weighing 25 grams with a circumference of 6 inches that have exactly the same position in space and time, or space-time? Think again of the little balls produced in a factory. What distinguishes or individuates them from one another are their positional properties; no two of them occupy exactly the same space at the same time. Independently of the truth or otherwise of the bundle theory, we know, or think we know, that it is not possible for two substances with all of the same properties to occupy exactly the same position in space and time. Substances are, so to speak, *substantial*: the occupancy of one in a given region of space and time, we think, excludes the simultaneous occupancy of another one with exactly the same properties in exactly that region. If this is right, then perhaps positional properties can ensure that no two substances that have them can have them in the same determinate form, thereby ensuring the necessary truth of (P).

However, it is no easy matter finding the right kinds of properties, namely pure ones, to do the work that needs to be done. In fact, the objection is that there are no such properties that can do this work. Consider, for example, spatial properties like those of being to the left of this apple, being beneath that cat, or being to the south of Detroit, or being in front of Joe. The attribution of any of these properties to a substance requires the existence of another contingent substance – an apple, a cat, a city, Joe. So spatial properties like these are not pure properties, and cannot be permitted in the range of properties associated with (P).

What about other spatial properties, like those of being 2 feet apart, or being equidistant from each other? There are two problems with appealing to these in order to preserve the necessary truth of (P). First, the attribution of them to a substance appears to require the existence of another contingent substance distinct from it, even if it does not require reference to that substance. Relations like being 2 feet apart are non-reflexive; they do not hold between a thing and itself (as, say, the relation of identity does), but rather, hold, if at all, between two or more things. This seems to rule them out as permissible properties in the range associated with (P) (we will return to this below). But second, and more importantly, even if they are admissible as pure properties, they cannot do the required work. The problem before us is how we are to ensure the necessary truth of (P), given that it seems possible that there could be two substances with exactly the same pure properties. The proposal is that we can do this by including the positional properties of those substances. But including such properties as being 2 feet apart cannot ensure the necessary truth of (P), since any two substances that are 2 feet apart both have this property! Each substance bears precisely this relation to the other.[34]

What, then, about 'pure' positional properties, ones that attribute a spatial and temporal, or a spatio-temporal position to a substance, like those of being at place p at time t or being at place-time pt? The attribution of these to any substance may involve relations to places and times, or to place-times, but it is not clear that this undermines the bundle theorist's reductive enterprise, since these are not substances. Further, this point can help to elucidate the idea that material substances are intimately connected to space and time, since it gives part of the sense in which material substances occupy places at times.

But this won't do either, for reasons that have already been hinted at above when discussing positional properties like that of being 2 feet apart. It seems that *either* these properties are also impure, and so cannot be included in the range of properties associated with (P), *or* they are not impure, but the attribution of them to a substance cannot help to establish the necessary truth of (P). Either way, (P) turns out not to be necessarily true.

The problem arises in this way: it is necessarily true that space and time (or space-time) are either relational or absolute; they must be one or the other. On the relational understanding, positional properties turn out to be impure. On the absolute understanding, such properties aren't impure, but including them in the range of (P) does not help to establish its necessary truth.

Suppose that space is relational (similarly for time). That is, suppose that it is not possible for space to be extended (and so for there to be distinct places in space) without there being things that occupy places, such as, for example, substances (similarly for times and events).[35] On the relational view, in order for there to be spatial dyadic relations (relations such as x's being 2 feet apart from y), there must be things that occupy them. Suppose that these occupants are substances.

It follows that distinct places can only be distinguished by distinguishing their occupants, in this case, substances. So, if space and time are relational, the position of a substance, $S1$, say, its being at a particular place, p_1, depends on its relation to another contingent substance, given that its being in place p_1 rather than p_2 depends on there being another contingent substance, $S2$, which occupies p_2. So, positional properties are impure properties; their attribution to any given substance requires the existence of another contingent substance.

Suppose, then, that space and time are not relational, but absolute. Specifically, suppose that space is a thing that consists of places, and that space and its constituent places exist independently of there being any contingent substances that occupy them – and suppose that the same is true for time.[36] This, it seems, would make places individuals in their own right. Then, while it seems to be the case that we cannot distinguish one place (or time) from another – and hence that in order to pick out a place or time we must mention a substance – it also seems that the properties that substances have in virtue of which they have the positional properties they do are not impure.[37] They are not impure because, although the attribution to a substance of a spatial or a temporal property requires the existence of spatial or a temporal point, such points are not substances, even if they are contingent.

While these properties count as pure and admissible in the range of properties associated with (P), their possession by substances cannot individuate them from one another, and so their admissibility cannot help to establish the necessary truth of (P). For, as we have seen, spatial (and temporal) points on the absolute view are necessarily indistinguishable from one another. They could only be distinguishable then if the things that occupy them are distinguishable. The only way, then, that positions could individuate distinct substances is by virtue of those substances' differing with respect to *other*, non-positional properties. Indeed, if (P) is to be necessarily true, distinct substances *must* differ with respect to pure properties other than their positional ones on the absolute (substantival) conception of space and time. Since it is possible that there should be two such substances that do not differ in this way, (P) turns out not to be necessarily true.

To sum up: on the relational view of space and time, positional properties turn out to be impure and cannot be appealed to in defence of (P); and on the absolute view of space and time, although positional properties turn out to be pure properties, they cannot individuate distinct substances that are otherwise indiscernible with respect to all of their pure properties, and so cannot help to ensure the necessary truth of (P). Either way (P) turns out not to be necessarily true. Since the bundle theory is committed to the necessary truth of (P), then, the bundle theory is false.[38]

This completes our survey of the objections to the bundle theory. At least four charges remain unresolved. The first is that the theory cannot explain the unity of substances. The second is that it cannot account for substances' persistence and survival through change. The third is that it cannot account for the intuition that true subject-predicate statements about substances are not necessary truths. And the fourth is that the version of the Principle of the Identity of Indiscernibles that the bundle theory needs to appeal to, viz. that which is restricted to the pure properties, is not necessarily true. All of these objections stem from the fact that the theory is reductive. We turn now to the bundle theory's main rival, the bare substratum theory, to see if it fares any better under scrutiny.

The Bare Substratum Theory and the Principle of Acquaintance

Like the bundle theory, the bare substratum theory attempts to accommodate and explain certain of our firm convictions about the nature of substances. According to it, each substance is identical, not with the bundle of properties that constitute it, but with a bundle or collection that includes both its properties *and* a uniquely individuating constituent, an entity *that is not a property*. Each substance has one and only one such constituent making it the substance it is and distinguishing it from all other substances. So, according to the theory, for each substance, there is a constituent of it that is not a property but is both essential and unique to it, this constituent being referred to as a bare particular, or substratum.

One plausible line of reasoning that leads to the bare substratum view stems from difficulties with the bundle theory. Since, it might be argued, it is logically possible for two numerically distinct substances to have all of their pure properties in common, and impure ones are not permissible as individuators, the only other way of accounting for the numerical diversity of two indiscernible substances is by reference to a difference between them that is not due to a difference in their properties. The basis of this line of reasoning is to be found in the fifth objection to the bundle theory discussed above and ultimately in the bundle theory's commitment to the necessary truth of the Principle of the Identity of Indiscernibles. The bare substratum theory rejects this principle. The only principle of identity to which the theory of bare substrata is committed is that of the Indiscernibility of Identicals, which says that, for any objects x and y, if x is identical with y, then every property of x is a property of y and vice versa.

On this view, the difference between indiscernibility and identity is simply to do with number. According to the proponent of the bare substratum theory, since properties cannot alone do this, each substance must be constituted not only by a bundle of properties, but also by some non-repeatable entity, a bare substratum, to which we can attribute the identity of that substance. Since the substratum of substance x is different from the substratum of substance y, x and y can be distinct even if they share all the same pure properties (and the Principle of the Identity of Indiscernibles is satisfied). Thus, a bare substratum just is the bearer or carrier of numerical difference.

According to the bare substratum theory, the constituent that is both essential and unique to a substance serves a second crucial function in addition to providing a basis for numerical diversity. It provides a ground for, in the sense of being an exemplifier of, the properties with which it is associated. So the bare substrata of substances not only confer their identity upon those substances, they also serve as exemplifiers of the properties with which substances are typically associated.

It is this second feature of bare substrata that affords an explanation of the unity of substances. Recall that one of the main difficulties with the bundle theory is that it seems unable to account for the fact that, unlike mere collocations of properties, substances are natural unities. That is, the theory seems incapable of explaining why some logically consistent sets of properties constitute a substance while others do not. In order to explain this, some other unifying principle is needed.

Since the substratum of a substance is that in which all the properties that we would normally attribute to the substance actually inhere or exist, we have an explanation of the unity of substances: all of a substance's properties inhere in a single substratum, distinct from that in which the properties of other substances inhere. This explanation works precisely because the theory allows substrata to function as the exemplifiers of all of the properties associated with substances.

Moreover, the bare substratum theory seems better able than the bundle theory to explain the persistence and survival of a substance through change. The bundle theory seems to require that substances be changeless, since change involves alteration in the properties associated with a substance, but, according to the theory, all of a substance's properties are essential to it. This flatly contradicts our conviction that substances, in the course of persisting through time, can and do change while remaining numerically the same (think, for example, of the red, round apple that changes from being red to being brown as it rots). The bare substratum theory appears to avoid this problem by identifying the source of numerical identity of a substance with a constituent of it that, in itself, remains the same throughout the substance's acquisition and loss of properties. It remains the same just because the substratum of a substance has in itself no properties, it can be something that survives intact when a substance (e.g., an apple) undergoes change; the substance's substratum loses (or acquires) a property, and acquires (or loses) a contrary, while itself remaining unchanged (we will return to this).

So, the bare substratum theory seems able to account for at least two strong intuitions we have about the nature of substances. The theory is also on stronger ground than the bundle theory with respect to the issue of whether it makes all true subject-predicate statements about substances logical truths. To say that a substance has a property, say, that Felix the cat has forty teeth, is to say that Felix's substratum exemplifies the property of having forty teeth. Since, however, the substratum is a bare particular, it is a contingent matter whether it exemplifies any property, and we can be surprised to discover that it does. So it is a contingent matter whether Felix the cat has forty teeth, and the statement that Felix the cat has forty teeth, if true, is both contingently true and informative.

Finally, the bare substratum theory avoids the objection that it makes substances necessary beings because properties are necessary beings, and for the same reason as it avoids many of the other objections: substances are not, on this view, identical with their associated properties.

Objections to the Bare Substratum Theory

On the face of it, the bare substratum theory is on much stronger ground all round than the bundle theory, since it seems to avoid all of the objections that prove to be intractable for that theory. Unfortunately, the theory suffers from a crippling objection. We can begin to get a sense of how serious the problem it faces is by returning to the issue of how the theory accounts for a substance's identity through change. According to it, this is explained by the fact that a substance's substratum acquires (or loses) a property and loses (or acquires) its contrary while itself remaining unchanged. But what can be meant by saying that a substratum is property-less and yet is that in which a substance's properties inhere? It seems that in order to make sense of this we need to appeal to the idea of a substratum's being an unqualified possessor of properties.

However, it is unclear whether the concept of an unqualified possessor of properties can be made intelligible at all. To make it intelligible, we need to make sense of the following kind of claim: whatever exemplifies a property is itself bare. But any attempt to do so appears to lead to contradiction. The natural way of making sense of the claim is to understand it as saying that whatever exemplifies a property has no properties. But this quickly leads to contradiction, since it is normally understood that a thing has properties just by exemplifying them. Given this, we can move from the claim that whatever exemplifies a property has no properties to the claim that whatever has a property has no properties.

The problem, it seems, is that there is no way of identifying a bare substratum as that which is a possessor of qualities (or as that in which properties inhere) without qualifying *it* as bare. And to do this appears to require attributing a property to it (the property of being bare, perhaps, or the property of having no properties). But then one has qualified it, and so it is no longer bare.

The bare substratum theorist might, with justification, respond that this is not at all the way in which the above claim is to be understood. The objection foists on the theory the claim that the bare substratum has no properties. But the above claim says something weaker than this, namely, that the substratum is *itself* bare. In a similar vein, the theory handles the problems of unity and change by distinguishing what the substratum is *in itself* from what the substratum exemplifies. We can make this distinction more precise by invoking the distinction, mentioned earlier in this chapter, between accidental and essential properties. The claim that the substratum is itself bare can then be interpreted as the claim that the substratum has no properties *essentially*. What it is committed to is the claim that bare substrata could, even if in fact they do not, exist without their properties: that it is possible that they should so exist, even if they actually do not. All of the properties that characterize bare substrata they have accidentally, not essentially.

So, the response is that the theory is not committed to the contradictory claim that whatever has properties has no properties, but rather, to the claim, which is not contradictory, that whatever has properties *accidentally* has no properties *essentially*. However, the bare substratum theory is now vulnerable to a different version of the contradiction charge. The above manoeuvre has the consequence that although bare substrata are contingently possessors of properties, they are necessarily bare. This in turn appears to have the consequence that bare substrata have the essential property of having no property essentially. So, although the bare substratum theory can avoid commitment to the contradictory claim that whatever has properties has no properties, it cannot avoid commitment to the contradictory claim that whatever has no properties essentially has at least one property essentially, namely, the property of having no properties essentially.

Further, and equally seriously, if it is indeed the case that bare substrata are necessarily bare – that they could exist without any properties at all – then they cannot serve to individuate two otherwise indiscernible things. For bare substrata are now not just indiscernible, but *necessarily* indiscernible. It is logically impossible for them to individuate substances from one another because it is logically impossible for them to be individuated from one another. They *all* have exactly one essential property, namely, the property of having no properties essentially. This being so, they cannot be distinguished from one another, not only in this world but in *any* other possible world. Given that necessarily indiscernible things are identical, there *could* not be more than one such substratum.[39] But if this is so, then the positing of bare substrata cannot serve the function that they were designed to serve. They cannot serve as individuators.

An Alternative

We seem to have arrived at the following impasse. The bundle theory, on the one hand, is not viable because pure properties alone are insufficient to guarantee the individuation of two distinct substances while impure ones re-introduce substances into the account. The bare substratum theory, on the other hand, is not viable because bare substrata cannot serve the purpose for which the theory was designed: if necessarily bare, they are necessarily indiscernible and so identical. A plausible diagnosis of this impasse is that both theories suffer in their attempts to do justice to important common-sense beliefs about the nature of substances because they are reductionist. Whereas the bundle theory attempts to decompose substances into the bundles of properties that constitute them, the bare substratum theory attempts to decompose substances into bundles of properties each of which contains a non-repeatable constituent that is not a property and is necessarily bare. Each of these theories attempts to construct substances out of things that are not themselves substances. What emerges from our discussion is that neither bundles of properties, nor bare particulars can do the individuative work that is required of a theory of substances – the work of ensuring that there cannot be two such things that satisfy the conditions set out by them for a substance to be a single thing (i.e., to be self-identical).

One response to this might be to simply concede that no theory of substances can do the required work without appealing to *impure* properties of substances, properties like being identical with *a*, for some substance *a*. Effectively this would be to give up on the idea of producing a reductive account of substances, since such properties as being identical with *a* re-introduce substances into the account.[40] But this strategy, besides being non-reductionist, concedes that a non-circular account cannot be given of substances. It may be that, in the end, a non-circular account of substances cannot be given, perhaps on the grounds that they are basic entities in the world, in that all other entities can be explained in terms of substances but substances themselves cannot be explained. But, since circular accounts are generally to be avoided, short of exploring and failing to find a non-circular alternative account, this cannot be a desirable outcome.

Fortunately, there is another suggestion that can be pursued.[41] This begins by rejecting a key assumption upon which both of the two theories that have been considered rely. The assumption in question is that the only properties that are involved in the individuation and characterization of substances are properties, construed as abstract universals that can be wholly and completely in many different places at the same time and so are literally identical, properties whose exemplifications do not and cannot distinguish between two distinct substances. The bundle theory assumes that this is so, and, as a result, is faced with the problem that the pure properties of substances do not guarantee that there could not be two substances with exactly the same properties, and that the impure properties, which could provide this guarantee, presuppose rather than effect the individuation of substances. The bare substratum theory makes the same assumption, and, seeing that a theory based on it cannot individuate distinct but qualitatively identical substances, appeals instead to a constituent that is not a property in order to effect individuation.

However, not all properties are ones whose exemplifications in places at times are like this. Such properties as, perhaps, red, round, 25 grams, and so on, might be, since, as we saw earlier, it seems possible that there could be two substances with exactly these properties. But there seem to be properties that, by their very nature, ensure that when they are exemplified they are exemplified by a single thing.[42] The kinds of properties in question are what Loux (1978, 1998, 2002) and others (Wiggins 1967, 2001) call *substance kinds*, and what we shall call substance-kind properties. They are ones whose instances or exemplifications are individual things that are members of such kinds. Examples are properties such as *lion*, *apple*, *cat*, and *human being*. An exemplification of the property, *human being*, is a single, individual human being.

Call this view of substances the property exemplification account of substances (hereafter, PES). According to it, a substance just is, in the sense of being identical with, an exemplification of a substance-kind property at a time in a place.[43] The kinds of properties whose exemplifications are of interest here are not properties *of* substances. Rather, they are properties whose exemplifications just are substances.[44] So, for example, the red round apple on my desk, not only has properties, such as the property of being red, or the property of being round; it just *is* an exemplification of the substance-kind property, *apple*, in a place at a time. Similarly, the black cat in my garden not only has the property of being black; it just is an exemplification of the substance-kind property, *cat*, in a place at a time.

According to the PES, substances themselves have a kind of 'internal' structure. They are identical with the exemplifications of substance-kind properties at times in places.[45] The places in which and the times at which those properties are exemplified or instantiated uniquely individuate substances from one another. And the properties, whose exemplifications in places at times just are substances, are not properties *of* substances but properties whose exemplifications *are* substances. Such properties are sometimes termed *constitutive* properties, and are so termed because they are the properties whose exemplifications just are substances.

It must be noted, however, that, on the present understanding of properties as universals, the exemplification of a property is (i.e., is identical with) the thing that has it (e.g., the exemplification of the property, red, is the red thing).[46] It follows that a substance such as a black cat is an exemplification *both* of the property, cat, and also an exemplification of the property, black. So, an exemplification of the property, black, is the substance that has it, a substance that is in fact black (e.g., a black cat). Similarly for the red round apple: it too is (= is identical with) the exemplification, not only of the substance-kind property, *apple*, but also of the properties, red, and round.

In view of this, what does it mean to say that substance-kind properties are ones whose exemplifications in places at times *just are*, i.e., are identical with substances but are *not properties of substances*? What it means is that constitutive properties are importantly different from other properties of substances. The exemplification of the property, black, is the *black cat*. The exemplification of the property, *cat*, just is the *cat*. Using the terminology of the property exemplification account, this is to say that, unlike substance-kind properties, which *are* constitutive of substances, properties like the property, black, are *not* constitutive properties of substances. In more familiar terminology, it is to say that the property of being black is, unlike the property of being a cat, an accidental property of the cat, rather than an essential one. The cat could exist without being black. But the cat could not exist without being a cat.

Substances construed along the lines of the PES might be viewed as 'structured particulars' because they have not only constitutive substance-kind properties, but also constitutive places and constitutive times. That is to say, it is in the nature of any substance to be an exemplification of a substance-kind property in a place at a time. Further, each substance, which is an exemplification of a substance-kind property, such as the property, *cat*, occupies a particular position in a hierarchy of more general substance-kind properties, such as the property, *animal*, and so is essentially an exemplification of more than one such property. In order for the identity conditions for substances to ensure numerical identity within the kind (i.e., ensure that only one substance can satisfy those conditions in some determinate form), then, they must specify the most fundamental, or 'atomic', substance-kind properties that substances can have.[47] If they did not, the application of a criterion of identity for substances could deliver the conclusion that there can be two substances in exactly the same place at the same time, since it is true of my cat Felix that he is both an exemplification of the substance-kind property, *cat*, and an exemplification of the substance-kind property, *animal*.

Thus, two conditions on substances are essential to the account, one an existence condition and another an identity condition. We can formulate these for substances as follows:[48]

Existence Condition: Substance [x,P,t] exists if and only if the atomic substance-kind property P is exemplified in place x at time t.

Identity Condition: Necessarily, substance [x,P,t] is identical with substance [y,Q,t'] if and only if place x is identical with place y, the atomic substance-kind property P is identical with the atomic substance-kind property Q, and the time t is identical with the time t',[49]

where x and y, P and Q, and t and t' are variables ranging over places, substance-kind properties, and times, respectively, and P and Q are fundamental, or atomic substance-kind properties.

This account takes seriously the idea, articulated in early chapters of this book, that metaphysics tells us what it is to be, say, a material substance, or a person, or an event; that is, it tells us what it is to be a member of a metaphysical kind of thing. Science tells us which the substances, persons, or events are. That is, science tells us what kinds of material substances, or persons, or events there are in the world. It tells us this, in part, by telling us what kinds of properties substances, persons, and events have. So, which are the substance-kind properties, and of those, which are the atomic ones, is not a matter that can be determined a priori, but depends on empirical investigation into the natures of objects and their properties.

The claim that substances have constitutive objects, properties, and times, should not be confused with the claim that they are in some way constituted by or composed of objects, properties, and times. In this respect at least, describing substances as 'structured particulars' is misleading. Such terminology invites us to view substances as somehow composed of places, properties, and times, related to each other in something like the way that a chair or any other complex physical object is often viewed as composed of or constituted by its parts (molecules) arranged in a certain way (this is partly what is so misleading about both the bundle theory and the bare substratum theory). What is misleading about such remarks is that the relation that holds between substances and their so-called constitutive components cannot be viewed as of the same kind as that which holds between other physical things, say, artefacts or biological organisms, and their constituent parts. The relationships that the 'constituents' of substances bear to one another are simply very different from the relations that the parts of physical things bear to one another. In the case of a substance, one constituent is *exemplified in* another, *at* yet another; and it is clear that whatever the constituents of a biological organism or an artefact may be, they do not bear this relationship to one another.

Further, the fact that canonical descriptions of the form '[x,P,t]' contain as constituents expressions referring to places, properties, and

times in no way shows that substances themselves 'contain' or are constituted by the entities referred to by the constituent expressions of such
descriptions. Consider, by way of analogy, functional expressions like
'the father of x', which, when they combine with names or descriptions,
produce complex or structured expressions that map offspring on to their
fathers. In spite of the fact that such expressions as a whole literally
contain as constituents expressions that refer to or mention other entities, there is no temptation to suppose, on that basis, that fathers are in
some sense composed of their offspring. To do so would be to assume,
falsely, that the way in which complex referring expressions are structured is just like the way in which the entities referred to are structured.

The same point holds in the case of substances. It is true that canonical descriptions of the form '$[x,P,t]$' contain as constituents expressions
referring, or purporting to refer, to substances, properties, and times. But
it in no way follows from this that substances themselves contain or are
composed of the entities referred to by the constituent expressions of
such descriptions.

If this is right, then we can see why the PES has no clear reductionist
consequences for substances in the way that both the bundle theory and
the bare substratum theory do. But then it is difficult to see how the
claim that the so-called constituents of substances are constitutive of
them can amount to anything more than the claim that they are essential to them. Indeed, we have already seen that the distinction between
constitutive and other properties of substances is effectively a distinction
between essential and accidental properties of substances. Further, as
we shall see in chapter 5, when discussing the property exemplification
account of events, its main proponent, Jaegwon Kim, explicitly commits
himself to some version of this claim. According to him, canonical
descriptions of events (i.e., descriptions of the form '$[x,P,t]$') describe
them in terms of their 'constitutive components', and thus give (on the
condition that these components are given 'intrinsic' descriptions) 'intrinsic' descriptions of them. At least one essentialist consequence is implied
by this, namely, that events have essentially the structure they have. That
is, events are essentially exemplifications of event properties at times in
(physical) objects; and hence, for any event e, being an exemplification
of an event property at a time in an object is an essential property of e.
But notice that this would appear to follow from the two basic tenets of
the property exemplification account alone, irrespective of whether it is
taken to be an account of events or an account of substances. For irrespective of how the existence condition is interpreted, the mere existence
of the relevant x, P, and t is not enough to guarantee the existence of
either an event or a substance. No entity could be an event, according
to this account, unless it was an *exemplification* of a property *at* a time

in an object. Equally, no entity could be a substance, according to the account, unless it was an *exemplification* of a property *in* a place *at* a time.[50]

To say that substances have essentially the structure they have is at least to say that they have properties whose possession guarantees that they are things of a certain metaphysical kind, ones without which they would not, as things of that kind, exist. Earlier, in chapter 2, we called these properties, real, or kind, essences, in order to distinguish them from properties, like being Socrates, that can be had essentially by individuals that fall into kinds such as the kind, *human being*, but which are not had essentially (because not had at all) by other members of the kind. A real, or kind essence is a property that every object that falls into the kind has essentially. We then characterized an essence that determines a kind as a property such that (1) it is possible for a thing to have; (2) is one without which that thing could not exist;[51] and (3) is capable of figuring in a minimal criterion of identity for the things that have it, in the sense articulated in chapter 2 (Lombard 1986).

In addition to having constitutive properties, substances also have *characterizing* properties. These are properties that substances possess, some of which they have simply in virtue of having the constitutive properties they have. Thus for example, the round, red apple has the properties of being red and round, and also the property of being an apple. It has the latter property, but not the former two, in virtue of *being an exemplification* of the (constitutive) property, *apple*. Felix the cat has the property of having forty teeth, and also that of being a cat (and has the latter, but not the former, property in virtue of being an exemplification of the constitutive property, *cat*).

This kind of view of the nature of substances is inherently more plausible than either the bundle theory or the bare substratum theory in being a different kind of essentialist view altogether. Recall that an essential property is one that is inseparable from a substance in that to lose it is to cease to exist altogether, whereas an accidental property is one without which a substance may continue to exist. According to the present, essentialist view, proponents of the bare substratum theory are wrong in thinking that bare substrata can function as subjects of predication by virtue of being character-less constituents of substances, without which those substances would not exist. Ultimate subjects are, on the present view, essentially characterized. They are so because all of their characterizing properties – not just the accidental ones like being black or being round, but also the essential ones, like being a cat, or being an apple – are properties that they have by virtue of being (i.e., being identical with) exemplifications of substance-kind properties, such as *cat* and *apple*. However, bundle theorists are wrong to assume that all properties of a substance are equally important to their identity. Substances can and do change, losing certain of their properties and acquiring others. According to the present, essentialist view, they do this by changing with regard to their accidental properties.

If the properties constitutive of substances are ones whose exemplifications just are those substances, they ought to effect the individuation of substances, not presuppose it. According to the present suggestion, this is just what exemplifications of substance-kind properties in places at times do. Further, they do so without re-introducing substances into the account, since substance-kind properties themselves are not impure; they are not such that their exemplification in a place at a time requires the existence of another, distinct substance.[52]

Substance-kind properties may be constitutive of substances, but they are not unique to any individual substance and so do not seem to be capable of functioning as individuators (there are many dogs, many human beings). How do we escape the problem, to which the bundle theory is vulnerable on one interpretation of the Principle of the Identity of Indiscernibles, that there could be two substances indiscernible from one another? According to the present account's identity conditions for substances, necessarily, substances are identical if and only if they are exemplifications of the same atomic substance-kind properties in exactly the same places at exactly the same times. So, suppose the substance a (= $[x,P,t]$) is identical with substance b (= $[y,Q,t']$), because $x = y$, $P = Q$, and $t = t'$. Then a (= b) satisfies the antecedent of Leibniz's Principle of the Indiscernibility of Identicals, which says that if things are identical (i.e., if something is identical with itself), then they have all the same properties (i.e., it shares all properties with itself). Since the atomic constitutive properties are the same ($P = Q$), we know that a and b both have the property of being P (= being Q), but since $a = b$ we also know that they have all other properties in common, essential and accidental. a just is the exemplification of atomic substance-kind property P at place x at time t; but it has other, characterizing properties. Given the assumption, articulated earlier in this chapter, that a thing has a property by exemplifying it, it follows not only that substances are exemplifications of substance-kind properties in places at times, but that substances themselves exemplify properties – their characterizing ones. And this view of substances is both non-reductionist and different from both the bundle theory and the bare substratum theory. For the bundle theory takes substances to be (i.e., be identical with) exemplifications of all of their properties, and the bare substratum theory takes bare substrata to be the exemplifiers of the properties associated with substances.[53]

Because it is not reductionist, the PES does not suffer from the problems that both the bundle theory and the bare substratum theory face. In particular, it does not suffer from the problems of explaining how substances can be natural unities, how they can be contingent entities, and how true subject-predicate statements about substances can be informative, while it avoids incoherence and commitment to the necessary truth of the identity of indiscernibles.[54] In addition to all this, it can afford an explanation of how substances can persist through time and survive change while remaining numerically the same things. Substance a is identical with material substance b if and only if a and b are exemplifications of exactly the same atomic substance-kind properties (such as the property, *cat*), in the same place and the same time. Of course, as noted above, if a is identical with b, then a/b will have all other properties in common (at that, and at all other times during which a/b exists). And this will be true for any other time at which the question of the identity a/b might arise. But, since most of the properties that a/b *exemplifies* (not properties that a/b is the exemplification *of*) are accidental properties of a/b (the exceptions being properties a/b has by virtue of *being* an exemplification of the substance-kind properties it is), the persistence conditions require only that a/b be the exemplification of exactly the same atomic substance-kind property or properties in all the same positions at all the same times during which a/b exists. These conditions are compatible with change over time with respect to the accidental properties of a/b. Further, and finally, there is a clear connection between what a substance is (it is an exemplification of an atomic substance-kind property in a place at a time), what the identity conditions are for substances (for any material substances, a and b, $a = b$ if and only if a and b are exemplifications of the same atomic substance-kind property in the same place at the same time), and what it takes for a substance to persist through time, and so survive change while remaining numerically the same thing (a/b persists through time if and only if $a(= b)$ is an exemplification of exactly the same atomic substance-kind property in all the same places at all the same times).[55]

Notes

1 By 'substance' is meant 'material substance'. Immaterial substances will not form a part of our discussion.

2 Thus, Crisp (2003, p. 217) says (of persons, also assumed to be continuants), 'I also take it as obviously true that it was someone numerically identical with me who began typing this sentence. The stage-theoretic

perdurantist denies this: on her view, the person who began the previous sentence was someone numerically distinct from the person who ended it, though similar in many ways. The endurantist, on the other hand, is free to suppose that one and the same person, strictly speaking, started and ended the sentence.' The terms 'endurantist' and 'perdurantist' are Lewis's (1986). According to the perdurantist, at each moment there is or exists only a part, or a stage, of a particular such as a person. The position is motivated by problems endurantists have in accounting for the phenomenon of persistence through change, as we shall see when discussing Objection Four to the bundle theory in the present chapter. In keeping with the view of metaphysics outlined in chapter 1, this and the next chapter will, for the most part, assume the common-sense, endurantist view about material substances and persons. The notable exception is in the discussion of the bundle theorist's attempt to deal with Objection Four, in the present chapter. For more on the perdurantist view, see Armstrong (1980), Lewis (1976, 1986, 1988), Quine (1960, 1981), and, more recently, Sider (1996, 2001). For discussion and an excellent account of the standard endurantist position, as well as a reply to Lewis's (1986) argument for perdurantism, see Merricks (1994). For an exceptionally clear general discussion of the positions and debate, see Loux (2002, chapter 6).

3   The criterion of identity alone cannot be all that we need, as we saw in chapter 2. After all, we can give a criterion of identity for ghosts (necessarily, they are identical if and only if they are spirits of the same person), but still think that there aren't any such things. What we need, in addition, if we are to be justified in thinking that there are such things, is an adequate metaphysical theory of ghosts. That is the point of this paragraph.

4   Philosophers have different ways of referring to properties. So, for example, all of these ways of talking about the property of being red can be used: 'Red is a property', 'Redness is a property', and 'Being red is a property'. For the purposes of our discussion these different ways will not be distinguished, although the differences may be relevant to the debate between Realists and Nominalists with respect to the existence of universals: for more on this, see chapter 6.

5   The issue of reduction is a tricky one. Generally speaking, a theoretic reduction of the entities of one theory to the entities of another can be of two kinds. In the first, the entities of the reduced theory are identified with the entities of the reducing theory, and this is effected by way of 'bridge' or correlation laws (the *locus classicus* is Nagel 1961). In the second, the entities of the reduced theory are eliminated in favour of the entities of the reducing theory (the *locus classicus* being Kemeny-Oppenheim 1956). It is the first kind of reduction that is intended here. It should be distinguished from a third conception of reduction that is stronger than Nagel's in requiring property identities (Causey 1977), which is stronger than what is intended here. Finally, there is a sense of 'reduction' in which what is reduced is talk: talk of *F*s is reduced to talk of *G*s. This sort of reduction, however, has no ontological implications, and so is not at issue here.

6 'Nothing but' in the sense that there is no other constituent of them, no further element or component that constitutes them, that is not a property. Loux (1978) expresses this commitment of the bundle theory in terms of what he calls The Principle of Constituent Identity, which states:

> Necessarily, for any substance, *a*, and any substance, *b*, if, for any entity, *c*, *c* is a constituent of *a* if and only if *c* is a constituent of *b*, then *a* is identical with *b*. (1978, p. 131)

This principle entails the Principle of the Indiscernibility of Identicals, which Loux formulates, somewhat differently than we have in chapter 2, and *with* the modal operator, 'necessarily', as:

> Necessarily, for any substance, *a*, and any substance, *b*, if, for any property, *P*, *P* is an attribute of *a* if and only if *P* is an attribute of *b*, then *a* is identical with *b*. (1978, p. 131)

7 It follows trivially that the bundle theory is committed to the necessary truth of the Principle of the Indiscernibility of Identicals, since if indiscernibles are identical, then, necessarily, given that they are identical, it follows that they indiscernible.

8 On this conception of the bundle theory, the alternative to it (call this the bare substratum theory) is the view that substances are *other* than their properties. This seems to have been what Locke had in mind; see the quotation in note 9 below. But as we shall see, another way of understanding the alternative is as the view that substances are something *more* than their properties. More precisely, it is the view that substances are constituted *both* by their properties *and* by a further component or element, this further thing being a 'bare' particular rather than a property and the carrier of a substance's numerical identity. This second way of understanding the bare substratum theory is the one that prevails in our discussion on pp. 110–13.

9 Here, for example, is what Locke says:

> Though, in the meantime, it be manifest, and everyone, upon inquiry into his own thoughts, will find that he has no other idea of any substance, e.g., let it be gold, horse, iron, man, vitriol, bread, but what he has barely of those sensible qualities, which he supposes to inhere, with a supposition of such a *substratum*, as gives, as it were, support to those qualities, or simple ideas, which he has observed to exist united together. (Locke 1975, II, xxxIII.6, p. 298)

Locke includes as substances stuffs such as gold, and perhaps matter; others take the Aristotelian view that only particular *things*, such as horses, count as substances. Aristotle, in contrast, held that the underlying 'supporter' of properties is matter, but that matter is not a substance since it is not a thing. So, for Aristotle, matter is not substance, in the sense of being a substratum in which properties inhere. Still, he distinguished between substances, as subjects that possess properties, from the properties that they have. He also seemed to think that at least one property of a substance, the property of being of the kind it is, is not a property of that substance, but rather a property possessed by matter. Substances for him were combinations of matter and form (though cf. the discussion of Aristotle in chapter 1). For more on this, see Loux (1978 and 2002). The discussion of both the bare substratum theory and the bundle theory in this chapter draws on, but also furthers, Loux's excellent discussions.

10 This view is embodied in what is known as the Principle of Acquaintance. See Bergmann (1967) and Loux (1978, 1998). According to this principle, a theory may be committed only to the existence of objects that it is possible to be acquainted with by means of the senses. Empiricism is the doctrine that all knowledge of a factual kind is justified by appeal to sensory experience. Berkeley's views are not included here because, although it is commonly agreed that he held a kind of bundle theory with regard to the constituents of material substances in denying the existence of a material substratum, he ultimately embraced the view that the constituents of material substances, viz. ideas, need a mental substratum in which to exist. See Berkeley (1996).

11 One can imagine a Kantian, for example, maintaining that a 'bare' substance, being characterless, could not be a possible object of knowledge, since to be so is to be capable of being brought under a concept of some kind, where that concept is applicable to the experienceable world.

12 What about the property of being identical with Socrates? It seems that that property would not have existed if Socrates had not existed. If we are going to rule properties like these out as properties, then it might be very difficult to defend the view that the Principle of the Identity of Indiscernibles is necessarily true. But the bundle theorist does need to rule these out, at least for the purposes of formulating the theory. This is because the theory is designed to be a reductive account of substances; thus, the account cannot appeal to things that (like the property of being Socrates) already entail the existence of substances because they contain substances as constituents. We will return to this issue when discussing Objection Four.

13 Loux (1978) also makes this point.

14 Plantinga explains the notion of a possible world like this:

> A possible world is a state of affairs of some kind – one that could have obtained if it does not. *Hubert Horatio Humphrey's having run a mile in four minutes*, for example, is a state of affairs that is clearly possible in the relevant sense; *his having had a brother who never had a sibling* is not. Furthermore, a possible world must be what we may call a *fully determinate* state of affairs. *Humphrey's having run a four-minute mile* is a possible state of affairs, as perhaps, is *Paul X. Zwier's being a good basketball player*. Neither of these, however, is fully determinate in that either of them could have obtained whether or not the other had. A fully determinate state of affairs, *S*, let us say,

is one such that for any state of affairs, *S′*, either *S* includes *S′* (that is, could not have obtained unless *S′* had also obtained) or *S* precludes *S′* (that is, could not have obtained if *S′* had obtained). (Plantinga 1970, p. 463)

15 But this looks like it commits the fallacy of division, in assuming that what is true of a whole is true of its parts. There are clear examples where this assumption is false. Suppose, for example, that I stammer. I stammer because my tongue catches. Indeed, it looks as though my stammering just is my tongue's catching. And my tongue is a part of me. But although it is true that I stammer, it is not true that my tongue stammers. Nor is it true that any other part of me stammers.

16 This assumes that two substances can't be in the same place at the same time, and it assumes that places exist independently of substances (otherwise the account, for the bundle theorist, is circular). But both of these assumptions might be defensible.

17 For the purposes of this discussion, 'instantiated' and 'exemplified' are being used interchangeably, although there are differences between them. One is that properties are typically thought of as instantiated *in* but exemplified *by* particular things.

18 According to some people, to say this is to say that substances are bundles of tropes. See Simons (1994) and Lowe (1989a, 1998). Whereas Simons defends a tropist view, Lowe rejects it. Tropes, according to trope theory, are variously known as 'particularized properties' or 'concretized properties' (Strawson 1959; Honderich 1981, 1982; Bacon 1995, 2002). That is, they are properties-at-times-in-places. For instance, this whiteness is essentially this whiteness, whiteness-here-now. This whiteness of this sheet of paper before me is as particular as the sheet of paper is itself. On this understanding of substances, substances are identical with because constituted by bundles of tropes. In fact, since substances endure or persist through time, they are identical with all of the bundles of tropes that constitute them throughout all of the times at which they exist. It is not clear that one must be committed to viewing instantiations of properties as tropes in order to defeat this objection, however. Suppose that we treat substances as bundles of properties, construed as abstract universals, including spatio-temporal ones, which enter into a collocation relation or are bundled by being co-instantiated. Then exemplifications of properties such as that of being red will be in positions, but not because those exemplifications are essentially spatio-temporal. What gives them their positions is their being (contingently) co-instantiated with spatio-temporal properties, these being understood, not as tropes, but as abstract universals.

19 Russell (1911–12) speaks of compresence, which he describes as 'occurring together', Williams (1953) speaks of collocation, and Castañeda (1974) speaks of consubstantiation. For a sustained defence of a tropist conception, both of the nature of particulars and of the relation between a thing and its properties, see Campbell (1990) and Bacon (1995).

20 In fact, the objection is best understood as assuming that substances are complex things, since the role of the notion of unity in it would be difficult

to understand otherwise: the objection would simply amount to the claim that substances are not collocations of properties since substances are simples and collocations of properties are complex.

21 This is the idea that van Inwagen (1990) has in mind when he denies that artefacts are anything more than heaps, i.e., denies that they are material substances.

22 This is effectively the kind of option that was pursued by Leibniz: see his *Monadology* (1998). Also, see Ishiguro (1998) where the view is further clarified and elaborated. The strategy can be viewed as questioning the distinction between 'truths of meaning' and 'truths of fact'. Another way of pursuing the strategy would be to argue, as Quine (1964e) and, more recently, Burge (1986), do, that all truths are informative, even synonymies, since even these can be doubted.

23 Equally, it may be taken to show that no truths are logical ones, that there is no distinction in kind between the so-called logical truths and others because all truths are informative. This is the line that Burge pursues (see note 22).

24 This is what Van Cleve (1994) finds to be the real source of Objection Three.

25 For an excellent discussion and defence of the view that truths of this kind are necessary but knowable only a posteriori, see Kripke (1980).

26 A version of this objection will arise again, this time with respect to the property exemplification account of substances defended in the present chapter, in chapter 6, where the universalist conception of the relation between a particular and its properties is defended against Trope Nominalism. There, however, the objection will be defeated.

27 For an argument for this claim, see Lombard (1986, p. 251).

28 This is similar to what Loux (1978, p. 125) appeals to in his attempt to defuse this objection.

29 This is something like the way that properties are treated by trope theorists. See note 18.

30 This is a distinction that Loux (1978, chapter 7) draws. Elsewhere, he defines an impure and a pure property thus:

> a property, P, is impure just in case there is a contingent particular, s, and a relation, R, such that necessarily for any object, x, x exemplifies P just in case x enters into R with s and that a property is pure just in case it is not impure.' (Loux, 1998, p. 246).

31 Since we're talking about material substances, which are contingently existing things, here, we are only concerned with properties that do or do not require the existence of other contingently existing things.

32 However, there may be relational properties of substances that are not impure. As we shall see, the spatio-temporal properties of substances, such as being 3 feet high at time t_1, are arguably both relational and pure by the definition given here.

33 Black's (1952) argument uses the example of a perfectly symmetrical universe in which the only objects are two qualitatively identical spheres at

some distance from each other. O'Leary-Hawthorne (1995) argues, against Black, that if the bundle theory is understood as taking the constituents of bundles to be immanent universals (universals that are literally in space and time and can literally be in two places at the same time, so that, for example, they can be at some distance from themselves), the example fails to demonstrate that (P) is not necessarily true. However, Zimmerman (1997) defends Black against this response.

34   In connection with this, a variant on the example introduced by Black (1952) can be cited against the necessary truth of (P). Suppose that there is a perfectly symmetrical universe that contains exactly three qualitatively identical spheres, each one being 2 feet apart from the others. Here it looks like there is no property that could individuate any of the spheres from the others. For discussion of this example, see Forrest (2002).

35   Note that this does not establish that there must be more than one substance, or more than one event. So long as that substance has more than one spatial part, and that event has more than one temporal part, sense can be made of there being spatial relations between distinct places and temporal relations between distinct times.

36   This is the substantival as contrasted with the adjectival conception of space and time. Crudely, the substantival conception takes places to be individual things, rather than properties of individual things.

37   We could not distinguish places (and times) from one another since impure properties, such as being identical with that (where that = the place in question) are not permissible as individuators, and the only other obvious possibility, namely, individuating places in terms of their parts is circular (for discussion of this see Hoffman and Rosenkrantz 1994, chapter 5).

38   The discussion does not end here, since there are a number of responses that bundle theorists can make. For example, they can deny that the bundle theory is committed to the necessary truth of the Principle of the Identity of Indiscernibles, but only to its truth. However, these responses are themselves problematic. For more on this, see Loux (1978, 1998) and references therein.

39   Note that the use of the Principle of the Identity of Indiscernibles here is consistent with the rejection of that principle as necessarily true in general, for it is consistent with the claim that the principle is not necessarily true that things that are necessarily indiscernible are identical.

40   See, for example, Wolterstorff (1970).

41   See Loux (1978, 1998, 2002) for reasoning along these lines.

42   Thus, as Loux says,

> A substance-kind provides us with the concept of a fully-fledged concrete object; and its instantiation is by itself sufficient to ensure the existence of a substantial particular. The kind, *human being*, we have seen, is a universal whose instantiation results in the existence of an individual human being; and the kind *dog* is such that its being exemplified consists in the existence of one canine particular. (1998, p. 245)

But see note 44 below. For another, different account of substances that is roughly speaking Aristotelian, see Hoffman and Rosenkrantz (1996). See also Quinton (1973).

43 The full-fledged Aristotelian version would add: 'they are exemplifications of those properties in matter that is a suitable 'receptacle' for such properties'. It might be objected that this account presupposes the concept of substance, since whatever one's account of substances, every property of a substance will be a 'substance property' in the obvious sense (so long as there are properties). We can only get a non-vacuous account of substances if we drop the 'substance' qualification – but then the account is just false. Two points are worth making here. First, a complete filling out of the qualification would add 'static' to 'substance-kind', which the account contrasts with 'dynamic' (for more on this contrast, see note 45 below and the discussion of the property exemplification account of events in chapter 5). Second, although 'substance' is ineliminable in the account, it isn't vacuous since it is held that *which* properties of objects are static, and so which are the substance-kind ones, is not a matter that can be determined a priori, but depends on empirical investigation into the natures of objects and their properties. Finally, the 'definition' of substance by the account is not intended to be a conceptual truth, but a metaphysical one.

44 This kind of account is well known as an account of the nature of events (see Kim 1976 and Lombard 1986). For more on the account and its development in the case of events, see chapter 5 of the present text. Loux (1978, 1998) develops an account that is not unlike this, although it is not clear that he would endorse this version of it. He considers his to be an Aristotelian account and calls it a 'substance-theory' of substances. The similarity to this account is striking, for he says:

> In point of fact Aristotle did not first propose the relevant interpretation of universals for universals like whiteness or wisdom. His account of these universals appears to be an extension of the account he provides for universals from the category of substance, universals like *man* and *dog*. In the case of these universals, he thinks, the view that instantiations of the universal are numerically diverse is not just plausible, but inescapable. (Loux, 1978, p. 160)

One important difference between Loux's account and this one, however, is that Loux holds that it is sufficient for there to be distinct individual substances of the same substance-kind that there be distinct instantiations of that kind, without reference to anything else, places and times included. Thus he says:

> every kind is a universal whose multiple exemplification is by itself sufficient to ensure the existence of a plurality of substances. For the kind *human being* to be instantiated is for there to be at least one human being and for it to be instantiated twice is for there to be two different human beings. (1998, p. 244)

However, what accounts for two instantiations being two and not one? It seems that something further is needed in the account. For more on this, see pp. 116 and 121–2 in the text.

45 Where substance-kind properties are required to be what we might call 'static' ones. Intuitively, some properties are ones whose exemplification implies change whereas others are not. Lombard (1986) labels these two sorts of properties 'dynamic' and 'static', respectively, and argues that only exemplifications of the dynamic ones are events. Static properties are ones whose exemplification implies that something is in a certain state. Examples of such properties are colour properties such as red, and blue, weight properties such as 3 kg, and 6 kg, and positional properties, such as in Detroit at 3 p.m. on Saturday, 1 December 2001, and in Denver at 5 a.m. on Sunday, 2 December 2001. Dynamic properties, in contrast, are ones whose exemplification implies that something is changing at that time. Because dynamic properties are indicative of change, they can be possessed only during intervals of time, however short they may be. That is to say, change takes time. As we shall see in chapter 5, the distinction between static and dynamic properties is critical to the distinction between the ontological category of substances and that of events, even if a property exemplification account can be given for entities of both categories.

46 So, the exemplification of a property is *not* a trope of that property. On a universalist understanding of properties, the exemplification of a property, such as red, is the particular red thing, such as the red apple. For more on the distinction between properties as universals and properties as tropes, see chapter 6.

47 What makes a substance-kind property atomic? Here we need to refine the account by introducing the idea of a *quality space* (an idea due to Quine (1960, pp. 83–4) and exploited by Lombard (1986) in his version of the property exemplification account of events (PEE), discussed in chapter 5). This is a set of simple static properties that fall into kinds, and are mutually exclusive (that is, no two such properties can be had by the same material substance at exactly the same time). For example, the colour quality space is a set of simple colour properties (e.g., red, blue, yellow, etc.), the weight quality space consists of simple weight properties (e.g., 1 kg, 2 kg, etc.), and so on. Effectively, the kinds of changes material substances can undergo is determined by the kinds of quality spaces there are. A substance can only change by exemplifying first one, then another, property from within the *same* quality space. So, for example, a thing cannot simply change from red to square given that these are properties from distinct quality spaces. Atomic substance-kind properties themselves constitute a quality space, the quality space associated with the atomic substance-kinds. Just as an atomic substance, such as a cat, or an apple, can have no more than one colour property from the colour quality space at exactly the same time, an atomic substance can have no more than one atomic substance-kind property from the atomic substance quality space at exactly the same time. As this indicates, substance-kind properties, even atomic ones, are properties

by virtue of which the things that have them are things at all, and so ones capable of having other, first-level properties, such as particular colours and shapes. They are not constructed out of those first-level properties. (So 'atomic' in 'atomic property' does not mean 'lowest level'. Nor does 'atomic' in 'atomic substance' mean 'smallest'). An atomic substance (for a given theory *T*) is the exemplification of a property in an atomic substance-kind quality space (a substance-kind quality space that is atomic, according to *T*), in a place at a time.

The question of how properties are to be individuated into kinds – how quality spaces are to be individuated from one another – is not one that the property exemplification account takes to be answerable a priori. This is, of course, consistent with the (Aristotelian) view of metaphysics outlined in chapter 1, according to which it is the business of metaphysics to tell us what it is to be an object of a metaphysical kind, say, a material substance, or a property, whereas it is the business of science to tell us which are the substances, or the properties.

48 This is adapted from the existence and identity conditions given for events on the property exemplification account of events. See Kim (1973, 1976) and chapter 5.

49 Note that the modal operator 'necessariliy' in the identity condition does not appear in Kim's account of the identity conditions for events, but is in keeping with the form of a criterion of identity arrived at in chapter 2.

50 Suppose that the property exemplification account of substances and the property exemplification account of events are both true. There are still two important differences between substances and events. First, whereas substances are exemplifications of substance-kind properties, events are exemplifications of act- or event-properties. Second, whereas events are exemplifications of properties in objects (i.e., substances), substances are not. There may be a third, important difference, since it may be true of events but not of substances, that their actual times of occurrence are essential to them (for argument for this, see Lombard 1986). We are assuming here that the property exemplification account is an adequate account of events. But we shall see in chapter 5 that certain versions of it are not.

51 That is, is one such that it is necessarily true that if some entity has that property, then it is necessary that if that entity exists, then it has that property. The sense of 'necessarily' in use is that employed in a Kripke-type semantics for quantified S5 in which the Barcan formula fails. (1) rules out as essences inconsistent properties. (2) ensures that an essence is a property that an object of a kind must have in order to exist as an object of that kind. And (3) rules out as kind-determining essences properties that may be common to objects of more than one kind, like being an existent thing, or being a (merely) spatio-temporal thing. While any property that meets (1) and (2) is an essence of a class of things, the idea behind (3) is that no property can be a kind-determining essence if it is not unique to things of that kind. For more on the nature and purpose of a criterion of identity, see chapter 2.

52 Loux makes essentially the same point, though somewhat differently:

> On this view, the universals associated with a familiar particular are not con-
> stituents of it. The kind to which a substance belongs is not somehow in it or
> a part of it. Being a member of its proper kind is just what the substance is;
> and its belonging to the kind marks it out as a subject for other universals.
> (1998, p. 246)

53 The kind of contrast being marked here between substance-kind properties
    and others is broadly Aristotelian and in keeping with that used by Loux:

> We say that it is which objects which exhibit whiteness; whereas, the white-
> nesses present in them count as instantiations of the universal they all exhibit.
> Having this distinction before us, we can say that while the objects exhibiting
> whiteness are numerically different, the instantiations of whiteness in them
> are identical. In the case of substance-kinds, however, there is no distinction
> between the objects which exhibit a universal and the various instantiations
> of that universal. The individuals who exhibit the universal, *man*, just are the
> instantiations of that universal, so that in the case of substance-kinds, there is
> no alternative to construing instantiations of each universal as numerically
> diverse. (Loux, 1978, p. 161)

54 One might wonder how it solves the problem of how substances can be
    natural unities. Well, the different substance-kind properties that it is of the
    essence of a substance, such as a cat, to exemplify, are ones that it is natural
    to say it co-exemplifies. Just as it is natural to suppose that an exemplifica-
    tion of the property, red, just is (i.e., is identical with) an exemplification of
    the property, colour, so too it is natural to suppose that to be an exempli-
    fication of the atomic substance-kind property, *cat*, just is to be an exem-
    plification of the substance-kind property, *animal* – in exemplifying the
    former property, the cat just does exemplify the latter one. That is, there is
    just one exemplification of two properties. Since, in addition, the exempli-
    fication of a property is the thing that has it, the cat is (i.e., is identical with)
    a single exemplification of all of its properties, not just the ones that it is of
    the essence of the cat to exemplify.
55 Or, to put it another way, a/b persists from time t to time t' if and only if,
    during the period of time that includes both t and t' a (= b) is an exempli-
    fication of exactly the same atomic substance-kind property and share the
    same spatio-temporal history.

Suggested Further Reading

Bacon, J. (1995): *Universals and Property Instances: The Alphabet of Being.*
Oxford: Blackwell.

Bacon, J. (2002): 'Tropes'. In E. Zalta (ed.), *The Stanford Encyclopedia of Philosophy* (Fall 2002 edn). URL = <http://plato.stanford.edu/archives/fall2002/entries/tropes/>.

Bergmann, G. (1967): *Realism: A Critique of Brentano and Meinong*. Madison: University of Wisconsin Press.

Black, M. (1952): 'The Identity of Indiscernibles'. In *Mind* 61, 153–64. Reprinted in Loux (ed.) 1970, pp. 250–62.

Campbell, K. (1990): *Abstract Particulars*. Oxford: Blackwell.

Crisp, T. (2003): 'Presentism'. In van Inwagen and Zimmerman (eds) 2003, pp. 211–45.

Elder, C. (2004): *Real Natures and Familiar Objects*. Cambridge, Mass.: MIT Press.

Haslinger, S. (2003): 'Persistence Through Time'. In van Inwagen and Zimmerman (eds) 2003, pp. 315–54.

Heller, M. (1990): *The Ontology of Physical Objects: Four Dimensional Hunks of Matter*. Cambridge: Cambridge University Press.

Lewis, D. (1976): 'Survival and Identity'. In Rorty 1976, pp. 17–40. Reprinted with 'Postscripts to Identity' in Lewis 1983a, pp. 55–77.

Lewis, D. (1983a): *Philosophical Papers*, vol. I. Oxford: Oxford University Press.

Lewis, D. (1986): *On the Plurality of Worlds*. Oxford: Blackwell.

Lewis, D. (1988): 'Rearrangement of Particles: Reply to Lowe'. In *Analysis* 48, 65–72.

Loux, M. (ed.) (1970): *Universals and Particulars*. New York: Doubleday and Company, Inc.

Loux, M. (1978): *Substance and Attribute*. Dordrecht: D. Reidel Publishing Company, chapters 6–9.

Loux, M. (1998): 'Beyond Substrata and Bundles'. In Laurence and Macdonald (eds), pp. 233–47.

Loux, M. (2002): *Metaphysics: A Contemporary Introduction*. 2nd edn. London: Routledge, chapters 3 and 6.

Lowe, E. J. (1998): *The Possibility of Metaphysics*. Oxford: Oxford University Press, chapters 5–9.

Martin, C. B. (1980): 'Substance Substantiated'. In *Australasian Journal of Philosophy* 58, 3–10.

Merricks, T. (1994): 'Endurance and Indiscernibility'. In *Journal of Philosophy* 91, 165–84.

O'Leary-Hawthorne, J. (1995): 'The Bundle Theory of Substance and the Identity of Indiscernibles'. In *Analysis* 55, 191–6.

Sider, T. (1996): 'All the World's a Stage'. In *Australasian Journal of Philosophy* 74, 433–53.

Sider, T. (2001): *Four-Dimensionalism: An Ontology of Persistence and Time*. Oxford: Clarendon Press.

Simons, P. (1994): 'Particulars in Particular Clothing: Three Trope Theories of Substance'. In *Philosophy and Phenomenological Research* 54, 553–75. Reprinted in Laurence and Macdonald (eds) 1998.

Van Cleve, J. (1985): 'Three Versions of the Bundle Theory'. In *Philosophical Studies* 47, 95–107. Reprinted in Laurence and Macdonald (eds) 1998.

Wiggins, D. (2001): *Sameness and Substance*. New edn. Cambridge: Cambridge University Press, chapters 2 and 3.

Williams, D. C. (1953) 'The Elements of Being'. In *Review of Metaphysics* 7, 3–18 and 171–92. Reprinted in Williams 1966, pp. 74–109.

Williams, D. C. (1966): *The Principles of Empirical Realism*. Springfield: Charles C. Thomas.

Zimmerman, D. (1997): 'Distinct Indiscernibles and the Bundle Theory'. In *Mind* 106, 305–9.

4

Persons and
Personal Identity

In the last chapter we considered various theories of the nature of particulars of one kind, namely, material substances, and the principles and criteria of identity associated with them. In this and the next chapter, we shall consider two further categories of particulars, persons and events, respectively, and our ontological commitment to them. We'll consider the relation between these particulars and material substances, with specific reference to the question whether they are reducible (in the sense specified in the previous chapter) to material substances and their properties. We begin, in this chapter, with the ontological category of persons.

Our Ontological Commitment to Persons

In our day-to-day interactions with each other and with particulars of other kinds in the world around us, we talk about and refer to persons as well as to other material substances. We also quantify over and count persons: we speak, for example, of the number of people who turned up for the wedding reception, of how many people were in the lecture theatre this morning, and so on, as though persons are within the domain of objects to which we are ontologically committed.

Persons are distinctive in having not only physical characteristics but also psychological ones, in virtue of having thoughts and other attitudes both about things in the world around them and about themselves.[1] Because they have bodies, they can, like many other physical mechanisms, float on water, eat, and move parts of their bodies. Yet, unlike many other physical mechanisms, persons can also have beliefs, desires, thoughts, and wishes, not only about things other than them, but also about themselves. It is because persons possess these latter characteristics that they have been thought not only to be distinguishable from mere material substances but also to form a fundamentally distinct ontological category of particulars, or to constitute a genuine metaphysical kind (Wiggins 1967, 2001; Baker 2000). If persons are to have this status (or if they are not), we need to enquire more deeply into the nature of persons and their identity conditions.

Identity conditions for persons should provide conditions necessary and sufficient for distinguishing, at any given time, members of that kind from objects or entities belonging to other categories of particulars, such as material substances and events, and also for individuating, or distinguishing members of the kind, persons, from each other. Such conditions specify properties that are essential to the kind, at least some of which are also unique to it, properties whose possession, at any given time in some determinate form by any member of that kind, ensures its numerical identity.

In chapter 3, we arrived at such a specification for substances, on the basis of a particular, essentialist, theory of them. According to it, substances are exemplifications of substance-kind properties in places at times, and substance a is identical with substance b if and only if a and b are exemplifications of the same atomic substance-kind properties in the same place at the same time. A substance persists from one time to another if and only if it remains the same with regard to its atomic substance-kind property and has the same spatio-temporal history.

Thus, the identity conditions for substances, and what it takes for a material substance to persist over time, both have a clear connection with what it is to be a material substance in the first place. Now, persons, too, are continuants: they persist through time and survive change. This being so, any metaphysical theory of what it is to be a person will encounter the problem of accounting for how a person can persist through change – how a single person can change qualitatively (i.e., with respect to his or her properties) from one time to another while remaining numerically the same person.

Discussions of persons and personal identity often consider a number of different questions under the same general heading, two of which are of particular relevance (Olson 1997, 2002a; Baker 2000, 2001a). The first is the question of what makes any entity a person, a single thing of a particular kind. This is a metaphysical question, one that calls out for a theory of persons and a criterion of personal identity. The account, if adequate, will do more than just answer the question of whether, at any given time, an identity statement of the form '$a = b$' is true, where a and b refer to persons. Since identity is omni-temporal – that is, since, if a is identical with b at a given time, t, then a is identical with b at all other times – the account will also answer the question of whether, at any time during a period that includes t and t', a is identical with b. Sometimes this is called the question of *synchronic* identity for persons.

The second question of particular relevance here is a question about the persistence of a particular person from time t to time t'. Although it is often referred to as a question of personal identity (or as a question of *diachronic* identity for persons), this can be misleading (Olson 2002a; Baker 2000, 2001). As just noted, since identity is omni-temporal, if, at a given time, t, it is true that $a = b$, then, as long as a continues to exist at all, it is guaranteed that $a = b$ at all times. Still, there is a question of persistence that can be raised with respect to persons, just as there is with respect to substances, as we saw in chapter 3. Suppose that I point to you now, and then point to or refer to someone who exists at another time, say, the bank teller I spoke to yesterday, and ask whether I am pointing twice to two things or pointing twice to one thing. It is this kind of question that often takes centre stage in metaphysical discussions of personal identity.[2]

Thus, there are at least two different metaphysical questions that can be asked about persons, one about their identity conditions, and another about their persistence conditions. Given what has just been said above and in chapter 3, though, we can expect there to be a connection between what makes for personal identity (that is, what the identity conditions for persons are) and what makes for a particular person's persistence from one time to another. The former concerns the possession of properties that are essential and unique to the category of persons, whose possession in some determinate form at any given time makes for the numerical identity of a person within that category. The latter concerns the continued possession of those properties, in some determinate form, that make for a particular person's survival as that very person from one time to another.

There are three main theories of the nature of persons that will be touched upon in this chapter. First, there is the view that they are essentially psychological beings. This type of view typically takes persons to be immaterial beings (Swinburne 1984, 1997; Foster 1991; Robinson 1989), and is the kind of view taken by philosophers such as Descartes (1984). Second, there is the view that persons are essentially physical beings. A recent version of this view is known as animalism, the view that persons are essentially animals (Snowdon 1990, 1996; Olson 1997, 2002b). Both of these views are considered to be reductionist, since they attempt to account for the nature of persons, and, more specifically, the nature of human persons, by taking one or the other, but not both, of the two sorts of characteristics typically associated with persons (psychological ones and physical ones) to be essential to them. The third type of view says that persons are essentially psychological beings that are constituted by physical things, such as animals (Baker 2000; Shoemaker 1984; Wiggins 1967). While this may appear to be reductionist in its account of what it is to be a person (since, according to it, whatever actually constitutes a person is inessential to it), unlike both animalism and immaterialism, its account of human persons (i.e., persons that are constituted by human animals) is non-reductionist in requiring that they be *both* essentially physical and essentially psychological beings.

In what follows, we will eventually opt for a view of persons that is motivated by, but is not identical with, this third view (namely, a version of the property exemplification account), and suggest a criterion of identity for persons based upon it. Since, however, many discussions of personal identity begin with the question of persistence rather than with the question of identity conditions for persons, it will be useful and instructive for us to begin with this.[3] Bearing in mind the connection between identity conditions and persistence conditions discussed in chapter 3 and above, the aim of the discussion will be to attempt, on the basis of various candidates for what it takes for a person to persist through time, to formulate a plausible proposal about what the identity conditions for, and nature of, persons might be.

Candidates for Persistence Conditions for Persons

We've noted that persons are distinctive in having both physical and psychological characteristics. Many proposals for criteria of persistence for persons have focused on one or the other, but not both, of these characteristics. In what follows, we'll consider two well-known families of criteria. Those of the first can be loosely characterized as psychological criteria, which focus on various psychological characteristics of persons, and the second can be loosely characterized as physical criteria, which focus on various physical characteristics of persons. Both types of criteria are vulnerable to an objection known as the reduplication argument, and we shall consider various attempts to deal with the objection, concluding that these attempts do not succeed. We shall then consider and defend an alternative criterion, and explore the connection between it and the question of what persons are and what their identity conditions might be, coming up with a concrete proposal.

The Memory/Psychological Criterion

What makes persons seem so strikingly and uniquely different from material substances is that they possess psychological characteristics.

Certain of these characteristics at least appear to be both very different from physical ones and particularly important to a person's being a person. These are the intentional characteristics, properties persons possess in virtue of their capacity to have propositional attitudes, states such as believing, thinking, expecting, desiring, or remembering that p, for some propositional content p (such as, for example, the propositional content, *Graham will win the tournament*, which constitutes the content of my now hoping that Graham will win the tournament).[4] These psychological characteristics, unlike physical ones, appear to have a distinctive normative character. There are two aspects to this character, one having to do with its normativity, and the other having to do with its distinctiveness.

First, whether a person has a given belief or desire is not just a matter of what she is disposed to do, or tends to do in certain circumstances, in the way that, say, the solubility of sugar is a matter of what it is disposed, in the sense of what it tends, to do in certain circumstances. It is a matter of what, ideally, she ought to do in those circumstances, whether or not she actually does it or has any tendency to do it. That is to say, having a particular belief or desire is not, whereas possessing a physical property such as being soluble is, a matter of what one does or has a tendency to do, where this can be captured in statistical-cum-causal terms. If I believe that it is getting dark and I want to finish reading the newspaper, then I *ought* to switch on the light, whether or not I actually do or tend to do so. If I want a coke and believe that there is some coke in the refrigerator, then I *ought* to get up and go to the refrigerator. In both cases (and in countless others) my belief and my desire give me a reason for acting in a certain way. But we all know only too well that we do not always, or even sometimes, do what we have reason, even very good reason, to do. The force of this 'ought' persists, moreover, even when there is no tendency or propensity to act in accordance with such reasons, and so cannot be made intelligible simply in terms of the formula, 'will, all things being equal'. There may be no obstacles to my switching on the light, either physical or psychological; and yet I may simply fail to turn on the light (perhaps because I am feeling lazy, for example).

Further, as such examples indicate, the force of this 'ought' is of a particular, rational kind. Specifically, the possession of a belief is constrained by various principles or canons of rationality, such as, perhaps, those governing deductive and inductive inference, maximizing logical consistency, and so on. Such principles are constitutive of rationality in the sense that they at least partly define what it is to be a rational creature. It is rational to attempt to maximize logical consistency within one's network of beliefs, irrational to embrace ones that contradict one another. Thus, for example, it is rational, given that one believes that $p\&q$, for some propositional contents p and q, to believe that p. It is a breach of rationality to believe that $p\&q$, and yet not believe that p. Again, it is rational, given that I believe that my cat Felix is black, for me to believe that some cats are black. It is a breach of rationality for me both to believe that my cat Felix is black and to believe that no cats are black (Davidson 1970a, 1974; Kim 1985).

This kind of normativity seems to be distinctive of intentional characteristics. Many think that the possession of such properties is essential to persons' being persons. For it is in virtue of this that persons are capable of reasoning, deliberating and weighing up reasons for their beliefs and for their actions, and, partly as a result of this, of being capable of doing right and wrong, and so of being morally culpable for their actions. In view of all this, it is hardly surprising that intentional properties should be singled out as ones that make for a person's persistence through time.

For many, the question that is of vital importance regarding personal identity is that of the continued identity of a person over time, of what makes me the same person today as I was yesterday. The sorts of psychological characteristics typically considered to be critical to answering this question are ones that, like memory characteristics, provide a ground for continuity between a person's psychology at one time and at another. It is in the nature of an experience's being a memory experience that it is veridical, i.e., that memory experiences are of events in the past that actually occurred. Given this and the plausible assumption that a person can only have a memory experience of an earlier event if that person actually witnessed or experienced that event, there is a connection between memory experiences and past perceptions of events that actually occurred. Because of this connection, memory experiences have been mooted as the ground for the continuity of a person's psychology over time (Locke 1975; Garrett 1998; Lewis 1976; Noonan 1989; Parfit 1971, 1984; Perry 1976; Shoemaker 1970, 1984; Unger 1990). It is at least partly for this reason that the psychological criterion has often taken the form of a memory criterion for personal identity. Let us begin, then, by concentrating on this version of the psychological criterion.

The memory criterion: memory identity

We will discuss three versions of the memory criterion of persistence for persons. Two of them require memory identity in some form or another as a condition on the persistence of a person, whereas the third replaces this with the weaker requirement of memory continuity. We begin with the strongest version and work our way towards the weaker one.

In its crudest and strongest formulation, the memory criterion states that a person's persistence through time consists in the continued possession of all of his or her memory characteristics. According to it,

A person persists from time t to time t' if and only if that person has at t' all the same memories that she has at t.[5]

This is, however, clearly too strong for two reasons.

First, it requires that a person can only persist if she does not gain any new memories. But the experiences or conscious states of one moment, t, are the memories of the next, t' (Williams 1956–7). As a person grows older and has more experiences, then, she acquires more memories. Thus, I do not have exactly the same memories that I had yesterday, despite my having survived. Identity of all memories over time cannot, therefore, be a necessary condition on the persistence of a person.

Second, it requires that a person can only persist if she does not forget anything that she once remembered. But it is an essential feature of the identity relation that identity is transitive. Thus, if $a = b$, and $b = c$, then $a = c$.[6] The memory criterion formulated in terms of memory identity appears to breach this condition on identity. I, as an adult, can remember the experiences that I had as a teenager, and my teenaged self could remember the experiences that she had as a five-year-old child, but I can no longer remember the experiences that I had as a five-year-old child. But I am the very same person as the person who was this child. Thus, a criterion of persistence for persons formulated in terms of memory identity is too strong: it is unnecessary, since the condition of identity of memory may not, and often is not, met even when there is persistence of the very same person from one time to another.[7]

In short, the criterion requires, not only that I do not gain any new memories (the first objection) but also that I cannot forget anything that I once remembered (the second objection). One way of handling the second objection is to weaken the criterion so as to require the identity of only a suitably chosen sub-set of a person's memories over time, perhaps just those memories of being in a certain place at a certain time, since positions seem to uniquely individuate.[8] The resulting criterion states that

A person persists from t to t' if and only if that person has at t' a sub-set of the memories that she has at t.

Unfortunately, this version also has problems.

First, the criterion is still faced with the second of the two problems just mentioned. I, as an adult, may remember the experiences I had as a new mother, and as a new mother I may remember the experiences I had as a pre-school child. But I may not now remember the experiences I had as a pre-school child. Thus, this version of the memory criterion is as vulnerable as the stronger one to the charge that memory breaches the transitivity condition on identity.

In addition, this version, in weakening the conditions on personal identity, is vulnerable to the reduplication argument, an argument originally advanced by Bernard Williams (1956–7) and designed to show that the memory criterion, even in this weakened form, is insufficient for personal identity. Although Williams uses it for this purpose, the reduplication argument is a general one that can be applied to any situation in which the question of the continued identity of a thing over time arises, making it a very powerful form of argument.

The argument begins by supposing that the conditions for the identity over time of a continuant, such as a substance or a person, are both necessary and sufficient. It then attempts to show that the conditions permit what we might call 'branching', a situation in which two things at a later time, say, y and z, both meet the conditions for persistence with a thing at an earlier time, say, x. That is to say, the conditions permit a situation in which a single thing at one time, t, can be deemed to persist as two things at time, t', later than t. But, the argument continues, this is impossible. This is because to persist is to survive change while remaining the very same (i.e., identical) thing. And identity is a reflexive relation: it is a relation that can only hold between a thing and itself. In other words, identity is a one: one relationship, not a one: many one. It cannot therefore hold between one thing and two things. The argument concludes that, since y and z are not identical with each other, and since x cannot persist as both y and z (for to do so would be for x, a single thing, to survive as *two* things), x does not persist, either as y, or as z.

We might think of this as a case of *fission*, in which, the claim is, the original does not survive at all. Williams illustrates this with the help of a thought-experiment. He imagines a situation where a person, say, Charles, living in the twentieth century, undergoes a radical change of character while asleep one night and wakes up in the morning claiming to have experienced events in the life of Guy Fawkes (events such as, perhaps, attempting to burn down the Houses of Parliament). Bearing in mind that not all claims to remember are veridical, these claims would need to be checked. In this case it is none too easy a matter. For one thing, Charles's body is not the body of Guy Fawkes, and so attempting to check the veridicality of Charles's memories by locating the body occupied by Charles or the body occupied by Guy Fawkes will not get us anywhere (nor should it get us anywhere, if the memory criterion is right, since the persistence of the same body is not a necessary condition on the persistence of a person). For another, those who were alive when Guy Fawkes was alive are no longer alive to consult, and, even if they were, they would be relying on evidence concerning the body of Guy Fawkes and the body of Charles.

But suppose that we have access to historical records, personal diaries, and similar sources of information, and we are able to check and verify Charles's claims. All of the evidence points to Charles's being Guy Fawkes. According to the memory criterion, we should say that Charles is Guy Fawkes. But Williams claims not only that we are not forced to do this, but that to do so would be unjustified, for the following reason.

Imagine a situation where two people, Charles, and his brother, Robert, who are contemporaries of one another, both wake up one morning and make exactly the same memory claims about the life of Guy Fawkes. Any reason that we had to say that Guy Fawkes is Charles in the first case now applies equally to Robert. The memory criterion thus directs us to say that, in this situation, both Charles and Robert persist as Guy Fawkes. For both Charles and Robert, it seems, share the same sub-set of memories, not in the sense that the particular states are identical (given the physical distinctness of Charles and Robert from one another, the states that are instantiated in them must be distinct), but in the sense that they are of the same psychological types (where types are like universals in being capable of being instantiated in two places at the same time). But this is impossible: identity being a one: one relation, it cannot be that Charles and Robert are both Guy Fawkes. Since they are distinct from each other, and it cannot be that both are identical with Guy Fawkes, Williams's view is that we should conclude that neither Robert nor Charles is Guy Fawkes.

Williams further argues that we should deny that Charles is Guy Fawkes in the situation in which Robert is *not* present. For it is absurd to suppose that whether Charles is identical with Guy Fawkes depends on something other than their intrinsic properties, properties that they have only independently of any relations they might bear to anything else. It cannot depend on whatever else happens to exist. Identity, being reflexive, is a relation that a thing bears to itself and to nothing else, so whether something is self-identical and persists as the very same thing cannot depend on its relation to something other than it.

It would be futile to respond to this imaginary situation by denying that Robert meets the conditions set out by the memory criterion. Given that the memory criterion does not prohibit the transfer of memories from one body to another, it allows for the possibility that a person at one time might possess memories that, at an earlier time, were 'housed' in another body. The point of Williams's imaginary situation is to demonstrate that if the memory criterion allows this much, it cannot prohibit a situation in which two persons at one time might possess memories that, at an earlier time, were 'housed' in a single body. That is to say, it cannot prohibit a situation in which memories, which are originally housed in a single body, undergo something like fission, and are as a result replicated in two later bodies. The memory criterion, in short, permits 'branching', and in so doing presents serious problems to its acceptability as a criterion of persistence for persons.[9]

Memory continuity

Williams's example is directed against a version of the memory criterion which makes it a requirement on personal identity that there be identity of memories from one time to another, even if only the identity of a subset of all the memories possessed by a person at distinct times. Thus both versions of the memory criterion that require identity of memories for the persistence of a person are faced with intractable difficulties. There is, though, a final version of the memory criterion to consider that is weaker still, replacing the requirement on personal identity of memory identity with that of memory continuity.

Continuity is, on the face of it, a weaker relation than identity. Two things may be continuous with one another from one time, t, to another, later time, t', even though they have no single feature in common, provided that there are times in between t and t' where at least some of the features of these two things overlap, or form a common sub-set. Suppose, for example, that at time t, x has features A, B, and C, and suppose that, at time t', y has features D, E, and F. Then, provided that there are times in between these two where x has features, at least one of which is shared by y, x is *continuous* with y. Thus, suppose that there is a time t^*, which falls within the interval of time that includes both t and t', during which x has, say, features B, C, and D. Then x is continuous with y throughout the period of time that includes t and t', by virtue of the fact that, at t^*, x has B, C, and D.[10]

Applying this now to the case of persons, the suggestion is this:

A person persists from t to t' if and only if that person has at t' memories that are continuous with the memories she has at t.

Given the requirements on continuity, this permits a person to persist from t to t', where the distance between t and t' is an interval, even though the memories that she has at t form an entirely disjoint sub-set from those that she has at t'. So, for example, at t she may have memories m_1, m_2, and m_3, at t^* (a time somewhere in between t and t'), she may have memories m_3, m_4, and m_5, at t', she may have memories m_4, m_5, and m_6.

Continuity is a transitive relation. Thus, if a person's memories at t are continuous with her memories at t^*, and her memories at t^* are continuous with her memories at t', then that person's memories at t are continuous with her memories at t' *even* if her memories at t' do not include a single memory that she had at t. And this fact makes memory continuity as a condition on the persistence of persons less vulnerable to one of the problems that beset both versions of the memory criterion formulated in terms of memory identity. The problem was that identity is a transitive relation, and a criterion formulated in terms of memory identity does not preserve transitivity.

As one might expect, however, a criterion formulated in terms of memory continuity is as vulnerable to the reduplication argument as is one formulated in terms of memory identity. For if it is possible for two persons at a given time, t', to have the same sub-set of memories with a single person at a time earlier than t', then it is also possible for two persons at a given time, t', to have memories that are psychologically continuous with those of a single person at a time earlier than t'. Thus, to return to Williams's example, if it is possible both for Charles and for Robert to have the same memory experiences as of the events witnessed by Guy Fawkes (as a result, perhaps, of a process of reduplication), then it must be possible for them each to have only *one* such experience in virtue of which each has memories that are psychologically continuous with the memories of Guy Fawkes. It need not even be the case that Charles and Robert have the *same* memory experience: Charles may have one memory in virtue of which his memories are continuous with those of Guy Fawkes, Robert another.

Again, the conclusion seems to be that a criterion of persistence formulated in terms of memory continuity permits 'branching': it permits a situation in which a single person may persist as two persons. But, since persistence requires identity, this cannot be possible. Later on in this chapter, we will see that this argument is not as conclusive against all versions of the psychological continuity criterion of persistence. However, for the time being, and in the light of it, it is worth considering a criterion of personal identity formulated in entirely different terms. The obvious candidate here is a physical criterion.

The Physical Criterion

Like the memory criterion, the physical criterion of persistence for persons comes in at least three forms. The first two require the identity of physical characteristics. The third replaces that requirement with the requirement of physical continuity. We briefly consider these in turn.

Physical identity
In its strongest formulation, the physical criterion of persistence for persons takes as necessary and sufficient for a person to persist from one time to another that she retains exactly the same bodily characteristics over time. That is to say, it states that

> A person persists from t to t' if and only if that person has at t' exactly the same bodily characteristics that she has at t.

This condition is obviously too strong. First, people change in size and shape, sometimes lose limbs, hair, and so on, and yet we want to say that they are the very same people. I would not consider my friend, Sue, to be a different person from one time to the next, if she were to lose a limb, or to change in physical respects in a host of other ways. But the requirement of sameness of bodily characteristics would force me to conclude that she is indeed a different person (i.e., that she is not Sue!).

Second, and perhaps less obviously, what seems to matter for the persistence of a person is the continued possession of *whatever* physical characteristics are necessary for the persistence of that person's *psychology*, and many think that something less than those that attach to a person's body may be required for this. Indeed, they think that only those concerned with the brain are necessary. If they are right, then the continued possession of the very same body is not necessary for a person to persist from one time to another, and a person could persist from t to t' without any of the bodily characteristics she has at t.

This claim has been supported by the following imaginary situation. Suppose that two persons, Brown and Robinson, were to undergo surgery at the same time, and Brown's brain were to be exchanged with Robinson's, with an accompanying exchange of psychological characteristics (Shoemaker 1963). Who, if anyone, would we say is Brown afterwards? The person with Brown's body but with Robinson's brain and psychological characteristics? Or the person with Robinson's body but with Brown's brain and psychological characteristics? Williams, who discusses this example, thinks that the answer is clear: those who love Brown, his nearest and dearest, will consider Brown to be the person with Brown's brain and psychological characteristics. They will describe this as a case where Brown has acquired a new body.

A better, although perhaps more bizarre, case for the claim is this. Suppose that Brown begins to lose bits and pieces of his body, retaining somehow the ability to manifest his psychological states, until he is reduced to a brain in a vat. At that point, apparently, people will still identify that brain, with its accompanying psychology, as Brown's. Then suppose that, bit by bit, Robinson's body parts are attached to Brown's brain. This seems to be a case for Williams's view that what seems to matter to the persistence of a person is the continued possession of only the brain (with its accompanying psychology).[11]

If Williams is right, two points need to be made about the strongest version of the physical criterion. The first is that the continued possession of the same body, or all of one's bodily characteristics, is not necessary for the persistence of a person: only those bits of the body whose continued possession is necessary and sufficient for psychological persistence are necessary. This illustrates the sense in which the strongest version of the physical criterion is too strong.

The second point that needs to be made is that physical characteristics matter to a person's persistence only insofar as they are necessary and sufficient for the preservation of psychological identity and/or continuity. Physical characteristics thus matter to the persistence of a person as a means to a further end, namely, guaranteeing psychological persistence.

This suggests that even the strongest version of the physical criterion is too weak, and so insufficient for the persistence of a person. Dissociated from any claim about psychological characteristics, even the strongest of physical conditions on its own is compatible with the failure of a person to remain the same person over time. We would not consider a person who lost all of their memories and also her other attitudes and character traits to be the same person from one time to another. This is because persons are at least psychological beings, and one cannot be the same psychological being from one time to another if one is not a psychological being at all. One need not hold that persons are essentially psychological beings (that would require commitment to a view about the nature of persons, viz. that their natures are psychological rather than physical); one need only appreciate that anything that is in fact a person is a psychological being, and this is compatible with the view that persons are essentially physical beings.

So we must reject the strongest version of the physical criterion as a criterion of persistence for persons. But the difficulties with it point to a weaker version that looks, at first sight, to be more acceptable. According to this, a person is the same person over time if and only if s/he has the same brain, thereby preserving psychological identity. That is to say:

A person persists from t to t' if and only if that person has, at t' exactly the same brain characteristics that she has at t.

Although this is an improvement on the strongest version, again it is too strong. Imagine a situation in which Brown and Robinson undergo surgery, but that Brown is brain dead. Robinson's brain is separated into its two hemispheres, the left one and the right. As it happens each half possesses the full complement of Robinson's psychological characteristics. One hemisphere is removed from Robinson's body. The surgeons remove Brown's brain, but when they proceed to replace it with the one half of Robinson's brain, a tragedy occurs. The surgeon drops the organ, and it (along with its accompanying psychology) is destroyed. The other half remains in Robinson's body and continues to function normally.

This situation is logically possible.[12] It is conceivable that a person might continue to survive, psychologically intact, with half of her brain. But then the identity of the entire brain, with all of its physical characteristics, is not necessary for a person to remain the same person over time. It is possible for a person to be the same person over time without meeting this condition.

Could we simply weaken the present criterion by replacing 'exactly the same brain characteristics' with 'a sub-set of the brain characteristics', hoping that it preserves all the same psychological characteristics and that this will be both necessary and sufficient for a person's persistence from one time to another? A little reflection shows that this will not work either. Suppose, to vary the example slightly, that both halves of Robinson's brain, each with their full complement of psychological characteristics, remain intact, and that the surgeons safely remove Brown's brain and replace it with one of the halves. The operation is successful, and both halves function normally in their respective bodies. It is a (logically possible) situation in which, again, we might say, fission has occurred: whereas, before surgery, there was one person, Robinson, after surgery, there appear to be two persons, both of which can be deemed to be Robinson. For we have two brain hemispheres with the same psychological characteristics, not in the sense that the particular states are identical (given the physical distinctness of the hemispheres, the states that are instantiated in them must be distinct), but in the sense that they are of the same psychological types (where types are like universals in being capable of being instantiated in two places at the same time). We know that it is impossible for one thing to be identical with two things. But then the problem with weakening the above criterion is not that the conditions are not necessary, but that they are now insufficient, for the persistence of a person from one time to another. It does not suffice for persistence, since persistence requires identity, and this proposal does not meet the condition that identity be a one: one rather than a one: many relation.

Physical continuity

In the face of the problems faced by criteria of persistence that require physical identity of the body or some part of it, it is tempting to think that replacing this condition with the weaker one of physical continuity will work. The suggestion, then, might be that

> A person persists from t to t' if and only if that person has at t' physical characteristics that are continuous with physical characteristics that she has at t.

As one might expect, though, this suggestion suffers from the same difficulties as its psychological counterpart does.

Although we will have reason to question the conclusion derived from it, the example that is typically cited is one that involves, not persons specifically, but a physical continuant with parts, the Ship of Theseus. Here we are to imagine a man, Theseus, who owns a ship and decides that this ship needs a complete overhaul. He takes it out to dock to dry out, and begins systematically replacing planks in the ship, eventually replacing every old plank with a new one. The original planks lie in a warehouse, and are not used by anybody to construct anything.

Here there does not seem to be a problem about whether the ship with its old planks remains the same ship throughout the replacement of all of its planks. It undergoes continuous change from one time to another, later one, but it seems right to say that the ship with the old planks is the same ship as the ship with the new ones.

But now imagine that Theseus has a competitor who hoards the original planks of the ship and decides to use them to build his own ship. He does this, and one day both he and Theseus put their ships out to water, each claiming that his ship is the original Ship of Theseus. Who is right here?

Well, in this second situation (call it situation 2, the former being situation 1), there is continuity between the original ship, composed of the old planks, and the ship composed of entirely new planks, since, for any two times in between the two which include the ship with only old planks and the ship with only new ones, the sets of planks constituting the ship overlap with one another. It is because of this that we are able to track the ship from one time to another. So one set of intuitions tells us that the original ship is the ship composed of entirely new planks (Theseus's ship, in fact).

But another set of intuitions tells us that the original ship is the ship composed of all of the old planks (Theseus's rival's ship). This is because there is also continuity in this case. As the original planks are replaced, one by one, by Theseus, a ship is gradually constructed by his competitor, plank by plank. It is true that, at the beginning of the competitor's construction of his ship, there is only one member of the set of planks constituting the two ships in common, and so at this time Theseus's ship and his competitor's ship are only very weakly continuous with one another. But it is also true that, at the end of Theseus's reconstruction, when the last old plank is about to be removed, his old ship and his new ship are only very weakly continuous, and for the same reason: there is only one plank in common between them.

So we have two sets of intuitions here, and they support judgements that conflict with one another. They conflict with one another if, that is, we take physical continuity to be both necessary and sufficient for identity over time. For this situation is one in which the continuity criterion supports the view that one thing (the original Ship of Theseus) is identical, at a later time, with two ships.

Now, the imagined situation of brain fission considered previously is an example of a similar kind in the case of the persistence of persons. Here we are to imagine that the brain of one person is split in half, each with its full complement of psychological characteristics of the person whose brain it is, one half of which is relocated in another body, and functions normally, and the other of which remains in the original body. Here there is physical continuity in both cases, since each of the later persons has half of the original brain. Moreover, in this situation it is taken as given that only the brain, and not the entire body, is necessary and sufficient for personal identity. So one cannot favour the person whose body contains the original half of the brain over the one with the new body as the better candidate for identity with the original person possessed of a whole brain. Here, as in the case of the Ship of Theseus, it seems that the physical continuity criterion permits us to say that the original person is identical with two later ones.[13] Since this conflicts with identity's being a one: one relation, it is unacceptable as a criterion of personal identity.

The Closest Continuer Theory and Its Problems

Let us take stock. All versions of the criteria considered thus far have assumed that conditions necessary and sufficient for the persistence of persons can be given in terms of either psychological/physical identity or psychological/physical continuity. But we have seen that the stronger versions are too strong (they provide conditions that are not necessary) and the weaker versions are too weak (providing conditions that are not sufficient) for the persistence of persons.

Some have resisted the latter conclusion, insisting that a version of the continuity criterion can be made to work (Garrett 1998; Nozick 1981; Shoemaker 1984; Wiggins 1967; Unger 1990). As they see it, the problem that is generated by continuity criteria is not that they permit branching; rather, it is that, in cases where branching occurs, they appear to provide no means by which to determine which of the various candidates is the original person. If some version of a continuity criterion could yield conditions sufficient to determine, in cases of branching, which of two or more candidates is the one with whom a single person at an earlier time is identical, then there would be no problem with branching. We could justifiably maintain that although many distinct persons might be continuous with a single person at an earlier time, only one of these can satisfy the stronger condition(s) required for identity, and so for the persistence of that person.

The Closest Continuer theory of persistence is designed to provide just such a condition. According to it, the persistence of a person from one time to another involves nothing more than continuity, psychological and/or physical. It is just that continuity comes in degrees, and not every person that is continuous with a person at an earlier time qualifies thereby as being identical with that person. Specifically, according to the closest continuer theory, although there may be many future persons who are continuous with me, only one of these will be my closest continuer and so the person with whom I am identical. The other 'continuers' will not be me.

As just noted, this theory trades on the fact that continuity comes in degrees. In the case of the persistence of persons, the criterion of persistence it generates typically takes the form of a psychological one (although it can take the form of a physical criterion also). In this form, the persistence of a person requires overlapping chains of psychological states that are strongly connected. Nozick's (1981) formulation comes in two versions, a 'local' one and a 'global' one. According to the local version, that future person who has the greatest degree of spatio-temporal and qualitative continuity with me will be me. What makes for qualitative continuity are psychological factors, where these include not only memories, but also other psychological attitudes such as beliefs, desires, perceptual experiences, and so on. Continuity will have to do with the strength of the connections between preceding and succeeding states (for example, that successive states are causally connected with states immediately preceding them in such a way that, had the preceding states not been as they were, the successive ones would not be as they are). Should there be no future person sufficiently closely continuous with me, then no future person is identical with me.

According to the global version, that future person who is the longest living closest continuer of me will be me. Such a continuer may not, at early stages continuous with me, be my closest continuer. But in the long run, by surviving longer than other continuers of me, it will be overall a closer continuer than one who does not live as long. Here, unlike the local version, longevity is a factor in whether a future person is my closest continuer.

Whether or not a future person is my closest continuer depends, not just on that thing, but on what other competitors are around. So, whether a future person is identical with me depends, on this theory, on what else happens to be around. A future person could be me in one situation but not in another; clearly, the consequence is that the question of whether a future person is identical with me does not depend solely on the intrinsic properties of that person and me.

This does not actually conflict with the requirement that identity be a one: one relation: *according to the theory*, in any given situation there will be at most one closest continuer. But it does conflict with the intuition, closely associated with that requirement, that since identity is a relation between a thing and itself, and not anything else, it should not depend on whatever else happens to be around.

It does seem, though, that a situation could arise in which there are two closest continuers of a single person at an earlier time. If this is true, then irrespective of whether the theory conflicts with an important intuition concerning identity, it cannot be an acceptable theory of persistence for persons.

Return to the example of the Ship of Theseus. In situation 1, Theseus docks his boat and rebuilds it plank by plank, but the original planks are not reconstituted to form another ship by his adversary, so there is only one closest continuer of the original ship. However, in situation 2, where Theseus's rival does use the original planks to reconstitute another ship, there are two candidates for the closest continuer, so, in this situation, neither has a better claim than the other to be the closest continuer. This is a consequence of the theory's commitment to the view that whether a future thing is a closest continuer of a present one depends on what else happens to be around. In the just considered example of the Ship of Theseus, where there are two candidates, the question of identity is problematic. But the reason why it is problematic can only be fully appreciated by considering a possible third situation, one that we have not yet considered.

In this third situation (situation 3), we are to imagine that Theseus dismantles, rather than renovates his ship. Rather than replacing each old plank with a new one, he simply takes the thing apart, plank by plank. He stores the planks in a warehouse, and, disenchanted with the shipping business, takes up a new occupation altogether. His rival discovers the planks in the warehouse, and decides to build a ship with them. Plank by plank, he reconstitutes the original ship.

In this third situation, as in the first, there is only one candidate for a closest continuer with the original ship, and that is the reconstituted one. Hence there is only one candidate for identity with the original ship. Intuitively, moreover, this reconstituted ship is sufficiently continuous with the original for it to be a candidate for identity with it. But, surely, if this reconstituted ship is sufficiently continuous with the original, and a close enough continuer to be deemed identical with it in this situation, then it must be sufficiently continuous with the original to be deemed a close enough continuer to be deemed identical with the original in the second situation too. For, our grounds here parallel those given for thinking that the renovated ship in the second situation is a close enough continuer of the original ship to be identical with it. These grounds are based on the fact that, in the first situation, it is the only candidate for a closest continuer of the original ship.

In short, if our reasons for thinking that the renovated ship is the Ship of Theseus in the first situation are good enough for us to consider the renovated ship to be the closest continuer of the original ship in the second situation, then our reasons for thinking that the reconstituted ship in the third situation is the Ship of Theseus must also be good enough for us to consider the reconstituted ship to be the closest continuer of the original ship in the second situation too. But there cannot be two closest continuers of the original ship if being the closest continuer is to be a sufficient condition for identity.

Can we tighten the conditions on being a closest continuer further, so as to avoid the conclusion that there are two closest continuers in the second situation? Maybe we could insist that the identity of a thing is not independent of its causal history, so that a thing's origin, and the events that comprise its development, matters to its identity. On this basis it might be argued that the reconstituted ship in the third situation is not the same ship as the reconstituted ship in the second situation, given that in the third situation, the reconstituted ship, although discontinuous with the original, is a stage in the life of the original and so has a causal history which includes the original ship. In the second situation, it is the renovated ship that has this relation to the original, not the reconstituted one.

Alas, not even this is satisfactory! For one wants to ask why we should think that, in the second situation, the renovated ship, but not the reconstituted ship, is a stage in the life of the original. It cannot simply be that, in the first situation, the renovated ship is the only closest continuer of the original and so is, in that situation, identical with it. For equally, in the third situation, the reconstituted ship is the only closest continuer of the original and so is, in that situation, identical with it. And it cannot simply be that in the first situation, the renovated ship is a stage in the life of the original ship, for, equally, in the third situation, the reconstituted ship is a stage in the life of the original ship.

In short, it looks like any reason that we might have for thinking that, in the second situation, the renovated ship is a stage in the life of the original we also have for thinking that, in the second situation, the reconstituted ship is a stage in the life of the original ship. Apparently, this way of attempting to patch up the closest continuer theory just won't work. It seems to have the consequence that neither the renovated ship nor the reconstituted ship is identical with the original ship in the second situation, or else both are identical with the original.

The problems with the closest continuer theory were discussed with specific reference to the example of the Ship of Theseus, but the results are easily applicable to *any* version of the closest continuer theory. So they are applicable to closest continuer theories of the persistence of persons formulated in psychological terms (Charles and Robert both being candidates for being closest continuers with Guy Fawkes). And they are applicable to closest continuer theories formulated in physical terms (Brown and Robinson, each of whom has half of Robinson's brain and with it the full complement of Robinson's psychological characteristics, both being candidates for being closest continuers with the original Robinson). The strategies invoked to deal with the reduplication argument as it applies to the example of the Ship of Theseus are also applicable to these other versions of the continuity criterion, but they are no more successful.

What to do? We have considered a number of suggestions for tightening up the continuity criterion so as to yield conditions that are not only necessary but also sufficient for identity. None of these appears to have succeeded. The reason is that the reduplication argument needs to be effectively countered, and so long as it is not, there is no way to prevent two or more rival candidates from being equally good candidates for identity with a single thing at an earlier time.

In the next section we will offer a plausible way out of what seems to be an impasse, beginning with the example of the Ship of Theseus. However, before moving on, it is worth considering briefly a final suggestion. This is simply to add a 'no rival candidates' constraint to the continuity criterion. Applied to persons, a future person will be identical with me if and only if that person is the closest continuer of me and there is no other continuer that is equally close or closer.

This does the trick, but it is unacceptable, and that is because identity is a reflexive relation, i.e., a relation between a thing and itself, and so should not depend on what else happens to be around. One of the points of the reduplication argument is to show that, because the continuity criterion cannot respect this feature, it is insufficient for identity.

Adding a 'no rival candidate' rider to the criterion may guarantee that only one thing can satisfy the conditions for identity, but only by sacrificing the principle that identity should not depend on what else happens to be around. But to sacrifice this principle is effectively to concede victory to those who view the reduplication argument as decisive against the continuity criterion.

Before we consider, and defend, a way out of this apparent impasse, it is worth considering two much more radical strategies.

Does the Concept of Identity Apply to Persons?

In the face of all of the difficulties that have plagued attempts to formulate an adequate criterion of persistence for persons, some have conceded defeat and claimed that the concept of identity does not apply to persons, so that persons do not literally persist from one time to another. Derek Parfit (1971, 1984) has defended this view at length. His view involves two claims, a negative one and a positive one. The negative one is that concerns with persistence and one's future well-being are in fact derivative concerns. The positive claim is that what they are derivative from – what matters to the persistence of a person – is not whether some future person will be identical with me but whether I shall survive. These claims need some explaining. Let's begin with the negative one.

Parfit takes it as given that identity is a one: one relation, and that this is a logical condition on a relation's being the identity relation. He accepts two further commitments. One, which we have already noted, is to the principle that because identity is a one: one relation, it should not depend on what else happens to be around. The other, which we have not yet mentioned, is that because the issue of persistence of a person has great significance, it cannot rest on a trivial matter of fact.[14]

Parfit views continuity criteria of persistence, and specifically, closest continuer forms of it, as the most likely and plausible of the candidates for acceptable criteria of persistence for persons. And in fact he endorses a psychological version of the closest continuer criterion since he thinks that psychological continuity is what matters to whether a future person will be me. But he acknowledges that it cannot rule out the possibility of branching and so violates the logical condition on identity, so he accepts that it cannot suffice as a criterion of persistence for persons. Predictably, he also rejects versions of this criterion that attempt to ensure identity by ruling out the possibility of branching by means of 'no rival candidate' clauses (Garrett 1998; Shoemaker 1984; Wiggins 1967; Unger 1990), since they fall foul of the requirement that identity should not depend on what else happens to be around.

Parfit notes that there are ways of avoiding recourse to 'no rival candidate' clauses in closest continuer criteria, while at the same time specifying conditions that could only be met by at most one continuer in any given situation. Take a version of the closest continuer theory requiring brain continuity for persistence. This requirement could be specified in such a way as to ensure that only one future person could be me, say, by requiring that, in order for a future person to be me, that person must have slightly more than half of my brain. Since there could not be two such persons, we seem to be able to formulate a persistence condition for persons in terms of physical continuity, which (provided that it preserves psychological continuity) would be sufficient for the persistence of a person from one time to another without the need for a 'no rival candidate' clause.

However, this way of attempting to secure conditions sufficient for the persistence of persons will not work. The reason why is that the issue of persistence now rests on a trivial matter of fact. How could it matter to whether a future person is me whether that person has slightly more, rather than exactly half of my brain, say, .00000000000000000001 per cent more? Surely such an insignificant difference cannot matter to something so important! A similar problem arises for the psychological analogue of the physical criterion formulated in such terms. Just as it is true that no more than one thing can have more than half of my brain, it is true that no more than one thing can have more than half of my psychological characteristics. But why should it matter to whether a future person is me whether she has one memory less, or one memory more? How can this trivial fact make such an enormous difference to whether a future person is me?

Parfit's radical conclusion is that we should simply concede that no acceptable criterion of persistence for persons is forthcoming; that there simply are no conditions that are both necessary and sufficient for such persistence. There is psychological continuity, but as we all know by now, continuity permits branching. So whether a future person will be me will depend, as identity cannot, on what else happens to be around. Given that the concept of identity does not apply to persons, and this is required for persistence, it is possible for two or more future persons to be me. But, according to Parfit, this should not worry us. Why?

The claim is that what really matters to persons is survival, and persistence does not matter for survival. Provided that I survive, it should not matter whether someone else, continuous with my earlier self, also survives. Clearly, by 'survival' Parfit does not mean what is ordinarily meant, since, ordinarily, one's survival is assumed to require one's continued persistence as the very same (i.e., identical) thing. We will address this issue more fully in a moment, when we discuss the positive aspect of his thesis. For now, we will continue with the negative aspect.

According to Parfit, we are only concerned about our persistence because we are concerned about our survival. So our interest in our continued identity is derivative from our concern for our own survival. But, given that our survival does not depend on identity, it just shouldn't worry me whether more than one future person will be my closest continuer. Further, it would be irrational for me to take a greater interest in one of these continuers than another. That there is a continuer is all that matters.

Consider the following analogy. We value our eyes because they are a source of an enormous amount of information about the world around us, and this information is valuable to us. So our concern about our eyes is a derivative concern, derivative on our concern for the information they provide. If they were to be replaced with some mechanical device that provided us with the same information, our eyes would cease to be valuable to us, their value depending only on the information they provide. What matters is the end: the information. The means – the eyes – matter only derivatively.

Similarly, Parfit argues, for identity and survival. We are concerned about our continued identity – our persistence – because we value our survival. But if we could achieve that end without those means – without identity – then we would cease to worry about identity. Luckily (he claims) we can achieve that end without those means (cf. also Shoemaker 1970; Martin 1990, 1998).

Go back to the split-brain case of Brown and Robinson. In one imagined situation, half of Robinson's brain is removed and relocated, intact, in Brown, both halves continuing to function normally with their full complement of psychological characteristics. In another, the surgeon slips after she has removed half of Robinson's brain and drops it, destroying it. According to Parfit, these situations elicit two corresponding, but conflicting, intuitions.

On the one hand, we want to say that, in the first situation, because branching has occurred, the original Robinson has ceased to exist and two new people have come into existence, but that, had only one half of Robinson's brain survived, as in the second situation, the original Robinson would have continued to exist. This suggests that whether Robinson continues to live or not depends on what happens to the other half of his brain.

On the other hand, we want to say that it would be irrational for Robinson to take any interest in what happens to the other half of his brain. This is because Robinson has nothing to gain or lose by having the other half of his brain destroyed. For his survival is ensured *whatever* happens to the other half of his brain. It would be quite wrong, for example, for Robinson to view the resulting situation as one in which he has died.

These intuitions appear to conflict, since one apparently instructs Robinson to take an interest in what happens to the other half of his brain, whereas the other instructs him otherwise. However, the claim is that both intuitions can be accommodated without conflict if we accept that what matters to survival is not identity. The first intuition ties the question of whether one continues to live or die to the question of whether one's literal identity is preserved – to the question of whether one persists. Since, ordinarily, we think of our continued existence in terms of our continued identity, our persistence as the very same person, this is a natural intuition. But the second intuition raises the question of whether we are right to view the issue of whether we continue to live or die as an issue that non-derivatively concerns our continued identity. That it would be irrational for Robinson to be concerned about what happens to the other half of his brain, and that it would be wrong for him to view a situation in which, were the other half of his brain to survive in Brown, he would die, indicate that what matters to survival is something less than identity.

If we accept this, and that we are only concerned about our continued identity because we are concerned about our survival, then we can accommodate both of the above intuitions. Understood properly, the first intuition tells Robinson that he is concerned about whether the other half of his brain survives because he concerned about whether he will continue to live or whether he will die. Here his continued identity, or persistence, matters, because it matters to whether he will continue to survive. The second intuition, however, tells Robinson that whether the other half of his brain survives cannot make a difference to his survival. This is confirmed by the realization that he would have nothing to gain or lose by arranging for the surgeon to destroy the other half of his brain. The two intuitions are reconcilable if we accept that our concern with persistence, and so with identity, is derivative on a more fundamental, non-derivative concern, the concern for whether one lives or dies.

The second intuition suggests that we would not view a situation like the one in which each half of Robinson's brain, with its full complement of Robinson's psychological characteristics, survives in two different bodies, as a situation in which Robinson dies. This indicates that one's continued survival does not depend on whether branching occurs. That a future person will be me is what matters, not how many future persons will be survivors of me. A situation in which only one future person happens to be the best candidate for psychological continuity with me will be one in which I continue to exist. And this will be true even if it is possible that there should be more than one such continuant. If there should be more than one, it would be irrational for me to take any greater interest in the survival and well-being of one over another.

On this story, what matters to survival is not identity but what might be called 'Parfitian survival'. A person is a Parfitian survivor if she meets certain conditions on psychological continuity and/or connectedness and the way in which states that meet these conditions are caused. Psychological connectedness has to do with the holding of direct psychological connections. Experiential memory, or a memory experience of an earlier event witnessed at an earlier time is one such direct connection. The continued holding of a belief, or a desire, from one moment to another, is another such direct connection. Psychological continuity is the holding of overlapping chains of states that have direct psychological connections. For Parfit, any cause that forges these connections is the right sort of cause. So, for example, my apparent memory experience of an event witnessed by a very close friend, which she told me about in great detail so often when I was young that I began to think of it as an event that occurred to me, could be enough to make me psychologically continuous with my friend.

Parfit's thesis requires that, in any situation in which I will have more than one Parfitian survivor, it cannot be rational for me to take a greater degree of interest in one survivor over another. So, if it can be shown that there are situations in which it is rational to take a greater interest in one rather than another Parfitian survivor of oneself, then this will undermine Parfit's claim that only our interest in Parfitian survival, and not our continued identity as well, is of non-derivative importance.

Noonan (1989, citing Nozick 1981) describes one such situation, which he calls the branch line case. Suppose, to begin with, that advances in technology make possible the construction of a machine that enables those who enter it to enjoy a kind of *Star Trek* type of space travel (the example is Parfit's). As in the *Star Trek* television series and films, this machine allows for a kind of teletransportation. There is this difference, however. Whereas the participants in *Star Trek* believe that the machine literally transports them to other parts of space by a kind of disassembly/reassembly process, in this case the travellers know that they are not literally transported. What happens instead is that the machine creates a duplicate of the person who enters it in another part of space.

In a simple case of the second kind of teletransportation, what happens is that, when the machine creates a duplicate, the original is destroyed in the process. We can imagine such a situation occurring, and imagine people in it moving various things, such as animals and vegetables, from one place to another by this means. It would be rational for them not to be concerned that the original objects do not literally survive the process, but only their duplicates do. It surely could not matter to me, for instance, whether the oranges that are teletransported to me to eat from another place are literally the original oranges, or whether they are duplicates of the originals.

But it is very difficult to imagine people in this situation taking a similar attitude towards themselves. We would think that there would be something wrong with them if they were to willingly enter the machine, knowing that although a duplicate of them would survive, they would be destroyed in the process. Does this not show that Parfit is wrong about what matters in survival?

Parfit argues that it does not. According to him, this attitude is simply irrational. The people in this situation would be right to enter the machine willingly, since they would survive, not die. There could be no rational reason for their unwillingness to enter the machine, any more than there could be a rational reason, in the split-brain Brown/Robinson case discussed earlier, for Robinson's concern about what happens to the other half of his brain. This, of course, is because what Parfit means by saying that Robinson survives is not that *Robinson* survives. He means that someone (perhaps Robinson, but perhaps not) who at least appears to remember what Robinson remembered, who has many if not all of the beliefs, hopes, fears, intentions, etc., that Robinson has, exists.

But now let us vary the simple teletransportation case slightly. Suppose that the original people in this situation, when they enter the machine, are not destroyed in the teletransportation process. Imagine that I enter the machine, and am told that if I stay in it for an hour, I will be able to actually see and hear myself (i.e., my future duplicate) on another planet. I am amazed, thinking it impossible, but decide to wait to see it. While I am waiting, I am handed a slip of paper by the machine operator. It says that something has gone wrong with the machine. While my duplicate will be unaffected, and will continue to survive where she is, I will suffer a very painful and massive heart attack within a few days, from which I will not recover.

Compare these two cases. In the first, simple teletransportation situation, there is no branching and so no problem about which future person is (in Parfit's terms) me. The duplicate survives, but the original does not, and so the closest – indeed, the only – continuer of me is my duplicate. This situation seems to accord with Parfit's intuition that since what matters to questions of persistence is not literal identity but survival, it is rational for me to be interested in what happens to my duplicate (cf. also Martin 1998; Shoemaker 1970). The fact that the original me will be destroyed shouldn't worry me, since I know that I shall survive. This is just a kind of reincarnation. But in the branch line case, the original me continues to survive along with my duplicate. What should my attitude be towards these two persons?

According to Parfit, I should have no greater degree of interest in the fate of the original me than I should have in the fate of my duplicate. If anything, because my duplicate will live longer than the original me, it would be more rational for me to take a greater interest in my duplicate. But in fact, it seems that my interest in the original me will be far greater than my interest in my duplicate will be. I will feel sad and distressed about what I will view as my impending death. And I will view this as my death. It is unlikely to be a comfort to me to know that my duplicate will live on.

The fact that I will take different attitudes to these two people, and that my concern for the original me will be far greater than my concern for my duplicate's fate strongly suggests that my concern for my persistence, where this requires my continued identity, is not a derivative concern, but one of fundamental importance. Think, for example, of what my reaction would be if I were to be told, not that the original me will suffer a massive heart attack, but that my duplicate will suffer this while the original me continues to flourish. The fate of my duplicate will not worry me. And it will be rational for me not to be concerned about it. For, after all, as long as the original me continues to survive and flourish, I will rest assured that I shall continue to live on.

So Parfit seems to be wrong in his claim that our concern with our continued identity is only of derivative importance, and hence that what matters to survival is not identity. Where do we go from here? We shall consider one final radical strategy before suggesting a solution.

The Multiple Occupancy Thesis

Identity, it seems, does matter to survival. Therefore, the conditions on identity – in particular, that it be a one: one relation and that it should depend only on the intrinsic properties of the things related – also matter to survival. How are we to square this with the fact that continuity, either psychological or physical, permits branching?

Some have argued that the most promising way to square these facts is to endorse what is known as the multiple occupancy thesis. Branching presents a serious threat to a continuity criterion of personal identity only because it appears to flout the conditions on identity. But there is a way of meeting these conditions consistently with endorsing a continuity criterion and with it the possibility of branching. The way to do so is to hold that, in cases where branching is possible, there is no single original thing, but rather two things that happen to occupy the same position.

Consider once again the example of Theseus's ship. In the first situation, where Theseus rebuilds his ship, plank by plank, but no other ship is constructed from the original planks, our opinion is that there is one ship throughout. Similarly, in the third situation, where the original ship is dismantled and then, at a later time, reconstructed from the original planks, we judge, again, that there is only one ship throughout.

According to the present suggestion, in both of these cases our intuitions are mistaken. This is not apparent until we consider the second situation, where it seems that there are two ships at a later time that are equally close continuers of the original: the renovated ship and the reconstructed ship.

Knowing, as we now do, that identity matters to survival, it is not really an option for us to say that the concept of identity does not apply to continuants like Theseus's ship, which persist from one time to another. (Even if it is an option in this case, it is not really an option in the case of persons, who are also continuants, since our concern for inanimate objects does not match our concern for ourselves.) Nor is it an option to say that, when branching occurs, the original ship ceases to exist and two new ships come into being. But there is a third option. This is to say that, appearances notwithstanding, in both the first and the third situation, there are in fact two ships present throughout which happen to be spatio-temporally coincident with one another. This is the multiple occupancy thesis.

The multiple occupancy thesis is counter-intuitive, since it certainly doesn't look as though, in the first situation and in the third situation, there are two ships present throughout. But is it any more so than Parfit's thesis that the concept of identity does not apply to persons? Lewis (1976), Noonan (1989), and others think not. In their view, it is more counter-intuitive to hold that the conditions on identity do not apply to persisting things at all than it is to hold that the conditions on identity do apply to continuants, and so, in cases where branching is possible, it must be that where we think that there is only one thing there are in fact two things occupying the same position. It is more counter-intuitive because the concept of a continuant is inseparable from the idea that continuants persist by retaining literal identity.

But actually, things are much worse for the multiple occupancy thesis than Lewis, Noonan and others encourage us to think. Examine more closely the second situation, in which branching occurs. If the reason why the possibility that there should be two ships at all in this situation is consistent with the conditions on identity is that there are two ships to begin with which happen to occupy the same position, then there is no limit to the number of ships that there are in that situation and which happen to occupy the same position. For, the possibility of branching does not prohibit the number of ships that might, at a later time, be continuous with the original ship; there could be two, or three, or four, or an infinite number of them. And if the mere possibility of branching is what poses the problem for the multiple occupancy theorist committed to meeting the conditions on identity, then, since there is no limit to the number of branchings, there is no limit to the number of ships that happen to occupy the same position in the original.

To make this more graphic, think of a slightly more complicated version of the Ship of Theseus example. Here, there are the three situations as described above, but there is also a further one. In this fourth situation, Theseus only replaces two-thirds of the planks of the original ship, and he has two rivals. The rivals decide to team up to do Theseus out of his shipping business. They divide the original planks between them, each using their third to help build a new ship. We can even imagine that the original planks are placed in positions in the new ships that correspond to the positions they occupied in Theseus's original ship.

We now have a situation in which there are, not two, but three closest continuers of the original ship. In keeping with the strategy of the multiple occupancy theorist, we must say here that, corresponding to the three closest continuers, there must be three distinct ships occupying the same position in the original.

But it is clear that there is no limit to the number of closest continuers there might be. To limit them to just three would be as arbitrary as it is to limit them to just two. The situation is yet more obvious in the case of persistence of persons. For, if there might be two persons, Charles, and his brother, Robert, that are psychologically equally close continuers of Guy Fawkes, there might be any number of such persons. Why limit the possibilities to just two? And if there might be any number of such persons, then, by parity of reasoning, there are *in fact* any number of persons in the position originally occupied by Guy Fawkes. Just as there are any number of ships where we thought there is only one, there are any number of persons where we thought there is only one.

In short, the multiple occupancy thesis has the consequence that, in the case of any continuant, there are any number of things of the same kind in any given position at any time. These are not merely possible things, moreover. If branching is possible, it can only be because, in actuality, there are these things whose positions could fail to coincide. For, according to the multiple occupancy thesis, the reason why branching is possible is because in actuality, two or more things which happen to occupy the same positions could come to occupy distinct positions. That very *possibility* requires distinct occupants in actuality, for one thing cannot become two things.

This result is unacceptable. To allow it, I would have to believe that there is not just one me, but rather, where there seems to be one me, there are any number of 'me's' at any given time that I exist. But this is beyond credulity.[15]

Back to Basics: Continuity and Fission

We've canvassed a number of suggestions for criteria of persistence for persons, and all of them have turned out to be problematic in a variety of ways. Fortunately, the suggestions that take psychological and/or physical continuity to be necessary and sufficient for the persistence of a person are more promising than those that require psychological and/or physical identity, since these latter require persistence conditions that are far too strong for persons to meet. Short of concluding that persons do not persist from one time to another, we cannot find these criteria acceptable. The main problem with continuity criteria is that they seem to be too weak, and the imagined situations of branching and fission are designed to show this. We have considered some ways in which the conditions specified by these criteria might be further strengthened so as to rule out counterexamples based on branching and fission, but these ways have seemed not to work. But, in the light of the discussion of Parfit's view and the multiple occupancy thesis, it is time to reconsider the steps that lead from these imaginary situations to the conclusion that continuity criteria are inadequate. In this section we will identify those steps in the arguments against continuity criteria for persistence that are suspect and should be rejected. This should free us up to explore the role that continuity might play in criteria of persistence for persons, on the basis of which we can indicate what the nature of, and identity conditions for, persons might be.

The Ship of Theseus

Let's start by reconsidering the second situation in the example of the Ship of Theseus, since it provides us with the clearest case of branching. Recall that this is a situation in which Theseus first builds a ship with planks that are members of set S, and then, over a period of time at some later stage in the history of the ship, he renovates it, rebuilding it plank by plank with members of set S' and discarding the old ones in the dockyard. Meanwhile, someone else, say, Fred, comes upon the discarded planks and begins to build a second ship out of them, so that, at some stage (t_2) further along in the process, there are two ships, one of which Theseus sails and the other of which Fred sails. The question is, which is the original Ship of Theseus at this later time, t_2? Is it the ship that Thesus sails, with planks that are members of S'? Or is it the ship that Fred sails, with planks that are members of S?

According to the argument considered earlier when discussing this example, the physical continuity criterion supports *both* the view that the original Ship of Theseus persists as the ship that Theseus now sails, with planks that are members of S', *and* the view that the original Ship of Theseus persists as the ship that Fred now sails, with planks that are members of S, both ships being continuous with the original. Theseus's ship is spatio-temporally continuous with the original, while Fred's is continuous with the original, because its planks are continuous with the planks of the original. The conclusion is that, because continuity is preserved in both cases but branching has occurred, the conditions specified by the continuity criterion are insufficient for persistence because persistence requires identity over time, and in this situation one thing persists as two things, which is inconsistent with identity.

But we need to look more closely at the reasons for thinking that both of the later ships are continuous with the original, for it is not at all clear that this is so. In particular, during the time that Fred's ship is being constructed from the original ship's original parts, and while the original ship is having its parts removed and replaced, there is only one ship, the original one. It is true that after the first plank of wood is removed, the original ship is flawed, since it is missing a part, and this is true at every time during the process of replacement that a plank is removed. But it is still a ship. So, up until the time that the original planks begin to compose another ship, the original ship still exists and is composed of some of its original parts and some – perhaps many – new ones. But even then there is no competitor, and so, although it may be faulty, it is the original ship. If at some stage later than this, say, at t_2, when there is a competitor and it is a ship, composed of all – or even most – of the members of S, then it can only be claimed to be the original ship by claiming that the original ship moved instantaneously and discontinuously from one place (where the original is) to another (where Fred's ship now is). But this is an unacceptable result.[16]

One point that emerges from this is that what matters to continuity is not just the beginning and end states of the process by which a thing persists, perhaps through change, but the process itself. Without attending to this, it looks as though there are equal competitors for the title of the original ship. But it isn't really until very near the end of the process that there are two *ships*. And, once we realize this, we have to wonder *why* anyone should think that, at some point during the period of time from t_1 to t_2, when the renovating and reconstructing occur, the title simply transfers from a ship that has remained a ship throughout the period of time from t to t_2 to a ship that has not.

A second, related, point that emerges is that the identity of a thing over time is not independent of its causal history. This shouldn't surprise us, since the issue is one of persistence, perhaps through change. Further, what we are concerned with here is the question of the persistence of the original ship. For this to persist is for it to persist *as a ship*. The only *ship* that persists through change, from t to t_3, is the one that Theseus now sails. So, quite independently of the unacceptability of supposing that a thing could move instantaneously and discontinuously from one place to another, there is no reason to think that there is a competitor for the title of the original ship. And, without a competitor, we do not have a case of branching that constitutes a counter-example to the continuity criterion of persistence.

Fission

This deals with one of the main arguments against continuity criteria for persistence. Counterexamples based on the possibility of fission present another. One kind of case concerns the Charles–Robert situation, in which there seem to be two people, contemporaneous with and distinct from one another, who have the same types of memories as those originally had by Guy Fawkes and so are equal competitors for the title of Guy Fawkes. Another kind of case concerns the Brown–Robinson situation, in which Robinson's brain is split into two hemispheres, each of which 'houses' the full complement of his psychological characteristics, and one hemisphere remains in Robinson's's body while the other is transplanted into Brown's body, replacing his original brain. Both of these imagined situations put pressure on the continuity criterion of persistence by providing a special case of branching: one thing 'survives' as two things. In both cases the memory continuity criterion for the persistence of persons proves too weak, as fission shows that one thing can persist as two things, which is inconsistent with identity (and persistence requires identity). What are we to make of these counterexamples?

Let's begin with the Charles–Robert case, and move on to the Brown–Robinson one, since the latter ultimately turns on issues concerning psychological continuity. Why should we think that these people are equal competitors for the title of Guy Fawkes? The only thing stipulated in the case is that each make the same claims to remember, and, since we are not talking about memory types, but, rather, of particular memory experiences (after all, each of Charles and Robert has his own), it is open for us to insist that only one of Charles and Robert actually has Guy Fawkes's memories. It is true that we might not know which is Guy Fawkes, and so we might not have any reason to choose Charles over Robert as the one whose apparent memories are real; but we can assume that there is a right answer. And, if there is, this case does not constitute a counter-example against the criterion.

Suppose, on the other hand, that we insist that because both Charles and Robert have (the same) apparent memories, and each is equally well supported by all available evidence, in both cases their apparent memories are real. Here we do have a case of fission. But this in itself does not force us to conclude that one thing (Guy Fawkes) persists as two things (Charles, and Robert, for it is open to us to claim that in cases of fission, the original does not survive the process *at all*. What happens is that the original divides in half, and two new things come into existence. These new things may have features very like the original, but they are not identical with the original. The original ceases to exist altogether.

This response is not simply an ad hoc one, invoked in order to protect the memory continuity criterion from counterexamples. Recall that Parfit's argument for his own position begins with the Brown–Robinson case, concerning which, he claims, we have two conflicting intuitions, concerning two imagined situations. In the first, half of Robinson's brain is removed and relocated, intact, in Brown, and both halves continue to function normally with their full complement of psychological characteristics. In the second, the surgeon slips after she has removed half of Robinson's brain and drops that half, destroying it. We want to say that, in the first situation, because branching has occurred, the original Robinson has ceased to exist and two new persons have come into existence, but that, had only one half of Robinson's brain survived, as in the second situation, the original Robinson would have continued to exist. The intuition this relies on is that whether Robinson continues to live or not depends on what happens to the other half of his brain. On the other hand, we want to say that it would be irrational for Robinson to take any interest in what happens to the other half of his brain, since he has nothing to gain by having the other half of his brain destroyed. The intuition this relies on is that Robinson's survival does not depend on what happens to the other half of his brain.

Parfit, we now know, argues that these conflicting intuitions can be reconciled by accepting that what matters to survival is not identity, and further, that the concept of identity does not apply to persons. But let's look again at these 'intuitions' and how they are supported. The first one relies on the thought that, in the second situation, but not in the first, Robinson continues to live. But if this is a genuine case of fission, and if fission results in the original going out of existence and two new things coming into existence, then what happens to the other half of Robinson's brain is irrelevant. Robinson does not continue to live on, once fission has occurred. He does not live on if both halves of his brain survive, and he does not live on if only one half of his brain survives. Once fission occurs, Robinson ceases to exist. Of course, this may not be a genuine case of fission. But if it is not, then there are not, in the case where both halves of the original survive – one in Robinson, and one in Brown – two equal competitors for the title of Robinson. There is just one, Robinson, and the imagined situation is not one that constitutes a counter-example to the continuity criterion for the persistence of persons.

The second intuition – that Robinson's survival does not depend on what happens to the other half of his brain – relies on the thought that, so long as one half survives, he will survive. But once again, if this is a genuine case of fission, Robinson will not survive once it occurs, so it should not matter to Robinson what happens to either half of his brain. To take an interest in either half would be irrational. For *Robinson* – he himself – will not persist; only someone who appears to remember what Robinson remembered, who has many if not all of the beliefs, hopes, fears, intentions, etc. that Robinson has, exists. Again, if it is not a genuine case of fission, then there are not two competitors for the title of Robinson, one of which survives and the other of which does not. There is just one, Robinson, and there is no need to explain why it is not irrational for him not to be concerned about the fate of the other half of his brain.

So, in neither of the two imagined situations, the Charles–Robert one, and the Brown–Robinson one, do we seem to have a clear case of fission where the original survives as two things. It is open to us to say either that fission has occurred, but the original does not survive, or that the situations are not ones in which fission has occurred. The result is that neither situation constitutes a counter-example to a continuity criterion of persistence for persons.

A Suggestion

Given that a continuity criterion of persistence remains viable, let us see, first, what role it might play in an account of the persistence conditions of items like ships, using the example of the Ship of Theseus, and, second, whether an analogous role might be given to it in an account of persistence conditions for persons. Our discussion of the Ship of Theseus case revealed that persistence is a process that some thing or entity undergoes that results in the survival of that very thing. So the persistence of the Ship of Theseus is a process that that *ship* undergoes and survives. One property that the ship cannot lose, then, while still persisting, is the property of being a ship. Given that ships are things of the kind that have spatial and temporal properties, a natural and plausible suggestion for a criterion of persistence for them is this:

> A ship persists from t to t' if and only if that ship has, at t', the same spatio-temporal history up to t as it has at t, and has, at t', a spatio-temporal history that is continuous with that history at t.[17]

By this criterion, the ship that Theseus sails at t persists as the ship he sails at t_3, after it has been renovated; and it is compatible with that ship's having the *same* spatio-temporal history up to t at t' as it has at t that the spatial history of the ship is a history of spatio-temporal *continuity*.[18] Given that there is a connection between what makes for the persistence of a thing from one time to another and what it is to be that thing in the first place, we should expect this persistence condition for ships to have something to do with what it is to be a ship in the first place. And indeed it does: the theory of material substances advanced in chapter 3 tells us that a substance is an exemplification of an atomic substance-kind property in a place at a time. So a ship is an exemplification of the (atomic) substance-kind property, *ship*, in a place at a time; this much follows from the account of what it is to be a material substance and the assumption that ships are material substances. The persistence conditions for ships should also have something to do with their identity conditions. And they do: ship *a* is identical with ship *b* if and only if *a* and *b* are exemplifications of the same atomic substance-kind property (*ship*) in the same place at the same time, and ship *a/b* persists from *t* to *t'* if and only if it is an exemplification of the atomic substance-kind property, *ship*, in all the same places at all the same times, i.e., if and only if it has the same spatio-temporal history.

Can this treatment be extended to the case of persons? Two points have emerged from our discussion. First, because persons have both physical and psychological characteristics, and because (as we've discovered in our discussion of the case of the Ship of Theseus) persistence conditions are conditions for them to persist *as* things of the kind they are, physical criteria for the persistence of persons must, to be adequate, ensure their psychological persistence. Second, since there is a connection between what makes for the persistence of a person from one time to another and what it is to be a person in the first place, we should expect an answer to our question to have something to do with the nature of persons and their identity conditions.

At the outset of this chapter, we noted that what seems to make persons so distinctive is that they have psychological characteristics in virtue of having beliefs and other attitudes, not only about the world around them, but also about themselves. They have, in other words, both other-regarding attitudes and self-regarding ones, where these latter require having what might be called a first-person perspective – a perspective on one's own psychological states. This suggests a criterion of persistence for persons, namely, that:

> A person persists from *t* to *t'* if and only if that person has, at *t'*, the same psychological history up to *t* as she has at *t*, and has, at *t'*, a psychological history that is continuous with that history at *t*,

where a person's having the same psychological history from one time to another is compatible with that history's being a history of psychological continuity. We can test the adequacy of this criterion by means of a variant of the Robinson-Brown example. Suppose, in this variant, that there is no Brown to consider and that Robinson's brain is not split, but that the two hemispheres of Robinson's brain each contain the full complement of his psychological states. Now suppose that, during a period of time that includes both *t* and *t'*, he loses bits of the left hemisphere of his brain, due to some kind of brain disease that only affects the left hemisphere of his brain, so that, at t' his brain is constituted by the right hemisphere alone. During this period of time, he has new experiences, forms new beliefs, and acquires and loses other psychological states. By the criterion of persistence for persons just given, Robinson persists from time t to t', having at t' the same psychological history up to t as he does at t, and having, at t', a psychological history that is continuous with that history up to t.[19] And this is just the result we would expect an adequate criterion of persistence to deliver. The criterion does not deliver a result in cases of fission, but this is not a shortcoming given that these are not clearly cases where the original survives at all.

We opted for a criterion of persistence framed in terms of psychological characteristics because it seems clear that *any* acceptable criterion of persistence for persons needs to ensure their psychological persistence, and it seems that physical criteria alone cannot ensure this. Now, given what we have said about the connection between identity conditions and persistence conditions, we can expect there to be a connection between what makes for personal identity (that is, what the identity conditions for persons are) and what makes for a particular person's persistence from one time to another. As noted at the outset of this chapter, the former concerns the possession of properties that are essential and unique to the category of persons, whose possession in some determinate form at any given time makes for the numerical identity of a person within that category. The latter concerns the continued possession of those properties, in some determinate form, that make for a particular person's survival as that very person from one time to another.

It follows from this that to opt for a criterion of persistence framed in terms of psychological characteristics is to opt for the view that persons are essentially psychological beings. And this immediately rules out one of the three theories of the nature of persons mentioned at the beginning of this chapter, namely, the view that persons are essentially *only* physical beings (a variant of which is animalism, the view that persons are essentially animals). Does it follow, though, that persons are essentially immaterial beings? No, and that is because it may be that in order to be psychological beings, persons must be embodied. Even the physical criteria of persistence for persons that we have discussed have required that only those physical characteristics that are required for psychological persistence are necessary for the persistence of persons.

What follows from the view that persons are essentially psychological beings is just that – they cannot exist without psychological characteristics or properties. But it is compatible with this that persons are *also* essentially physical beings. Given that human persons have bodies, even if they are not identical with them, and given that we typically track persons by tracking their bodies, the view that persons are essentially psychological beings that requires them to be embodied is both natural and plausible.

One version of this is the view that *human* persons are psychological beings that are constituted by physical things, in something like the way in which a statue is constituted by the matter that makes it up, or a ring is constituted by gold. On this view, constitution is not identity – the statue is not identical with the matter that constitutes it, because the statue can be destroyed while the matter continues to exist, and the ring is not identical with the gold that constitutes it, since the ring can be destroyed while the gold continues to exist. Because these things – the statue and the lump of matter that constitutes it, the ring and the lump of gold that constitutes it – have different persistence conditions, they are not identical. It may be, though, that while the particular lump of matter that constitutes a thing such as a statue or a ring may not be identical with it, it might also be that no statue or ring can exist without being constituted by some matter or other.

If this constitution view is right, then, although the physical matter that actually constitutes a human person may not be essential to her, it is essential to her that she is constituted by some matter or other. This being so, human persons are essentially physical things, even though their actual physical constitution, and so actual physical properties, may be accidental, rather than essential, to their being persons. This is not a version of the purely psychological view of persons mentioned at the outset of this chapter, because that view holds that persons are essentially *only* psychological beings, and this view holds that although this might be true of some persons it is not true of human persons. However, it is close enough to that view to attract those who think that persons are essentially psychological beings (and so who reject animalism), while avoiding the problems with the view that persons are immaterial beings.[20]

According to the constitution view, human persons are humans because they are constituted by physical things, namely, human beings. One consequence of it is that persons (*simpliciter*) fall into kinds, depending on the natures of the things that constitute them. There are human persons, persons that are human because they are constituted by human beings, which are material substances of a particular kind. So there might be bionic (electrically powered) persons, or cat persons, or dolphin persons. Of course, on the present understanding of the nature and scope of metaphysics, it is not the business of metaphysics to determine what kinds of persons there are.

The constitution view of persons has many virtues, one of which is, in the present context, that it has clear affinities with the property exemplification account of substances (see chapter 3). Indeed, some version of the constitution view is compatible with, and can help to motivate, what we might call the property exemplification account of persons (PEP).[21] According to this, persons are exemplifications of person-kind properties (properties such as *human person*) at times in material substances (such as human beings). The properties, whose exemplification in material substances at times just are persons, are characterizing (or accidental) properties of material substances, but constitutive properties of persons. It is of the essence of a person to be an exemplification of a person-kind property at a time in a substance.

If the property exemplification account of persons is true, then claims analogous to the ones that hold for substances on the PES hold for persons on the PEP. Thus, there are two conditions that are essential to the account, one an existence condition and another an identity condition:

> *Existence Condition:* Person [x,P,t] exists if and only the material substance x has the person-kind property P at time t.

> *Identity Condition:* Person [x,P,t] is identical with person [y,Q,t'] if and only of $x = y$, $P = Q$, and $t = t'$.

where x and y, P and Q, and t and t, are variables ranging over material substances, person-kind properties, and times, respectively.

Is it of the essence of any particular person to be an exemplification of the person-kind property she is in fact an exemplification of? It seems so. Suppose that Fred is an exemplification of the person-kind property, *human person*. Then, given the existence condition on persons, Fred is essentially an exemplification of that property in a human being. Suppose that parts of Fred's body are replaced, bit by bit, by electronically powered parts, so that eventually Fred's body is not human but bionic. Then Fred not only ceases to be an exemplification of the property, *human person*, but ceases to exist altogether.

It follows from this that Fred could not persist as the same person from one time to another if he were to 'change' from being an exemplification of the person-kind property, *human person*, to being an exemplification of, say, the person-kind property, *bionic person*, for the persistence conditions of persons, according to the property exemplification account, are importantly connected to their identity conditions. Given that person a is identical with person b if and only if a and b are exemplifications of the same person-kind property in the same material substances at the same times, the persistence conditions for persons are these:

A person persists from t to t' if and only if that person is an exemplification of the same person-kind property in all the same material substances at all the same times,

and this will be true if and only if that person has, at t', the same psychological history up to t as she has at t, and has, at t', a psychological history that is continuous with that history at t. Thus the property exemplification account of persons delivers persistence conditions for persons that are just what our discussion in this final section has led us to expect.

Notes

1 Thus, for example, Locke defines a person as something that has certain mental characteristics: specifically, a person is 'a thinking intelligent being, that has reason and reflection, and can consider itself as itself, the same thinking thing, in different times and places' (1975, p. 335).
2 For classic discussions of this kind of question, see Lewis (1976), Parfit (1971, 1984), Perry (1976), Quinton (1962), Swinburne (1997), Unger (1990), Wiggins (1967, 2001), and B. Williams ((1966, 1970). These not only focus on the issue of the persistence of persons, but also approach them in the same spirit that dominates Locke's discussion (Locke 1975). Zimmerman (2003), following Johnston (1987), calls the approach 'the method of cases', a method that uses imaginary cases, or thought-experiments, to help to determine answers to questions concerning the persistence conditions of persons. In the face of some recent scepticism about the value of this method (Johnston 1987; Wilkes 1992; Rovane 1997; Gendler 2000), and also about the centrality of questions concerning the adequacy of psychological vs. physical criteria of persistence compared with more abstract questions about the ontological status of persons (van Inwagen 1990), those such as Zimmerman (2003) focus on the more abstract question about the ontology of persons. Zimmerman does note, however, that there is 'no sharp divide' between the work that occupies those concerned with the specific criteria of persistence for persons and those concerned with the more abstract ontological question, and that those who have been interested in this latter question have also been interested in the more specific criteria (e.g., Lewis 1976; Parfit 1971, 1984; and Shoemaker 1963, 1970). In this chapter, we will be concerned with both sorts of questions, beginning with the ones about specific criteria of persistence for persons, using 'the method of cases', and then moving on to the more basic question about the ontology of persons, of what makes for personal identity. These questions overlap in the discussion of physical criterion of persistence and the case of the Ship of Theseus where the question of persistence gets entangled with that of the relation between a thing and its parts (see the discussion in the text of this chapter). Like Zimmerman, we here take the view that persons, like mate-

rial substances in general, can gain and lose parts, and that an account of how it is that persons can survive changes of this kind should be one that generalizes to material substances in general. The account in this chapter meets this constraint.

3 Baker does not begin with the question of persistence, but takes her account of the nature of persons to be based on considerations about persistence: 'the view rests on what I claim to be a difference in persistence conditions between persons and animals' (Baker 2001b).

4 What about sensations, such as pain? These too seem to be characteristic of conscious creatures and this fact separates them from other material substances, so why are they omitted? One reason is that the mere capacity to have sensations seems to be insufficient for the capacity for rational thought and agency, a capacity that many believe is essential to being a person. Descartes (1984), for example, believed that to be a person was to be essentially a thinking thing. Further, many of those who believe that the capacity of rational thought and agency is essential to being a person also believe that that capacity can be possessed by mere machines, such as robots, which may or may not be capable of having sensations (see, for example, Pollock (1989) and Baker (2000)).

5 Another way of phrasing this, which is of a more familiar, but also more misleading form in discussions of persistence (Olson 2002a), is this:

> Person x, at time t, is identical with person y, at time t', if and only if x and y have all the same memories.

This way of phrasing criteria of persistence for persons is problematic in a number of ways. Most importantly, for present purposes, is that expressions like 'x at time t' look as though they refer, not to continuants (persons), but to temporal parts of continuants (temporal parts, or stages, of persons). But the view that persons have temporal parts is emphatically not being endorsed in this chapter. The alternative is to take 'x at time t' to be a referring expression in which 't' attaches to 'is identical with'. But, as has already been noted, identity is omni-temporal. The suggested phrasing in the text is intended to avoid this kind of problem.

6 More generally, a relation, R, is transitive if and only if, given any three things, x, y, and z, if x bears relation R to y, and y bears relation R to z, then x bears relation R to z.

7 There is a third objection to this, and to all other, formulations of the memory criterion, one that Locke himself (1975) voiced against Bishop Butler, who advocated this criterion. The claim is that, because it is part of the concept of remembering that one can only remember one's *own* past experiences the memory criterion is uninformative or trivial. I can know whether I remember a past experience only if I know that I am the one that had it. Some say, as a result, that the criterion presupposes, rather than gives an account of personal identity. However, it is possible to introduce a notion that is weaker than that of memory, that of 'quasi-memory' that does not suffer from this objection (Penelhum 1970; Shoemaker 1970; Parfit 1984;

but cf. McDowell 1997 for criticism of this way round the problem). For discussion of the objection and strategy for avoiding it, see Noonan 1989.

8   This might have the consequence of requiring that persons be embodied, (since persons seem to be positional in virtue of their bodies being positional), but this in itself would not undermine the memory criterion or any version of the psychological criterion in general. The reason is that the requirement that persons be embodied is compatible both with (a) persons being distinct from their bodies (so that physicalism – the view that everything is either physical or is constituted wholly by what is physical – is false) and (b) the persistence of a person not requiring the persistence of that person's body. For more on this see the final section of this chapter.

9   Or so Williams argues. However, the argument is not as conclusive as Williams suggests. Part of the problem with it is that the only thing that is fixed in the Charles–Robert case is that they both make the same memory claims. But we are not talking about memory types or kinds here – the sorts of thing that can, like universals, be instantiated in different places at the same time – but, rather, of particular memory experiences. For, after all, each of Charles and Robert has his own memory experiences. So it seems that only one of them actually has Guy Fawkes's memories. Of course, from an epistemological point of view, we might not have any reason to choose Charles over Robert as the one whose apparent memories are real; but this does not show that there isn't a right answer. And, if so, Williams's argument collapses. There is also the problem that a staunch defender of the criterion can respond by saying that in a case like this, where there is memory 'fission', the appropriate conclusion to draw is not that one person persists as two later ones, but rather, that the original person simply does not persist at all. We will return to this issue later in the chapter.

10 As this illustrates, although the features possessed by things that are continuous with one another at two distinct times may overlap (that is, form a common sub-set), the sets themselves may differ quite radically in many other ways. In the limiting case of continuity, there may be only one feature in common between two such sets.

11 Thanks to Larry Lombard for this example.

12 It seems to be more than just logically possible. See Rey (1976), who cites experimental work published by Gazzinaga, Bogen, and Sperry (1962) in support of this possibility. Their experiments seem to suggest that not only is it false that the entire body is necessary for psychological continuity and persistence, but that it is false that the entire *brain* is necessary. As Rey describes the work:

> The Sperry experiments on epileptics whose *Corpora Collosa* have been cut present fairly persuasive evidence that the human brain exists as a pair of very similar hemispheres, each one of which could in principle exist and (with a little tampering) function fully independently of the other. Only technological (and perhaps some moral) difficulties prevent a brain being divided into two, one hemisphere being transplanted to one new skull, the other to another. In

such a case, our usual criteria of personal identity [*sic. persistence for persons*] – bodily or psychological continuity – would break down. For they would present us with two (over time) equally eligible, but (at a given time) bodily and psychologically quite distinct candidates for the continued identity of the original person. (Rey 1976, p. 41)

13 But again, as we shall see, just as in the Charles–Robert example discussed in connection with the memory criterion, it is open to a defender of this criterion to insist that fission results, not in one person's persisting as two later ones, but rather, in the original person's failing to persist altogether.

14 Parfit actually speaks of personal identity, but it is clear that the issue he is concerned with is that of persistence. We have noted that persistence requires identity, in that it requires that an object or entity survive as the very same object from one time to another, even though it may change in a variety of ways. But we've also noted, very early on in the present chapter and in chapter 3, that the issue of persistence is a different issue from that of identity. So here, where Parfit would speak of personal identity, we speak instead of the persistence of a person.

15 There is also the following objection. In chapter 3 it was argued that no two material substances of the same atomic substance-kind can have the same spatio-temporal history. Now, suppose that no branching ever occurs with Theseus's ship. Then the hundreds or thousands (or more) ships that must actually exist in order to account for the possible branchings all have the same spatio-temporal history. It follows that if the identity conditions for material substances are right, ships are not material substances. The same reasoning can be applied to persons. Of course, in this case one might respond that this just shows that persons are not material substances.

16 Here I am indebted to Larry Lombard.

17 This criterion might seem to be circular, since it looks as though it purports to give conditions under which a ship can persist (i.e., exist as the very same ship), but nothing could meet those conditions unless it was the very same ship. But it is not circular. From the outset it was made clear that persistence requires identity; it requires that some thing or entity continues to exist as the very same thing or entity from one time to another. But the conditions for persistence are not the conditions for identity; see pp. 135–8 of this chapter. The question of persistence is a question about the conditions under which identity over time is ensured. The claim here is that sameness of spatio-temporal history ensures identity over time. That nothing can meet that condition without being self-identical just goes to show that the conditions for persistence are adequate.

18 Why is continuity important at all? It is important because we may not be able to tell whether an object or entity has persisted from one time to another except by tracking it, and continuity relations – spatio-temporal, for things like ships, and for material substances in general – between characteristics of that thing at one time and characteristics of it at another are typically the means by which we do it. This may be the only way in which

we can do it, given that persistence is a matter of process, and so is not just a matter of beginning and end states, but of how those end states are arrived at.

19   Again, it might look as though the criterion is circular; but it is not (see note 17). What might give the appearance of circularity is that we might not be able to know whether the conditions are met – in this case, that Robinson does persist from t to t' because he has the same psychological history – unless we know that, at t', Robinson is the very same person as the Robinson that exists at t. But this just goes to show that persistence requires identity, not that the conditions for persistence are the conditions for identity. See pp. 135–8 of this chapter. Further, we've noted that persistence is a *process*, something that takes place over time, and so not something that we are able to determine has occurred just by looking at the beginning and end states of that process. This, by the way, is why it is important that the persistence conditions for items like ships (and material substances in general) and for persons are compatible with continuity criteria. We may not be able to tell whether an object or entity has persisted from one time to another except by tracking it, and continuity relations between characteristics of that thing at one time and characteristics of it at another – spatio-temporal, psychological – are typically the means by which we do it.

20   One of the features of that view that is problematic is that since, according to it, psychological states are not physical ones (and so dualism is true), it cannot easily explain the phenomenon of causal interaction between mind and body, a phenomenon that has made many turn away from dualism and the purely psychological view of the nature of persons.

21   But not Baker's (2000) version. This view advanced here departs in some important ways from it. Specifically, there are these differences: (1) whereas Baker holds that so long as x constitutes y, x has no independent existence from y (although it might come to have independent existence, if, say, y ceases to exist), the property exemplification view does not; (2) whereas Baker holds that 'what the thing really is' when x constitutes y is y, the property exemplification account does not; (3) whereas Baker holds that Fred might remain the same person if his human body parts were replaced bit by bit by bionic ones, with the result that his body is no longer human, the property exemplification account does not. Both the property exemplification account and Baker's version of the constitution view hold that human persons are essentially *human*. But Baker's account allows, whereas the property exemplification account does not, that a human person could persist as the same person but not the same human person, from one time to another. (The account allows this because Baker thinks it possible that a person could maintain the same first-person perspective, the same perspective on herself, even if she were to come to be constituted by an entirely different body or material substance.) Still, the property exemplification account is compatible with a constitution view, where constitution is not identity, because the persistence conditions of person are different from

the persistence conditions of the material substances that constitute them. Further, although the property exemplification account of persons takes them to be both essentially physical and essentially psychological, whereas Baker's constitution view does not (though human persons are essentially both), it does not collapse into any version of the physical view (including animalism) because, on that view, persons are essentially *only* physical (or animal) beings. All of these points are merits of the property exemplification account, and advantage it over the general constitution view favoured by Baker.

Suggested Further Reading

Baker, L. (2000): *Persons and Bodies: A Constitution View*. Cambridge: Cambridge University Press.

Barresi, J. and Martin, R. (eds) (2003): *Personal Identity*. Malden, Mass.: Blackwell.

Garrett, B. (1998): *Personal Identity and Self-Consciousness*. London: Routledge.

Kolak, D. and Martin, R. (eds) (1991): *Self and Identity: Contemporary Philosophical Issues*. New York: Macmillan.

Lewis, D. (1976): 'Survival and Identity'. In Rorty 1976, pp. 17–40.

Loux, M. and Zimmerman, D. (2003): *The Oxford Handbook to Metaphysics*. Oxford: Oxford University Press.

Lovibond, S. and Williams, S. (eds) (1996): *Identity, Truth and Value: Essays for David Wiggins*. Oxford: Blackwell.

Martin, R. (1998): *Self Concern*. Cambridge: Cambridge University Press.

Noonan, H. (1989): *Personal Identity*. London: Routledge.

Nozick, R. (1981): *Philosophical Explanations*. Cambridge, Mass.: Harvard University Press.

Olson, E. (1997): *The Human Animal*. Oxford: Oxford University Press.

Olson, E. (2002a): 'Personal Identity'. In Zalta, E. (ed.), *The Stanford Encyclopedia of Philosophy* (Fall 2002 edn). URL = <http://plato.stanford.edu/archives/fall2002/entries/identity-personal/>

Olson, E. (2002b): 'An Argument for Animalism'. In Barresi and Martin (eds) 2002, pp. 318–34.

Parfit, D. (1984): *Reasons and Persons*. Oxford: Oxford University Press.

Perry, J. (ed.) (1975): *Personal Identity*. Berkeley, California: University of California Press.

Perry, J. (1976): 'The Importance of Being Identical'. In Rorty 1976, pp. 67–90.

Rorty, A. (1976): *The Identities of Persons*. Berkeley, California: University of California Press.

Rovane, C. (1997): *The Bounds of Agency: An Essay in Revisionary Metaphysics*. Princeton: Princeton University Press.

Shoemaker, S. (1963): *Self-Knowledge and Self-Identity*. Ithaca, New York: Cornell University Press.

Shoemaker, S. (1970): 'Persons and their Pasts'. In *American Philosophical Quarterly* 7, 269–85. Reprinted in Shoemaker 2003, pp. 19–48.

Shoemaker, S. (1984): 'Personal Identity: A Materialist Account's. In Shoemaker and Swinburne 1984, chapter 2.

Shoemaker, S. and Swinburne, R. (1984): *Personal Identity*. Oxford: Blackwell.

Shoemaker, S. (2003): *Identity, Cause, and Mind*. Expanded edn. Oxford: Clarendon Press.

Snowdon, P. (1996): 'Persons and Personal Identity'. In Lovibond and Williams 1996, pp. 33–48.

Swinburne, R. (1997): *The Evolution of the Soul*. 2nd edn. Oxford: Oxford University Press.

Unger, P. (1990): *Identity, Consciousness, and Value*. Oxford: Oxford University Press.

Wiggins, D. (1967): *Identity and Spatio-Temporal Continuity*. Oxford: Blackwell.

Wiggins, D. (2001): *Sameness and Substance*. New edn. Cambridge: Cambridge University Press.

Williams, B. (1973): *Problems of the Self*. Cambridge: Cambridge University Press.

Zimmerman, D. (2003): 'Material People'. In Loux and Zimmerman (eds) 2003, pp. 491–526.

5

Events

We have now considered two basic categories of particulars, material substances and persons, and explored their natures and relations to one another. We've concluded that the ontological category of persons is not reducible to that of material substances, but, rather, is a sub-category within the larger ontological category of substances. So material substances form one kind of substance, and persons form another. Neither of these kinds is reducible to a kind more basic still: not even to the kind, *substance*, since to be a substance is to be a member of a substance kind. Finally, we've concluded that substances themselves are reducible neither to bundles of properties nor to bare substrata.

Later, in chapter 6, we will consider whether, in addition to those various kinds of substances whose members are concrete and particular, there might also exist things of a very different kind, whose members are abstract and universal. As noted in chapter 3, concrete particulars are particular in being wholly and completely in a given place at a given time, and concrete in that no other thing of the same kind can be in the same place as them at the same time. In contrast to this, abstract universals are universal in that they can be wholly and completely in many places at the same time, and are abstract in that many of them can be in the same place at the same time. In this chapter, we will consider whether, in addition to material substances and persons, there might be dated particulars (i.e., particulars whose natures are at least partly temporal) of another basic or fundamental ontological kind. The particulars in question are events.

In a seminal paper, Donald Davidson (1970b) raises the question 'Things change; but are there such things as changes?', where, by 'changes' he means 'events'. This may sound like a very strange question, since we don't normally speak of changes as things. However, we can all agree that events aren't things, if what is meant by 'things' is 'substances'. Still, we think and speak about events all the time – as often, in fact, as we think and speak about material substances and persons.[1] We talk about wars, earthquakes, avalanches, deaths, and explosions, as well as birthdays, weddings, and funerals. Our day-to-day conversations are riddled with such talk. We even use singular terms to refer to many of these occurrences. We say such things as 'the Second World War was a gruesome war', 'The attack on the World Trade Center was the second act of war against the US on US soil', and so on. We typically identify these occurrences in ordinary talk in just the same way as we identify persons and material substances, by using singular terms in order to facilitate such talk. If 'events exist' is not the appropriate way in which to speak of our ontological commitment to events, then perhaps 'events occur' is. When we say that things happen, then, what we evidently really mean, at least sometimes, is: there are happenings. And, as awkward as it may sound to say it, occurring may well be a way of existing.

We could, perhaps, dismiss talk of events as things if we could make sense of the idea of happenings simply in terms of talk about material substances and their properties. When an object, say, a chameleon, changes from being brown to being green, for example, this is a happening. It is tempting to think of this change as consisting in the chameleon's being brown at one time, and that same chameleon's being green at another. However, if we consider this chameleon at each of these two times, taken separately, we seem to be unable to capture the chameleon's *changing*. At the earlier time, it is brown, and at the later time, it is green. And, no matter how small we take the intervals of time to be between the latest time at which it is brown and the earliest time at which it is green, we seem unable to capture its *changing* from red to green, the happening itself. In order to do this, we seem to need to talk, not just of objects and their properties, but also of events, or changes, that these objects undergo.

This chapter will begin by considering one powerful motivation for thinking that we are ontologically committed to events, one that is consistent with our choice, in chapter 2, of a broadly referential criterion of ontological commitment that focuses on the bound variables of existentially quantified sentences of a language. The discussion will then turn to various candidates for criteria of event identity. We will eventually settle on one that flows from a particular version of a theory of events, a version of the property exemplification account. We won't consider all of the theories of events that are available; notably absent from our discussion will be trope theories.[2] One reason for omitting them is that trope accounts of the relation between particulars and their properties will come up for discussion in chapter 6, where they will be shown to be unsatisfactory. This has ramifications for trope theories of events, since these take events to be tropes (or complexes of tropes) of properties (Ehring 1997; Bennett 1988, 1996, 2002; Cleland 1991).

The theory of events that we settle on needs to be sophisticated and worked out in fine detail in order to generate a satisfactory criterion of event identity. Readers without a fair amount of philosophical expertise on theories of events may find that a degree of patient attention to these details is necessary in the final section of the chapter.

Our Ontological Commitment to Events

We noted in chapter 2 that part of what is involved in doing metaphysics is doing semantics. It should come as no surprise, then, that one motivation for thinking that there are events derives from attempts to arrive at an adequate semantics for what appear to be event-describing sentences, many of which contain singular terms purporting to refer to individual, particular events. But these sentences are not very promising, since it seems that we can easily rewrite a sentence such as 'Julia's birth occurred' as 'Julia was born'. The interest in Davidson's strategy comes from seeing that, even after one has done these paraphrases, the sentences that remain (e.g., 'Julia was born') seem to entail that there are events. There are many sentences, such as, for example, 'Sally shattered the window', that do not involve singular terms purporting to refer to events, but which we nevertheless understand as involving talk about events because they involve the use of event-verbs.

One of the interesting things about sentences of this latter type is that they are capable of augmentation by adverbial modifiers in an indefinite number of ways. Thus, for example, 'Sally shattered the window' is capable of augmentation as 'Sally shattered the window, swiftly, with a rock, at 5 p.m., in the cellar', as 'Sally shattered the window with a rock', and so on. There appears to be no limit to the number of adverbial modifiers that can be meaningfully attached to, or detached from, a sentence of this type. Intuitively, we can see that there are not only grammatical connections between such sentences, but also semantic ones. How do we capture the semantic connections?

Davidson (1967) argued that the usual way of representing the semantic structure of such sentences as

1 Sally shattered the window in the cellar at 5 p.m. with a rock.
2 Sally shattered the window in the cellar at 5 p.m.

and

    3   Sally shattered the window in the cellar.

respectively, makes it impossible to capture the entailment relations between them, specifically the entailments, which we take to be intuitively correct, from 1, to 2 and 3, from 1 to 3, and from 2 to 3. The usual way, in standard quantification theory, to represent these sentences is as having, respectively, the semantic structure of a 5-, a 4-, and a 3-place relational predicate, each of which is a semantic primitive (i.e., not further semantically analysable), thus,

    4   Shattered (Sally, the window, the cellar, 5 p.m., rock)
    5   Shattered (Sally, the window, the cellar, 5 p.m.)
    6   Shattered (Sally, the window, the cellar).[3]

However, this way cannot preserve the intuitively correct entailment relations between such sentences.[4]

Davidson suggests that events be included among the values of the variables of quantification, and that event predicates, which appear to be n-place, have an extra $(n + 1)$ argument place taking variables ranging over events. The introduction of a repeatable variable makes possible a conjunctive analysis of event-describing sentences; one according to which 1, 2, and 3 receive something like the following form:

    7   There was an event, and it was a shattering, and it was done by Sally, and it was done to the window, and it occurred in the cellar, and it occurred at 5 p.m., and it was done with a rock.
    8   There was an event, and it was a shattering, and it was done by Sally, and it was done to the window, and it occurred in the cellar and it occurred at 5 p.m.
    9   There was an event, and it was a shattering, and it was done by Sally, and it was done to the window, and it occurred in the cellar.[5]

The fact that the same variable ranging over an event can be repeated accounts for the entailments by simplification.

In other words, in standard quantification theory,

    10   There is something that is F and G.

entails

    11   There is something that is F.[6]

But we would not understand how this was so if the object which made 10 true were not the object which made 11 true. Applying this reasoning to 7–9, we can see how 1 entails 2 and 3. It does so because the same event makes all three sentences true.

The positing of events accounts both for the preservation of entailment relations and for the possibility of re-description, since, from

3   Sally shattered the window in the cellar,

which has the form

9   There was an event, and it was a shattering, and it was done by Sally, and it was done to the window, and it occurred in the cellar,

we can validly infer

12   There was something, and it was a shattering, and it was done by Sally, and it was done to the window, and it occurred in the cellar,

from which it follows that

13   Sally did something in the cellar.

This is important, since, as Davidson points out, it seems that we can only make sense of certain patterns of behaviour, for example, excuses, if events can have more than one description. Thus, he says,

> I flip the switch, turn on the light, and illuminate the room. Unbeknownst to me I also alert a prowler to the fact that I am home. Here I do not do four things, but only one, of which four descriptions have been given. (Davidson 1963, p. 686)

Given that events can have more than one description, we can re-describe, say, a particular stabbing as a killing, and a particular killing as a murdering, a signing of a cheque the paying of a bill, and a movement of a hand the greeting to a friend. It seems that behaviour, and actions in particular, are capable of being re-described in many different ways, and this is essential to the possibility of rationalizing and, more generally, of explaining behaviour and other events.[7]

This solution to a semantic problem requires ontological commitment to events. Since semantic considerations are only part of what is involved in doing metaphysics, however, this raises the question of whether the semantics provided by Davidson is correct. And that depends, at least in part, on whether an adequate criterion of identity for events is forthcoming. So let us turn to this issue.

Three Criteria: Spatio-temporal Coincidence, Necessary Spatio-temporal Coincidence, and Sameness of Cause and Effect

A good way to begin our discussion of possible criteria of identity for events is to consider what pre-theoretical intuitions or beliefs we might have about events. And, although it may not be immediately apparent, we do have some. Here are a few of them.

An event seems to be a happening, and many happenings are ones that occur in or to something. When my arm breaks, something happens to me, and I am the subject of this happening. When an explosion occurs, it occurs to something: something explodes. When an earthquake occurs, it occurs to something (the earth). One intuition we have about events, then, is that many, if not all, of them have subjects.[8]

Events also seem to take time or last for a certain period of time, however short. The breaking of my arm lasts for a certain amount of time, before which it is unbroken, and after which it is broken. (This may explain why it is that, if we consider an object and its properties at one time, and then consider it and its properties at another, later time, we seem not to be able to capture its *changing*.) Explosions, earthquakes, wars, weddings, and downpours all take time. So many, if not all, events seem to have temporal *parts* – they have beginnings, middles, and ends. In this way they seem to be very unlike substances, which take up space rather than time. Substances, we think, have spatial parts, but not temporal ones; at any given time, however short, they are wholly and completely in the places that they occur. This is not the way things seem to be with events. At any given moment during the occurrence of an avalanche, we think, only part of the avalanche is wholly and completely taking place. We might capture this perceived difference between substances and events by saying that, whereas substances have spatial parts, and persist *through* time, events have temporal parts, and last *for* a period of time.

Finally, events, in being happenings that take time, seem to involve change. Their subjects are a certain way before these events happen to them, and are a different way afterwards. Their subjects are altered by, changed by, the events that happen to them. These changes are typically changes in the properties of the subjects that undergo them. A metal rod, for example, expands when heated. Its size before being heated is different from its size after it expands. Events, whatever else they are, seem to be essentially connected with changes in the properties of things.

So, we seem to have at least three intuitions about events on which we might base a criterion of event identity. We shall briefly consider three criteria of event identity that focus on one or another, or all, of these before passing on to two further ones (for further discussion of all of these, see Macdonald 1989). These final two criteria flow from different versions of the property exemplification account of events, which we have already encountered in chapters 3 and 4. The first three criteria are, respectively, de facto (or actual) spatio-temporal coincidence, necessary spatio-temporal coincidence, and sameness of cause and effect.

De Facto Spatio-temporal Coincidence

It seems evident even from the brief discussion above that events bear important relations to space and time. A natural first suggestion for an adequate criterion, then, might be that events are identical if and only if they occupy exactly the same positions at exactly the same (periods of) times (Lemmon, 1966). That is, it states that

Necessarily, for any events, x and y, x is identical with y if and only if x and y they occupy all the same places at all the same times.[9]

However, this suggestion immediately faces two objections. Both have their source in the requirement mentioned in chapter 2, that any acceptable criterion of event identity must specify properties of events that are both necessary and sufficient (1) to individuate events from particulars of other kinds, and (2) to individuate events from one another. Spatio-temporal coincidence has been thought insufficient to satisfy either (1) or (2). Thus, for example, imagine a sphere that both continuously rotates and becomes continuously warmer throughout its existence (Davidson 1969). Here it seems that continuously rotating and continually increasing in temperature are indiscernible spatio-temporally from one another (and, indeed, from the sphere itself).

De facto spatio-temporal coincidence also fails in its attempt to specify conditions sufficient to individuate events from one another (i.e., to satisfy requirement (2)). Thus, suppose that John swims the English Channel, and, while swimming it, catches a cold. Here it seems that the event that is John's swimming of the Channel occupies the same spatio-temporal region (namely, that occupied by John) as that occupied by John's catching of a cold. We want to distinguish between these events, but it seems that by the lights of the criterion we cannot.

One way of attempting to avoid this kind of counter-intuitive consequence might be to invoke a notion of a minimal location of an event.
Suppose that one locates events by locating those objects within or to
which they occur. Then one might specify a minimal location of an event
by specifying the smallest object within or to which it occurs. It would
probably be necessary to define a notion of a minimal location for events
for any version of the spatio-temporal criterion, since without it the conclusion that all simultaneous events have the same spatial location and
are therefore identical is not easily avoided, because every object is part
of another, the universe.

However, it is doubtful whether this will suffice. For one thing, the
notion of a minimal location for events helps to individuate them only
in cases like Davidson's example of John's swimming the English Channel
and John's catching cold (if it helps even with these). It fails to be of any
use in cases like that of the rotating sphere, where the changes involved
encompass the whole of the objects that undergo them. In these latter
types of case, the changes – of temperature, of rotation – arguably cannot
be more minimally located than by locating the entire sphere. But more
importantly, there is no obvious a priori reason to think that, no matter
how minimally one locates events, *only* one event can occupy exactly the
same spatio-temporal region.

This suggests that the spatio-temporal criterion gives an incomplete
account of the nature of events, in the sense that, although spatio-
temporal properties are essential to events, they are not all of what is
essential to them. This is reinforced by doubts of the kind mentioned
earlier, namely, that de facto spatio-temporal coincidence does not suffice
to individuate events from particulars of *other* ontological categories
(i.e., that it fails to satisfy (1)). Doubts of this kind reveal that we know
no more about events when we know that they have spatio-temporal
properties than we know about *any* other non-repeatable dated particular of any kind; for it is true of any such particular that it has spatio-
temporal properties. Take any spatio-temporal region wholly occupied
by any material substance, and suppose that object to be undergoing a
continuous change that encompasses the whole of it – our continuously
rotating sphere, perhaps. There is nothing in the notion of a non-
repeatable dated particular itself by which to individuate events qua particulars of one kind from material substances qua particulars of another
(this of course also indicates what we know from chapter 3 in any case,
namely, that spatio-temporal coincidence does not suffice for material
substance identity).

It is tempting to respond by insisting that we do know something more
about events than we do about particulars of other distinct kinds simply

in virtue of knowing that they have spatio-temporal properties. We know, for instance, that events relate to space and time *differently* than do physical objects. Physical objects take up space and persist through time. Events, however, take up time rather than space.[10]

But this knowledge is not derivable from a criterion formulated merely in spatio-temporal terms. If the criterion is right, events as well as material substances can be said to occupy spatio-temporal regions. It is true, of course, that we do often speak of events as *occurring in* places at times, in contrast with physical objects, which we typically speak of as *occupying* places at times. But it is not clear what to make of this difference independently of a full-fledged theory of events, something the criterion of de facto spatio-temporal coincidence alone does not supply. Short of this events cannot be assumed to relate to space and time differently from the way material substances do, since it assumes, rather than justifies, the claim that the de facto spatio-temporal coincidence criterion is false.

Necessary Spatio-temporal Coincidence

The idea that events do not exclude one another in space and time suggests that the spatio-temporal criterion might suffice for event identity if it were strengthened to require *necessary* spatio-temporal coincidence, that is, if it were to state that events are identical if and only if they necessarily occupy the same spatio-temporal region. Thus, Brand (1976, 1977) proposes the following criterion:

> Necessarily, for any events x and y, x is identical with y if and only if, necessarily, x and y occupy all the same places at all the same times.[11]

That is, events are identical if and only if they not only do, but must, occur in exactly the same places at the same times. This is equivalent to saying that events are identical if and only if it is not logically possible that they should *fail* to occupy the same spatio-temporal region.

This version of the spatio-temporal criterion would appear to deal effectively with one of the doubts raised in connection with de facto spatio-temporal coincidence, viz., whether it suffices to individuate events from one another (condition 2), though we shall return to this. Even if the criterion does not deal effectively with that question, it does seem to suffice to individuate events from material substances (condition (1)). The difference between members of the two kinds can now be marked by reference to their differing criteria of identity: in addition to identity of substance-kind properties, de facto spatio-temporal coincidence might suffice for material substance identity, whereas necessary spatio-temporal coincidence is required for event identity.

Of course, de facto spatio-temporal coincidence guarantees that there cannot be two substances – say, two cats – that are exemplifications of exactly the same atomic-substance property (and so of all other properties) in exactly the same place at the same time. But then, since things that are identical are necessarily identical (i.e., the thesis of the necessity of identity is true), substances that are identical and in fact occupy the same spatio-temporal regions *must* (in being identical) occupy the same spatio-temporal regions. Further, since the criterion of necessary spatio-temporal coincidence entails the criterion of de facto spatio-temporal coincidence, the de facto criterion applies to events. So the difference between events and physical objects is not that different criteria of identity apply to them. It must be, rather, that entities of the two kinds have different *minimal* criteria of identity associated with them. The suggestion is that whereas substance-kind property identity plus de facto spatio-temporal coincidence is the minimal criterion of identity for physical objects, necessary spatio-temporal coincidence is the minimal criterion of identity for events.

Why is it that one fact, that physical objects that are exemplifications of the same atomic substance-kind properties happen to occupy exactly the same spatio-temporal region, suffices to ensure that they must do so, whereas de facto spatio-temporal coincidence does not similarly ensure this for events? An intuitively plausible explanation, perhaps, is that material substances exclude one another in space whereas events do not. But it is unlikely that this can be justified without appeal to some such notions as those, say, of solidity or impenetrability. The idea of impenetrability is bound up with the idea of what it is for a thing to occupy its spatial location: to be impenetrable is to occupy a location to the exclusion of anything else. However, the notion of occupancy is involved in the identity criterion for material substances, as we saw in chapter 3, since that criterion states that material substances are identical if and only if they are exemplifications of the same atomic substance-kind properties in the same places at the same times. So, it looks as though we can appeal to this difference between material substances and events in order to explain why different minimal criteria of identity apply to them.

What about the doubt as to whether it suffices to individuate events from one *another* (condition (2))? Here events are deemed distinct if it is *possible* that they should diverge in their spatio-temporal positions, regardless of whether they in fact coincide. So, for example, the continuous rotation of the sphere can be deemed distinct from its continuous increase in temperature because these events might have failed to occupy the same spatio-temporal region even if in fact they did not.

But why should we think that events that in fact occupy the same spatio-temporal region might nevertheless have failed to do so? Independently of considerations that tell us more about the nature of events than that they occupy spatio-temporal regions (such as, perhaps, the property exemplification account), the claim seems to beg, rather than to answer, the question of whether events that in fact occupy the same spatio-temporal region might have failed to do so. The reason is that we know no more about events when we know that they occupy spatio-temporal regions than that they are particulars, i.e., spatio-temporal things. But knowing this isn't enough to justify the modal claim that it is possible for events that are spatio-temporally coincident to diverge in their spatio-temporal positions. Let us turn, then, to a third possibility.

Sameness of Cause and Effect

Davidson and others have emphasized that the causal relation is best understood as a relation between events (Davidson 1967, 1969; Brand 1976; Lombard 1979a, 1986; Ehring 1997). If they are right, events typically bear causal relations to one another and so have (relational) causal properties. Such properties are plausible candidates for ones that might figure in an acceptable minimal criterion of event identity. For, on the one hand, it seems clear that not every spatio-temporal thing has causes and effects: material substances, for example, though subject to change, do not themselves seem to bring changes about and so seem not to be causal in the way that events seem to be. And, on the other hand, any entity that has causal properties seems sure to have spatio-temporal ones, and this guarantees that any criterion framed in the former terms will entail one framed in the latter ones. If causal properties are unique as well as essential to events, then a criterion of event identity that specifies such properties will offer support for the view that events constitute an ontological category of particulars distinct from substances.

The suggestion is that events are identical if and only if they have all the same causes and effects. That is, it states:

Necessarily, for any events, x and y, x is identical with y if and only if x and y have exactly the same causes and exactly the same effects.[12]

Despite its intuitive appeal, this criterion has suffered from a number of well-known complaints. The majority of these focus on the doubt (associated with requirement (2)) as to whether it does manage to individuate events from one another. The objections have been of two main sorts.

The first, most frequently voiced sort of objection to the causal criterion is that it is unacceptable because it is circular. The kind of circularity referred to cannot be formal since, as Davidson (1969) points out, no identities between events appear in the definiens of the criterion (the part of the criterion that gives the identity conditions for events). But those who endorse the objection do not have a formal circularity in mind. Rather, the criterion is said to suffer from a conceptual circularity and a logical circularity.

The conceptual-circularity objection is that the idea of cause includes the idea that causes are distinct from effects and causes and effects are events. Consequently, the notion of a causal relation already presupposes a notion of event identity. According to the logical-circularity objection, the definiens of the criterion requires quantification over events; and events can only be legitimately quantified over if there already exists an adequate criterion of event identity. Both sorts of circularity arise because the conditions specified for event identity in the definiens of the criterion can only be satisfied if events are already individuated. Quine (1985), for example, points out that the causal criterion is no different from one that states that events are identical if and only if they are members of the same classes of events.[13] The problem with this is that it makes sense only if classes can be individuated from one another; and because classes are individuated by their members, it effectively has the consequence that events cannot be individuated from one another. The fault with the causal criterion is the same but more straightforward, since, instead of quantifying over classes of events, it quantifies over events directly.

These circularity objections are instructive, since they indicate that, even if it is true that events and only events bear causal relations to one another, this, in addition to the fact that they are essentially spatio-temporal, cannot be the whole truth about their nature. Causal properties are relational; they require for their attribution the existence or occurrence of at least two things. But then, on pain of circularity, they cannot suffice to individuate events from one another.

This conclusion is reinforced by the second sort of objection based on the doubt as to whether the criterion meets requirement (2). Brand (1976), for instance, argues that it is possible that a single particle, split by a process of fission, should later be reunited by a process of fusion. If so, then it is possible that there should be two events, distinct because the particles' parts from the onset of fission to the completion of the process of fusion are distinct from one another, with exactly the same causes and effects. Brand also points out that the causal criterion commits one to the view that there can be at most one causally isolated event (an event with neither causes nor effects).

In fact, the situation is worse than this, because the criterion eliminates the possibility of even this isolated event occurring. This is because the criterion requires the identity conditions for events to be fixed by their relations to events distinct from those whose identity conditions are in question. If these conditions specify properties essential to events, i.e., properties without which no event could occur, then it follows that the very occurrence of an event depends upon the occurrence of other events distinct from it that are its causes and its effects. This forces us to rule out on a priori grounds alone both the possibility of there being a universe in which only one event occurs and the possibility of there being events that are uncaused, ineffectual or both. But neither seems impossible. If, on the other hand, the properties specified by the criterion are not understood as being essential to events, then the criterion has the counter-intuitive consequence that all uncaused, ineffectual events are identical, since, in cases like these, the criterion is trivially satisfied. Further, the criterion must identify all ineffectual events whose causes are identical, and all uncaused events whose effects are identical.

All of these problems strongly suggest that the causal criterion, no less than the two spatio-temporal criteria, is inadequate. All three criteria fail to suffice either to individuate events from one another, or to individuate them from material substances, or both. These failures repeatedly point to the need for an underlying theory of events, in terms of which an acceptable criterion of event identity can be formulated. In the remaining sections of this chapter we consider two such accounts, with their respective criteria of identity. Both are versions of what is known as the property exemplification account of events (Macdonald 1989).

The Property Exemplification Account of Events (PEE)

As mentioned earlier we often speak of events by using sentences that attribute an empirical, change-indicating, property to an object at a time, such as 'The window shattered yesterday'. According to the property exemplification account of events (hereafter, the PEE), such events not only have properties (e.g., the property of being a shattering event) but just are (i.e., are identical with) the exemplifications, or exemplifyings, of properties of objects, such as the property, shatters (a property of the window), in those objects, at times. This being so, there can be no subjectless events, events that are not changes in any thing.[14] They are commonly construed as having a kind of 'internal' structure (though we will return to this). Events are identical with exemplications, or exemplifyings, of (n-adic) act-or event properties at (or during intervals of) times in objects.[15] For present purposes, we shall speak in terms of exemplifications, although, as we shall see, the difference between exemplifications and exemplifyings marks a critical difference between the two versions of the account that will be the focus of our discussion, Jaegwon Kim's (1976), and Lawrence Lombard's (1979b, 1986).) The objects in which such exemplifications occur (such as the window) are the subjects of those events. And those properties whose exemplifications in subjects just are events are properties, not *of* events, but *of* their subjects. For example, the window's shattering now just is the exemplification (now) by the window of the property, shatters. Such properties are sometimes termed *constitutive* properties of events, and are so termed because they are the properties of subjects whose exemplifications by those subjects just are events.

Events construed along these lines are sometimes referred to as 'structured particulars' because they have not only constitutive properties, but also constitutive objects (or subjects) and constitutive times. That is to say, it is in the nature of any event to be an exemplification of a property (of its subject) in a subject at a time. As noted in chapter 3, two conditions on events are essential to the account, one an existence condition and one an identity condition. These are formulated for monadic events (i.e., events that have one subject only) as follows:[16]

Existence Condition: Event $[x,P,t]$ exists if and only if the object x has the property P at time t.[17]

Identity Condition: Event $[x,P,t]$ is identical with event $[y,Q,t']$ if and only if the object x is identical with the object y, the property P is identical with the property Q, and the time t is identical with the time t'.

Descriptions of the form '$[x,P,t]$' are known as *canonical descriptions* of events because they pick out events in terms of their constitutive objects, properties and times. Kim calls the constitutive properties of events 'generic events', since these determine the event types or kinds into which particular events fall. (It is worth noting that only on some versions of the PEE is the identity condition, as stated by Kim, correct. Kim assumes that events have only one, unique, constitutive property (see note 23). But the version of the account we will favour (Lombard 1979b, 1986, 1998) allows for an event's having more than one constitutive property.[18]

As we noted in chapter 3, when discussing the property exemplification account of substances, the claim that substances have constitutive objects, properties, and times should not be confused with the claim that they are in some way constituted by or composed of objects, properties, and times. The same point holds, and more obviously, for events. Describing events as 'structured particulars' is misleading, since it invites us to view events as somehow composed of objects, properties, and times, related to each other in something like the way that a chair or any other complex physical object or, perhaps, biological organism is often viewed as composed of or constituted by its parts, arranged in a certain way. But the relationships that the 'components' of events bear to one another are plainly very different from the relations that the components of physical things bear to one another. In the case of an event, one component is exemplified by another, at yet another; and it is clear that, whatever the constituents of a biological organism or an artefact may be, they do not bear this relationship to one another.

Further, that canonical descriptions of the form '$[x,P,t]$' contain as constituents expressions referring to objects, properties, and times in no way shows that events themselves 'contain' or are constituted by the entities referred to by the constituent expressions of such descriptions. Consider once again the analogy with functional expressions like 'the father of x', which, when they combine with names or descriptions, produce complex or structured expressions that map offspring on to their fathers. In spite of the fact that such expressions as a whole literally contain as constituents expressions that refer to or mention other entities, there is no temptation to suppose, on that basis, that fathers are in some sense composed of their offspring. To do so would be to assume, falsely, that the way in which complex referring expressions are structured is like the way in which the entities referred to are structured. A similar point holds in the case of events, since the structure '$[x,P,t]$' is to be read as a definite description (like 'the father of Smith'): the event which is an exemplification by x of P at t.

For these reasons, as well as others, talk of events as 'structured particulars' is probably best avoided altogether.[19] However, if events aren't literally composed of their 'constitutive components', the claim that the components of events are constitutive of them seems to amount to the claim that they are essential to them, i.e., that events have essentially the structure they have. Indeed, Kim explicitly commits himself to some version of the latter – specifically, to the view that events are essentially exemplifications of act or event properties at times in objects, and hence, that, for any event, e, being an exemplification of an act or event property at a time in an object is an essential property of e.[20] Notice, though, that this would appear to follow from the two basic tenets of the PEE alone. For, irrespective of how the existence condition is interpreted, the mere existence of the relevant x, P, and t are not enough to guarantee the existence of an event. No entity *could* be an event, according to this account, unless it was the exemplification of a property at a time in a substance. To say that events have essentially the structure they have, then, is at least to say that they have properties whose possession guarantees that they are things of a certain metaphysical kind; ones without which they would not, as things of that kind, exist. In the terminology of chapter 2, these properties are real, or kind, essences of events.

To say that an event that is a's P-ing at time t is identical with an event that is a's Q-ing at t is to say that an event that is (= is identical with) an exemplifcation of the property, Ps, by a at time t is identical with an exemplification of the property, Qs, by a at t. Given the identity conditions on events, the truth of this will require that the property identity claim, $P = Q$ is true, but only when P (= Q) are *constitutive* properties of those events.[21] When they are not, there may be true identity claims of the form 'a's P-ing at t = a's Q-ing at t', where there is just one exemplification of two *distinct* properties. One example where this might occur might be when an object's exemplification of the property, red, at time t just is its exemplification of the property, coloured, at t, since it is extremely implausible to suppose that, when an object's exemplification of the more determinate property (red) occurs, something *further* has to happen in order for it to be true that that object's exemplification of the determinable property (coloured) occurs.[22]

It is important to see that, although Kim himself maintains that events have one and only one constitutive property (see note 23), nothing in the basic tenets of the PEE commits him to this. Thus, Lombard says,

> Suppose that an event, e_1, is x's exemplifying of F at t, and that an event, e_2, is x's exemplifying of G at t, where F and G are distinct properties. Despite the fact that Kim's criterion of identity for events says that events are identical only if they are exemplifyings of the same property, that condition does *not* imply that e_1 and e_2 are distinct events. Nothing in that condition or in Kim's existence condition for events says that e_1 could not, in addition to being an exemplifying of F, be an exemplifying of G, and that e_2 could not, in addition to being an exemplifying of G, be an exemplifying of F. And if those were the facts, then e_1 and e_2 would be exemplifyings of the same properties by the same objects at the same times, and hence would be, according to Kim's criterion, identical. . . . that latter idea [that an event can be an exemplifying of only one property] is a consequence, not of the view that events are exemplifyings of properties by objects at times, but of the view that events are explicanda, a view from which Kim's property-exemplifying account is ultimately derived. (Lombard 1986, p. 55)

Lombard's version of the PEE differs fundamentally from Kim's in allowing that an event might be (identical with) the exemplifying of more than one property. Indeed, as we shall see, his version not only countenances that possibility, but actually requires it.

In addition to constitutive properties, events also have characterizing properties. These are properties that events possess, some of which they have simply in virtue of having the constitutive properties they have. For example, the event that is my having pain now has the property of being a pain. The event that is the exemplification of the property, runs, in Jones at time t, has as its constitutive property a property of Jones. That event has the property of being a running.

Kim takes the constitutive properties of events to be ones that figure in laws connecting events that are the exemplifications of them.[23] His reason may be that it is these properties whose exemplifications bring about, or cause, other events. However, it is a strange view to take. For the constitutive properties are properties of the *subjects* of events, not of events themselves. And, intuitively, laws connect events in virtue of *their* properties, the characterizing ones, not properties of their subjects. Of course, for each constitutive property of an event there is an associated characterizing property. Thus, if e is $[x,P,t]$, the constitutive property of e is the property, Ps, and the associated characterizing property is the property of being a P-ing. So, we could reformulate Kim's view in terms of those characterizing properties of events that are entailed by their having the constitutive properties they do.

The PEE construes properties as abstract, multiply-exemplifiable entities that can have, but are not identical with, their exemplifications (as universals rather than tropes).[24] How, then, does it interpret the claim that events *have* (characterizing) properties as well as *being* the exemplifications of properties? Well, according to the universalist conception, just as things exemplify properties, and a thing just is (i.e., is identical with) an instance of each property that it has, an event exemplifies its properties, and it is (i.e., is identical with) an instance of each property that it has.[25]

Kim's Version

Kim's version of the PEE has suffered from various objections. Condition (2) (chapter 2) is the source of the trouble: an acceptable criterion of identity must suffice to individuate things within a single metaphysical kind from one another. The most frequently voiced objection is that the account discriminates too finely between events that we might wish to say are identical, such as Sally's shattering of the window yesterday, and Sally's shattering of the window yesterday with a rock, or Sally's shattering of the window swiftly.[26] Because properties differ when their extensions do, and events are distinct when their constitutive properties are distinct, the criterion of event identity has been said to have the consequence, amongst others, that no shooting can be a killing, no arm-waving a signalling, and no signing of a cheque a paying a paying of a bill.

The reason why this charge arises is that Kim's criterion for uncovering the constitutive structure of an event is by means of sentences that attribute an empirical property to an object at a time (Kim 1969, esp. pp. 204–5). Because verbs like 'shot', killed', etc., express event (or, more specifically, act) properties in sentences attributing empirical properties to objects at times, they express properties that, given Kim's criterion, can be taken to be constitutive of events.

These consequences are avoidable, however, and so do not constitute serious objections to the PEE. Kim (1976) himself suggests two ways in which events like Sally's shattering of the window and Sally's shattering of the window swiftly might be accommodated by his version of the account. According to one of these, properties like that of shattering are construed as generic events (i.e., constitutive properties), with expressions like 'swiftly' and 'with a rock' being construed as modifying, not the generic events themselves, but rather, the individual events that are exemplifications of them (see also Thomson 1971). In this case, Sally's shattering of the window with a rock and Sally's shattering of the window swiftly would not be understood as involving different generic events, but rather as being exemplifications of the same generic event. If one were to pursue this strategy, it might also be possible for the PEE to accommodate more difficult intuitions, such as that particular stabbings may be identical with particular killings, or that particular signings of cheques may be paying of bills. It might do so by construing verbs like 'kills' and 'pays (a bill)' as expressing characterizing rather than constitutive properties of events. According to the second, events like Sally's shattering of the window swiftly are construed as including events like Sally's shattering of the window, with the consequence that, while the two events are non-identical, they are not entirely distinct.[27]

In fact, the real problem with this version of the PEE concerns, not condition (2), but condition (1). If the account is correct, the one crucial difference between events and particulars of other sorts is that the former have the essential property of being exemplifications of act or event properties of objects. The truth of the claim that events have essences that determine them as an irreducible kind thus rests on the issue of which of their properties are said to be generic – that is, ones whose possession by a material substance implies that a change has occurred, is occurring, or will occur. Specifically, it rests on the issue of how these properties are to be differentiated from other properties whose possession by a material substance does not imply change. This is the part of the account that is vulnerable to attack. As we have just seen, the main, if not sole, criterion used by Kim for identifying and individuating event properties is by reference to sentences that attribute an empirical property to an object at a time. This criterion cannot discriminate between properties constitutive of events, where these are narrowly construed as changes (such as the property of shattering (a window)), and ones constitutive of states, where these are construed as including persisting conditions (such as being blue). Kim does indicate that generic events might also be adequately identified and individuated from other sorts of properties by means of the laws or lawful regularities of a favoured scientific theory. It is clear, though, both from the kinds of properties he cites as figuring in such laws (for example, colour properties, temperature properties, and weight properties), and from his more general remarks (1969, 1976) that he intends any acceptable criterion to circumscribe not only those properties constitutive of events narrowly construed, but also those constitutive of states (which he dubs 'unchanges').

This result is acceptable only if one believes (as Kim does) that it is a mistake, in advance of producing a complete theory of events, to take the dichotomy between events and states, or changes and 'unchanges', too seriously. And it is clear that this view is not forced upon us by the essentials of the PEE. However, the failure to distinguish changes from other static conditions, more than any other single feature of this version of the PEE, threatens to undermine the claim that events constitute a fundamental metaphysical category, a claim to which Kim himself seems committed.[28]

A comparison here between Kim's position on events and the essentialist theory of material substances favoured in chapter 3 may help to illustrate this. Recall that, according to this, material substances are essentially characterized individuals; they are essentially exemplifications of atomic substance-kind properties in places at times. Their identity conditions are given in terms of some proper sub-set of the properties they are capable of possessing, without which they would not exist, and whose possession in some determinate form ensures that they form a kind. Further, these substances themselves aggregate into kinds that are mutually exclusive of one another (as, for example, plants, animals, and the like are normally conceived of as doing). So, each kind of material substance is essentially characterized by a distinct sub-set of properties (an atomic substance-kind property, a spatial property and a temporal property) whose possession by particulars ensures that they form the kind they do and which individuates them from one another.

This type of position bears more than a passing resemblance to the conception of events embodied in the PEE. Indeed, we have argued that it is the correct position to take with regard to material substances. It is natural to suppose, then, that substances have, as events do, a sort of 'internal structure'. Specifically, they are exemplifications of certain kinds of properties (atomic substance-kind properties, such as *cat*, or *tiger*) in various spatio-temporal positions, and thus have associated with them the essential property of being exemplifications of atomic substance-kind properties.[29] Given the conception of essences articulated earlier, it follows that although some essences may be shared by substances of different kinds (as are spatio-temporal properties by, say, animal kinds and vegetable kinds), each kind of substance must have associated with it at least one atomic substance-kind property whose possession ensures that it is of that kind *and no other*. The sorts of properties that immediately suggest themselves as essential to the kinds in this way are those that would figure in their identity conditions.

Couple this theory of material substances with a corresponding view of events and a question naturally arises. Of all the properties, accidental and essential, that animals of a certain kind – say, cats – might possess, which of these can be determined by Kim's criterion to be constitutive of events that cats might undergo, as opposed to kind-determining essences of cats themselves? If we were to consider only properties like brown, this might seem to be a relatively simple matter to settle, since these are typically viewed as accidental to a substance-kind such as the *cat* kind. Thus they can easily be construed as ones that are constitutive of events that might occur in or to cats without creating any tension in an essentialist account of the natures of these two supposedly distinct kinds of particulars.

But what about properties like being a cat, or being a human being? These emerge on an essentialist account of material substances as kind-determining essences of animals of certain kinds. Yet it is clear from what Kim has to say about events that such properties as being a cat, and being a human being are no less indicative of states or 'unchanges' that these substance-kinds undergo. It is clear that a property like being a cat cannot be one whose exemplification it is of the essence of both a cat *and* an event to be, if these are to constitute two irreducible metaphysical kinds of things. Yet Kim's treatment of events as exemplifications of empirical properties at times in objects cannot distinguish between them. So, the failure to distinguish exemplifications of properties from exemplifyings of properties obscures the distinction between the metaphysical categories of events and substances by allowing properties that an essentialist account of substances would hold are kind-determining essences of substances to be considered to be kind-determining essences of events. At root, Kim's failure to distinguish such properties is due to a failure to distinguish exemplifications from exemplifyings.

Proponents of a Kim-type view of events may insist that properties like the property, being a cat, are not ones that could be constitutive of both cats and events (or states that cats might be 'in'). Such properties, they might say, are possessed *by* cats, but are *constitutive* of events (where if a property, ϕ, is a constitutive property of an entity, x, then x is not ϕ). But since an exemplification of a property *is* a thing that has it, the principle being appealed to here is not, in general, true. The property, being a cat, for example, would seem to be both constitutive of my cat, Felix, and a property of him. For Felix is an exemplification of the property, being a cat, but he also has that property.

In short, substances would seem to have at least some of their properties in virtue of being exemplifications of them. It is true that the same does not appear to hold for events. The property, being a cat, may be constitutive of the state that is Felix's being a cat, but that state does not have that property, since a state is not a substance. However, for the objection to stand, the principle to which it appeals must apply, not to the case of events, but to that of substances.

Certain ways of developing the PEE, then, are actually at odds with the point of the account, which is to support the view that events form a fundamental ontological category of particulars. Evidently, the question of how the account is to be developed is much more important than it might seem to be, since it is here, rather than in the fundamentals of the account, where the view is most vulnerable to attack.

Lombard's Version

This is the point in the chapter where matters become much more complicated. A variant of the view of events embodied in the PEE, developed by Lawrence Lombard (1979b, 1986), is predicated on the assumption that events are paradigmatically and fundamentally changes, where these are *not* to be understood as states or persisting conditions. This assumption is founded on the intuition that some properties are such that their possession by an object at a time implies change, whereas others are not. Lombard labels these two sorts of properties 'dynamic' and 'static', respectively, and argues that only exemplifyings of the dynamic ones imply the existence of events.

Static properties are ones whose possession by a material substance at a time implies that it is in a certain state.[30] Examples of such properties are colour properties such as red, and blue, weight properties such as 3 kg, and 6 kg, and positional properties such as being in Detroit at 3 p.m. on Saturday, 1 December 2001, or being in Denver at 5 a.m. on Sunday, 2 December 2001. Dynamic properties, in contrast, are ones whose possession by a material substance entails that that substance is changing at that time. Examples of such properties are turns red, accelerates, and shatters. To possess a dynamic property is to go from having one to having a contrary property. Since no thing can possess contrary properties at the same time, a thing can possess a dynamic property only during an interval of time, however short that may be. That is to say, change takes time.

If a material substance has a dynamic property during an interval of time, then it will be true that that substance is changing during that interval from having one static property to having another. This will be true because a dynamic property just *is* the property of first having one, then another, static property. So, there are two clear differences between static and dynamic properties. Static properties may be possessed by a material substance at times that are not intervals, and their possession does not entail the existence of any other property, static or dynamic (other than properties entailed by their possession, as, for example, blue entails coloured). Dynamic properties, in contrast, may be possessed by a material substance only during intervals of times, and their possession entails the existence of at least two distinct static properties.

Lombard refines this account by introducing the idea of a *quality space* (whose origins are in Quine 1960).[31] This is a set of simple static properties that fall into kinds, and are mutually exclusive (that is, no two such properties can be had by the same material substance at exactly the same time). For example, the colour quality space is a set of simple colour properties (e.g., red, blue, yellow, etc.), the weight quality space consists of simple weight properties (e.g., 1 kg, 2 kg, etc.), and so on. Effectively, events are movements by material substances (and their constituents) 'through' quality spaces; and the kinds of changes material substances can undergo is determined by the kinds of quality spaces there are. A substance can only change by exemplifying first one, then another, property from within the *same* quality space. So, for example, a thing cannot simply change from red to square given that these are properties from distinct quality spaces.

The question of how properties are to be individuated into kinds – how quality spaces are to be individuated from one another – is not one that the account takes to be answerable a priori. Rather, it assumes that the classification of properties into such spaces will be dependent upon observations of changes that various material substances and their constituents can undergo. Moreover, many of these observations are likely to be affected by scientific theories, which dictate how at least some of these changes are to be described.[32] In other words, although what it is to be an event may be an a priori matter, it is not an a priori matter what kinds of events there are. This is, of course, consistent with the (Aristotelian) view of metaphysics outlined in chapter 1, according to which it is the business of metaphysics to tell us what it is to be an object of a metaphysical kind, say, a material substance, or a property, whereas it is the business of science to tell us which are the substances, or the properties.

In general, according to the account, scientific theories affect our ways of describing and conceiving things and phenomena by telling us, amongst other things, what material substances are ultimately composed or made of, and what properties these ultimate constituents have in virtue of which substances composed of them have the properties they do. In doing so, they tell us what changes these ultimate constituents can undergo in virtue of which substances composed of them can undergo the changes they do. In other words, scientific theories are theories about ultimate objects and the quality spaces through which they move when they change.

We might call the ultimate, or most basic, objects and quality spaces that they move through when they change 'atomic' objects and 'atomic' quality spaces. Then, correspondingly, we can call the 'movements' of objects through atomic quality spaces 'atomic' events.[33] Some events that are composed entirely of atomic events may themselves also be atomic. This is because, on this account, there is no such thing as an instantaneous event, an event that has no duration and so no temporal parts. Thus, atomic events cannot be construed as the 'smallest' events of a given atomic event kind. Rather, they are to be understood as the most basic or fundamental sorts of events that atomic objects may undergo. An atomic event (for a given theory T) is an object's moving from having first one, then another, property in an atomic quality space (a quality space that is atomic, according to T).[34]

Events, then, are either atomic, or non-atomic, where non-atomic events may be one or the other of two sorts. First, there are events that consist of simultaneous atomic events (either simple or complex). Consider, for example, the event of (a pot of) water's boiling. That event consists of a number of atomic events occurring simultaneously, these events involving the movements of hydrogen and oxygen molecules. It is a complex synchronic event, because it consists of atomic events, events that occur at the same interval of time, whose subjects are distinct from one another. If a synchronic non-atomic event were to be composed of atomic events, all of which were changes in the same atomic object, then it would be a simple synchronic non-atomic event. Second, there are events that consist of diachronic atomic events, events that occur one after another. These too can be either simple or complex. Consider, for example, an avalanche. This event consists of a number of movements of distinct particles of snow, one after another, over a period of time. This seems to be a complex diachronic event, since it consists of atomic events occurring over a period of time whose subjects are distinct atomic objects. But the movement of a single particle from one place to another during a period of time might be a simple diachronic event. Further, some diachronic non-atomic events may be continuous, whereas others may be 'gappy' or discrete. The case of an avalanche seems to be one where the event consists of continuous movements of particles of snow, with no temporal gaps between them. But a wedding, for example, may consist of atomic events that occur, not continuously, but with temporal gaps between them.

On the basis of these definitions of an atomic event, atomic quality space, atomic objects and simple properties, and further definitions of at least two varieties of non-atomic events, the following hypothesis is advanced:

(H) Every event is either

(i)   an atomic event, or
(ii)   an event composed of simultaneous atomic events (a synchronic non-atomic event), or
(iii) an event composed of a temporal sequence of events each of which is either an atomic event or a synchronic non-atomic event (a diachronic event). (Lombard 1986, p. 172)

Atomic events, we now see, are exemplifyings of first one, then another, static property in an atomic quality space during an interval of time. And, as noted earlier, because a dynamic property just is the property of having first one, then another, static property in a quality space, for every pair of static properties whose exemplifying during an interval of time by an atomic object constitutes an atomic event, there will be an atomic dynamic property which that object will have during that interval. In some cases a verb expressing such a property will already be present in the language of the theory (T). An *atomic event verb* is thus one that is synonymous with, or equivalent in the theory (T) to an expression of the form, 'exemplifies the property of first having P_i and then having P_j, where P_i and P_j are static properties in an atomic quality space whose exemplifying by an atomic object at a time (which is an interval) is an atomic event in (*T*). It is verbs like these and the dynamic properties expressed by them that are associated with (indeed, determine) atomic event types.

An atomic event is thus an event having the property of being a ϕ-ing, where ϕ-ing is an atomic event type. Only verbs like 'ϕ' figure in canonical descriptions of atomic events. A description of an atomic event will be canonical if and only if it is a singular term of the form, $[x,\phi,t]$', where 'x' stands proxy for a name or description of the atomic object involved in the event, 'ϕ' for the atomic event verb expressing the dynamic property involved in that event, and 't' for a name or description of the interval of time during which x exemplifies ϕ.

Now, since each atomic event belongs to some atomic event type, it is of the essence of an atomic event that it be an instance of the atomic event type of which it is in fact an instance. So, although it may be a contingent matter whether an atomic event of a certain type actually occurs, given that it does, it cannot be a contingent matter that it is of the type it is. We can tell what the essences of various sorts of atomic events are from their canonical descriptions alone, since these describe such events in terms of atomic-event verbs that express dynamic properties that it is of the essence of those events to exemplify. Of course, non-atomic events also have essences; and, apart from events whose subjects are not partless (see below), we ought to be able to tell what these are from the canonical descriptions of the atomic events that constitute them.

On this conception of a canonical description, not all descriptions of atomic events will be canonical, though for any atomic event there may be more than one such description, as the possibility of sequences of atomic events that are movements by atomic objects through atomic quality spaces that are dense shows. (For instance, an event may be both of the type 'moves from having P_i to P_j to P_k' and of the type 'moves from having P_i to P_k', since the second description does not imply that a movement of the type described involved no other property between P_i and P_k. The distinctness of the types is ensured by the distinctness of their exemplifyings.) To be a canonical description of an atomic event, a singular term must name or describe the dynamic property involved in that event by means of an atomic event verb. In fact, the vast majority of events that serve as 'test cases' for the adequacy of criteria of event identity are picked out by means of descriptions that are not, on this account, canonical.

This last point is very important, since the criterion of identity associated with this version of the PEE is formulated in terms of canonical descriptions as follows:

> Necessarily, for any events x and y, x is identical with y if and only if x and y have all the same canonical descriptions.

This criterion applies not only to atomic events, but also to the varieties of non-atomic events mentioned in hypothesis (H), both simple and complex. The criterion thus covers both atomic events whose canonical descriptions pick those events out in terms of their atomic objects, atomic properties, and times, and non-atomic events whose canonical descriptions pick those events out in terms of canonical descriptions of the sequences (synchronic or diachronic) of atomic events that compose them.

Some may object on the grounds that this formulation cannot apply to events in worlds unpopulated by people and/or scientific descriptions. In that case, though, we can, consistently with Lombard's general view, formulate it without reference to canonical descriptions thus:

> Necessarily, for any events, x and y, x is identical with y if and only if x and y are exemplifyings by the same atomic objects, of the same atomic dynamic properties at the same time, if x and y are atomic events, or, otherwise, x and y are composed of the same atomic events (in exactly the same order, etc.).

where an atomic dynamic property is equivalent to a pair of static properties in an atomic quality space.

It is unclear from what Lombard says how either of these versions of the criterion applies to such events as the sinking of the Ship of Theseus, since these are conceived of as macroscopic events composed of atomic events or sequences of atomic events from which the macroscopic ones are *distinct*. That is to say, they are non-atomic events whose minimal subjects are objects with parts, where these subjects are distinct from aggregates or sums of their parts. The minimally involved subjects of these macroscopic events are *non*-atomic and so do not figure in the specification of the atomic objects involved in the atomic events that compose them. Still, a change in a macroscopic object that is composed of atomic parts will be composed of the (relevant) changes in those atomic parts. So, the identity conditions for such macroscopic events can be given in terms of the identity conditions of the atomic events that compose them.

The distinction between subjects and minimal subjects itself represents a major departure from a Kim-type view of events. Because that view takes any sentence attributing an empirical property to an object at a time to be one from which a canonical description of an event is derivable, it is unable to avoid commitment to type-type identities between the so-called 'constitutive' properties of events in any case where a particular claim is endorsed. So, for example, if, in a particular situation we wanted to say that Jones's pulling of the trigger just was his shooting of the gun, we could only do so by committing ourselves to the claim that all pullings of triggers are shootings of guns – something we clearly do not want to do. This in turn has the result that, in cases where intuitions run counter to the type-type identities, proponents of the account are committed to denying the truth of particular identity claims linking instances of those types (in the situation envisaged, that Jones's pulling of the trigger just was his shooting of the gun).

However, this version refines the account by distinguishing between atomic and non-atomic objects, properties, and quality spaces, in such a way as to make it possible for us to see how certain identity statements, involving re-descriptions of events, could be true. For, the 'types' to which such events and actions appear to belong (shooting, killing) do not figure in the specification of the identity conditions for those events. And the reason is that the properties that such verbs as 'shoot' and 'kill' express are ones that objects can possess only if other objects possess other properties. Most of the identity claims that we are concerned to determine the truth or falsity of are ones involving descriptions of events that do not pick them out in terms of their atomic objects, properties, and times. Because one cannot simply 'read off', from a description of an event in ordinary everyday terms, its constitutive components, it is possible to maintain the truth of certain identity statements that we take to be intuitively true, by maintaining that they involve re-descriptions of the events described by them.

How do we know whether the criterion is satisfied in particular cases of non-atomic events that are not mere aggregates or sums of atomic ones, when the question of identity arises? Well, the way to argue that events are identical in cases like these, as well as many others, is not necessarily to show that the criterion is satisfied. As we saw in our discussion of the nature and purpose of a criterion of identity in chapter 2, providing identity conditions for events serves a metaphysical end, of justifying claims to the effect that there are entities of a given ontological category. But they typically do not serve an epistemological purpose, of providing a means of telling, in a particular case, whether there are two items of a given kind, or only one. Nor is it plausible to suppose that they should. In fact, often the best way of arguing that events are identical is to do something else. Consider the case of killing and shooting. There, one might argue, first, that to kill is to do something that causes a death, and then argue that the shooting was just that, something that caused the death. One does not 'decompose' the killing and the shooting into their atomic constituents, and then show that those are the same constituents.

Finally, and most importantly, this version of the PEE takes seriously the idea that events are fundamentally changes that objects undergo, as distinct from states or standing conditions to which they may be subject. As we saw in our discussion of Kim's version of the PEE, this is essential to the distinction between events and objects of other categories of particulars and so to the defence of the claim that events constitute a fundamental metaphysical kind. The idea of events as changes is further developed as the view that they are 'movements' of objects 'through' quality spaces.

So, this second version of the PEE both makes it possible for us to see how it could be that there can be re-descriptions of events and to defend the claim that events form a metaphysical kind distinct from others.

Notes

1 See Davidson (1967). Davidson in fact gives three reasons for thinking that there might be an ontological category of events, only two of which are mentioned here (that we often use sentences containing singular terms referring to events, or which imply the existence of events, and that we need to be able to explain the relationship that holds between event-describing sentences that seem to be semantically related). The third, which will come up when we discuss the two versions of the property exemplification account, Kim's (1973, 1976) and Lombard's (1979b, 1986), is that we can only make sense of certain patterns of behaviour, for example, excuses, if we can make sense of re-describing actions and events.

2 For useful surveys of the different theories of events that are available, see Lombard (1998) and Simons (2003).

3 More formally, they would receive the following analysis:

$$4^* \ (\exists x)(\exists y)(\exists z)(\exists w)(\exists u)(\text{Shatter}_{xyzwu})$$
$$5^* \ (\exists x)(\exists y)(\exists z)(\exists w)(\text{Shatter}_{xyzw})$$
$$6^* \ (\exists x)(\exists y)(\exists z)(\text{Shatter}_{xyz})$$

4 This is not to say that there are not other ways of preserving the entailment relations; Romane Clark's (1970) predicate modifier approach is one way that makes use of resources other than those of standard first-order quantification theory. For discussion of this approach and defence of the Davidsonian one, see Taylor (1985). A virtue of Davidson's approach is that it shows how such relations can be preserved in just the same way other entailment relations between sentences are, using only the resources of standard first-order quantification theory, and is thus the more economical and simple of the two methods of dealing with such sentences.

5 More formally, they would receive the following analysis:

7* $(\exists e)(\exists x)(\exists y)(\exists z)(\exists w)(\exists u)$(Event($e$) & Shatter($e$) & By($x,e$) & Of($y,e$) & In($z,e$) & At($w,e$) & With($u,e$))

8* $(\exists e)(\exists x)(\exists y)(\exists z)(\exists w)$(Event($e$) & Shatter($e$) & By($x,e$) & Of($y,e$) & In($z,e$) & At($w,e$))

9* $(\exists e)(\exists x)(\exists y)(\exists z)$(Event($e$) & Shatter($e$) & By($x,e$) & Of($y,e$) & In($z,e$))

Construed in this way, 3 follows from 2, and 2 and 3 both follow from 1 by straightforward simplification.

6 Put formally, $(\exists x)(Fx \ \& \ Gx)$ entails $(\exists x)Fx$.

7 There is an enormous amount of literature on the topic of events and their descriptions. For more on this, see Davidson (1963), Goldman (1970), Thomson (1977), papers collected in LePore and McLaughlin (1985) and papers collected in Casati and Varzi (1996).

8 One way to articulate this point is to say that events are changes, just as Davidson (1970b) suggests. This conception of events is the one that we will settle on in the final sections of this chapter.

9 Put formally: $\Box(x)(y)$[Event(x) & Event(y) $\rightarrow$ ($x = y \leftrightarrow (s)(xRs \leftrightarrow yRs)$)], where s ranges over spatio-temporal regions and R is the relation 'occurs within'.

10 Thus, Davidson (1966, 'Replies'), when reconsidering the spatio-temporal criterion, suggests that the way in which events relate to space and time might suffice to individuate them from particulars of other kinds, specifically, physical objects. However, in a later paper (Davidson 1985) he embraces the criterion as formulated here, but refuses to acknowledge that that amounts to reducing events to material substances (or temporal parts of them).

11 Put formally: $\Box(x)(y)$[Event(x) & Event(y) $\rightarrow$ ($x = y \leftrightarrow \Box(s)(xRs \leftrightarrow yRs)$)], where ·$s$ ranges over spatio-temporal regions and R is the relation 'occurs within'.

12 Put formally, $\Box(x)(y)$(event(x) & event(y) $\rightarrow x = y \leftrightarrow (z)(w)$(event($z$) & event($w$)) $\rightarrow$ (($zCx \leftrightarrow zCy$) & ($xCw \leftrightarrow yCw$))), where C is the relation 'causes'.

13 Put formally, $\Box(x)(y)$(event(x) & event(y) $\rightarrow$ ($x = y \leftrightarrow (z)(x \in z) \leftrightarrow (y \in z)$), where z is taken to range over classes of events.

14 The view that there are no subject-less events has come up for some criticism (Bennett 1988, 1996, 2002; Cleland 1991). Kim's version of the property exemplification account is more vulnerable to this charge than Lombard's because it does not take events to be, fundamentally, changes. If, however, the concept of an event is wedded to that of change, the view that there are no subject-less events is more defensible. Thus, Lombard says,

> I do not see how to get a grip on the concept of an event without seeing the concept of an event as bound up with the concept of change; and I do not see how to get a grip on the concept of change without seeing change as what objects undergo. But this is just to insist that the points from which my theory

starts (though perhaps not where it ends) are obvious truths. As I see it, to suppose that there are subjectless events is to suppose that there are events that are not changes. (1986, p. 242)

15 Kim's version of the account takes them to be exemplifications, but the version of the account that we shall favour takes them to be exemplifyings. As noted in the text, this is no mere terminological matter, as we shall see when discussing objections to Kim's version of the account. For an application of this general account to the category of substances, see chapter 3. It might be objected that the account presupposes the concept of event, since whatever one's account of events, every property of an event will be an 'event property' in the obvious sense (so long as there are properties). We can only get a non-vacuous account of events if we drop the 'act-or-event' qualification – but then the account is just false. In fact, a complete filling out of the qualification would replace it with 'dynamic', which the account contrasts with 'static'. And it isn't vacuous since it is held by the account that which properties of objects are static and which are dynamic (and also, which are atomic and which are non-atomic) is not a matter that can be determined a priori but depends on empirical investigation into the natures of objects and their properties. Finally, the 'definition' of event by the account is not intended to be a conceptual truth, but a metaphysical one.

16 The exposition of the PEE here is based on this work of Kim's (1973, 1976). According to him, although the first condition is indispensable to the theory, the second, as formulated, is not. He mentions that the theory could proceed by defining the predicate 'is an event' over ordered n-tuples of objects, properties, and times. In this case, the ordered triple, $\langle x,P,t \rangle$, would be an event if and only if x has P at t; and the principles of set theory would guarantee the existence of the triple (assuming, of course, that x, P, and t exist). But Kim himself favours the first method over the second, both in these works and in Kim (1991), where he says that expressions of the form 'the exemplification of P by S at t' are best understood as functors from ordered triples of substances, properties, and times, to property exemplifications (i.e., events). The first method is certainly preferable from the point of view of the phenomenon of causal interaction between events, where this is assumed to entail their positionality, since one does not want to claim that causes are sets. As we shall see, this issue can lead to confusions of the kind noted in the text concerning events' 'constitutive components'. The position taken here is in agreement with Kim that the second, identity condition on events is not, as formulated, indispensable to the theory, but for reasons that differ from those that he gives.

17 Given the possible inappropriateness of saying of events that they 'exist' (rather than 'occur'), this condition might better be called an 'occurrence condition', and reformulated as 'Event $[x,P,t]$ occurs . . .'

18 In this case, the identity condition (for atomic events) could be re-written as replacing '$P = Q$' with 'every property constitutive of x is constitutive of

y' and Kim's and Lombard's identity criteria (for atomic events) come out the same, as we shall see (ch.5, p. 206).

19 One is that it encourages the view that the PEE is a 'reductive' account of events, a view that Kim himself is quick to deny. Thus, he says:

> The account so far presented is not an 'eliminative' or 'reductive' theory of events; that is, it does not attempt to show that events are in some eliminative sense 'reducible' to substances, properties, and times. (It may be remarked, though, that a better case for the elimination or reduction of events might be made if we take the ordered triple approach sketched above.) I do not know exactly when a metaphysical theory is 'reductive'; the account, however, attempts to tell us something about the metaphysical nature of events by relating them to such other ontological categories as substances, properties, and times. (Kim 1976, p. 162)

20 Kim is also inclined, though not without qualification, to endorse the claim that each individual event has at least some of its constitutive components essentially, namely, its constitutive object and possibly its constitutive property (1976, pp. 166–7). Whereas the claim in the text says what, in general, events essentially are, this latter claim says what each individual is essentially. We are more directly concerned with the claim in the text. For more on kind-determining essences of events, see Lombard (1979b, 1986).

21 Kim claims on behalf of the PEE that both mental properties (of persons) and physical properties (of persons) are constitutive properties of events, and, in his early work (Kim 1972) concludes that token identity theories of the mind–body relation are false, on the grounds that mental properties are not identical with physical ones, but the PEE is *not* committed to this conclusion, for two reasons. First, Kim's version of it requires that an event cannot have more than one constitutive property, and the PEE need not be committed to this (cf. Lombard's version of the PEE, which rejects it). Second, even if one does suppose it, one might claim – as anyone committed to the contingent truth of physicalism is apt to do – that mental properties of persons supervene on the constitutive properties of physical events, and so are not essences of the events that are exemplifications of them. Further, this way of reconciling the PEE with token event identity is preferable because a proper physicalism should not only be committed to an ontology of physical events, but should also provide an explanation of the relation between mental and physical *properties* which shows them to be, if not physical, not worryingly nonphysical. The first way of reconciling the PEE with token event identity leaves the question of the relation between mental and physical properties completely open. For more on the details of Kim's position, see Macdonald (1989) and Macdonald and Macdonald (1995).

22 How is it to be determined which are the constitutive properties of events? This is an issue over which Kim and Lombard differ. We will return to it when discussing the different versions of the account.

23 See Kim (1973):

> Every event has a unique constitutive property (generally, attribute), namely the property an exemplification of which by an object at a time is that event. And, for us, these constitutive properties of events are generic events. It follows that each event falls under exactly one generic event, and that once a particular cause-effect pair is fixed, the generic events which must satisfy the constant conjunction requirement are uniquely fixed. It is important to notice the distinction drawn by our analysis between properties *constitutive* of events and properties *exemplified* by them. . . . once cause and effect are fixed, the generic events that must lawfully correlate are also fixed. (1973, p. 226)

24 Thus, Kim (1973) formulates the Existence Condition as follows:

> $[(x_n,t),P]$ exists if and only if the n-tuple of concrete objects (x_n) exemplifies the n-adic empirical attribute P at time t. (Kim 1973, p. 223)

and, later in the same paper, says, 'Generally, we do not allow "mixed universals" such as stabbing Caesar as constitutive attributes of events; only "pure universals" are allowed as such' (1973, p. 224). Bennett (1996, 2002) attributes to Kim a trope view of events, but it is plain from the above sources as well as others that he does not commit himself to the trope conception.

25 This is one reason why it is misleading to say that the account takes events to be 'structured' particulars. Given (1) the view that an event just is an exemplification of a property (of an object) by an object at a time, (2) the universalist view presumed by the account, and (3) the view that events have properties by exemplifying them, it follows that an event just is (i.e., is identical with) an instance of all of its properties. Any attempt to distinguish different 'instances' of properties would commit the account to a trope account of properties rather than a universalist one.

26 All of the expressions that we are using for events (actions) here, e.g., 'Sally's shattering of the window yesterday', are perfect nominals, and hence refer to events. But Kim uses imperfect nominals, e.g., 'Sally's shattering the window yesterday', exclusively in his writing on events. These refer, not to events, but to facts (see Bennett 1988). Because Kim uses imperfect nominals exclusively in his writings on events, it is no surprise that the identity-results do not bother him, since they are precisely the correct results if one were speaking of facts (or other proposition-like entities). So the objections to his view mentioned here presume that the entities referred to by such nominals are events, not facts, or other proposition-like entities.

27 This is akin to Alvin Goldman's (1970) account of level generation.

28 See, for example, his 1976 work and the quoted material in note 19.

29 It is properties of this latter kind, and not the constitutive properties of substances, such as the property, horse, that deserve the name 'kind-determining essence'.

30 That the subjects of events are material substances is not entailed by Lombard's view. On his account, any entity that can have and then lack non-relational properties can be the subject of an event. But Lombard does take material substances to be subjects of events.

31 Formally, a quality space is a set S of simple static properties, $\{P_0, P_1, \ldots, P_n\}$ satisfying the following conditions: (1) if at any time, t, any object, x, has $P_i \in S$, then at t for every $_j\neq_i$, it is not the case that x has $P_j \in S$, and (2) if any object, x, which has $P_i \in S$ at any time, t, fails to have P_i at a time t' $(t \neq t')$ (and still exists), then x changes in S (or in respect 'S'), that is, by t' x has, for some $_j$ $(_j\neq_i)$ $P_j \in S$. The effect of (1) is to restrict the kinds of static properties that are eligible for membership in set S to mutually exclusive ones. The point of (2) is to make explicit the fact that quality spaces consist of sorts or kinds of properties (e.g., colour properties, weight properties), so that, if any object changes with respect to one of its static properties, it can only do so by coming to have another property of the same sort. See Lombard (1986, p. 113). All references in this section are, unless otherwise stated, to this source.

32 See Goodman (1965). Suppose, to adapt Goodman's example, that an object, x, is grue if and only if it is green before time t, otherwise blue. Then, since x is grue throughout any interval of time during which it changes from being green to being blue, it would seem that the question of whether x has changed if it is green before t and blue thereafter cannot be settled independently of settling the issue of what to count as static properties of objects. As Lombard points out, this latter issue would appear to be incapable of being settled independently of settling the issue of what to count as an object; for only if there were such things as emerires – objects that were emeralds before t and sapphires thereafter – would it be true that some objects were grue.

33 On this basis Lombard (1986, p. 171) formulates the following definitions:

(D1) An object, x, is an *atomic object* for a theory, T, if and only if, in T, x exists, and there is no object, y, distinct from x, that is a part of x,

(D2) A set, S, is an *atomic quality space* for a theory, T, if and only if S is a dense quality space whose members are qualities that objects that are atomic in T can have, according to T,

(D3) An event, e, is an *atomic event* for a theory, T, if and only if:

(i) e's subject, x, is an object that is atomic according to T,

(ii) e is x's moving from having P_i to having P_k, at some interval of time, t, where P_i and P_k belong to a dense quality space, S, which is atomic according to T,

(iii) e is temporally continuous,

(iv) no event of which e is composed is a change in a quality space distinct from S, and

(v) there is no property, P_j, in S that x has at two or more times during t.

where a quality space is dense if and only if, for any two properties, P_i and P_k, which are members of the space, there exists another property, P_j, 'between' them (examples being time and spatial location spaces); and where an event e is temporally continuous if and only if e is a change in some object, x, through a portion of some quality space S during some interval of time, $t - t'$, such that at each instant in that interval, x has a different property in S (1986, pp. 119–20).

34   The *minimally involved subject* of e is defined in terms of the notion of an object's involvement and minimal involvement in an event, thus:

> If x is any object, e is any event, and t is a time, then x is *involved* in e at t if and only if it is the case that (a) if e occurs (or is occurring) at t, then x changes (or is changing) at t, and (b) a change in x at t is identical with e at t;

and

> x is the *minimally involved subject of e at t* if and only if (a) x is involved in e at t. and (b) x is the *smallest* object, a change in which, at t, is identical with e at t. (1986, pp. 122–3)

Suggested Further Reading

Bennett, J. (1988): *Events and Their Names*. Cambridge: Cambridge University Press.

Bennett, J. (1996): 'What Events Are'. In Casati and Varzi (eds) 1996, pp. 137–51.

Brand, M. (1977): 'Identity Conditions for Events'. In *American Philosophical Quarterly* 14, 329–37. Reprinted in Casati and Varzi (eds) 1996, pp. 363–71.

Brand, M. and Walton, D. (eds) (1976): *Action Theory*. Dordrecht: D. Reidel.

Casati, R., and Varzi, A. (eds) (1996): *Events*. Aldershot: Dartmouth.

Casati, R. and Varzi, A. (2002): 'Events'. In Zalta, E. (ed.), *The Stanford Encyclopedia of Philosophy* (Fall 2002 edn). URL = <http://plato.stanford.edu/archives/fall2002/entries/events/>

Davidson, D. (1984): *Essays on Actions and Events*. Oxford: Clarendon Press, contains several seminal papers by Davidson on events.

Kim, J. (1973): 'Causation, Nomic Subsumption, and the Concept of Event'. In *Journal of Philosophy* 70, 217–36.

Kim, J. (1976): 'Events as Property Exemplifications'. In Brand and Walton (eds) 1976, pp. 159–77. Reprinted in Casati and Varzi (eds) 1996, pp. 117–35.

Laurence, S. and Macdonald, C. (eds) (1998): *Contemporary Readings in the Foundations of Metaphysics*. Oxford: Blackwell.

Lemmon, J. (1966): 'Comments on D. Davidson's "The Logical Form of Action Sentences"'. In Rescher (ed.) 1966, pp. 96–103.

LePore, E. and McLaughlin, B. (eds) (1985): *Actions and Events: Perspectives on the Philosophy of Donald Davidson*. Oxford: Blackwell.

Lombard, L. (1979b): 'Events'. In *Canadian Journal of Philosophy* 9, 425–60. Reprinted in Casati and Varzi (eds) 1996, pp. 177–212.

Lombard, L. (1986): *Events: A Metaphysical Study*. London: Routledge & Kegan Paul.

Lombard, L. (1998): 'Ontologies of Events'. In Laurence and Macdonald (eds) 1998, pp. 277–94.

Loux, M. and Zimmerman, D. (eds) (2003): *The Oxford Handbook to Metaphysics*. Oxford: Oxford University Press.

Macdonald, C. (1989): *Mind–Body Identity Theories*. London: Routledge, ch. 4.

Rescher, N. (ed.) (1966): *The Logic of Decision and Action*. Pittsburgh: University of Pittsburgh Press.

Simons, P. (2003): 'Events'. In Loux and Zimmerman (eds) 2003, pp. 357–85.

Part III

Universals

6

Universals and the Realism/Nominalism Dispute

One of the oldest and most familiar problems in metaphysics is the so-called problem of universals. However, it is not entirely clear just what that problem is. Many say that it is the problem of how two individuals (whether concrete or abstract) can be of the same kind, or fall under the same linguistic type.

The problem can be introduced more simply and more directly as the problem that arises because things are alike. We often say that things that are alike are the same. However, two things, in being two things, are never the same. So, it seems that distinct things that are alike are both the same and not the same. But this appears to be a contradiction.

The idea that the problem of universals is about how things can be both the same and different is part of a larger view that philosophical problems are problems about how what is actual is possible, given that what is actual appears, because of some faulty argument, to be impossible. The solution to such problems is an explanation of how what is actual is possible by exposing the fallacy in the argument. When we say that different things are nonetheless, in some sense, the same, we must, if possible, say what it is that is the same. One way of attempting to do this is to distinguish what might be called numerical sameness from qualitative sameness. Numerical sameness is explained by the theory of identity; a theory that tells us which inferences involving the identity sign ('=') are valid, or truth-preserving, and why. What, then, explains qualitative sameness? That is the question that a solution to the so-called problem of universals is supposed to answer. According to the Realist – one who believes that there are universals – what is the same is the property, or attribute, that the different things possess. So, the Realist takes seriously the idea that there really is something the same (i.e., identical) when different things are truly said to be the same.[1]

Formulated in this way, the problem, to which the positing of universals is meant to be a solution, is a purely metaphysical one about how things are in the objective order, where by 'objective' is meant at least 'mind-independent'. However, there are other ways in which this problem has been, and is, formulated. Campbell, for instance, formulates it like this:

> Take two white things again. They deserve a common description, namely, 'white'. What is the link between them which underlies this linguistic fact? (Campbell 1990, p. 206)

In a similar vein, Armstrong says,

> It is asked how a general term can be applied to an indefinite multiplicity of particulars. (Armstrong 1978a, p. xiii)

This way of formulating the problem, in focusing on language, is semantic: it is concerned with how predicates can apply to an indefinite number of particulars. But since we know that part of what is involved in doing metaphysics is doing semantics, this way of formulating the problem gives some voice to the idea of a thing's being both the same and different.

Loux notes the semantic formulation of the problem is sometimes confused with an epistemological one about speaker-competence. Interpreting the semantic version as consisting of the claims that

> (I) Where a predicate term ... F is truly applicable to each of a number of objects, $a \ldots n$, there is some universal U which each of $a \ldots n$ exemplify,

and

> (II) When a predicate term ... F functions predicatively in a true subject-predicate sentence, it serves to pick out or refer to a universal U which each of $a \ldots n$ exemplify. (Loux 1978, p. 16)

he points out that those committed to (I) sometimes construe the problem as one concerning how it is that we can correctly apply a predicate to something that we have never encountered before on the basis of what we have applied it to in the past. Thus, he says,

> (I) should not be confused with a quite different claim about predicate-terms, the claim that a speaker's ability to apply predicate-terms correctly

is grounded in his ability to recognise in objects the presence of the universal that (I) tells us is exhibited by all and only the things of which that expression is truly predicable. This claim is an epistemological thesis about speaker-competence . . . Proponents of (I) have, of course, sometimes conflated (I) with this claim about speaker-competence; but as I am understanding it, (I) makes no claim at all about the kind of knowledge involved in a speaker's ability to use predicate-terms. (Loux 1978, p. 16)

These claims constitute different formulations of the so-called problem of universals. However, they aren't unconnected. Suppose that we take the first, metaphysical formulation, to be the correct one, the one that really does identify 'the problem of universals'. Then it really is something of a misnomer. For what the problem is, is how two or more particulars can be qualitatively the same: how they can agree in attribute, or have the same property. And universals are meant to be a solution to this problem. So if there is a 'problem' of universals, it can only be one of seeing how universals could solve the problem of how two or more particulars can possess the same property. One might say it is the problem *with* universals!

But then, put like this, the metaphysical problem is not worlds away from the semantic and epistemic formulations of the problem. According to the semantic formulation, the problem is how two or more particulars can satisfy the same predicate, how the same predicate can apply to two or more of them. This is a problem because the particulars are themselves distinct, and because, on the standard way of construing the relation between a thing and its properties, a thing has a property by exemplifying it. Together these imply that what makes for the satisfaction of a predicate by one particular is wholly different from what makes for the satisfaction of the same predicate by another. We seem unable to say what is the *same* about them that explains why the same predicate applies to them. According to the Realist, the solution is that distinct particulars can satisfy the same predicate if and only if each exemplifies or instantiates one and the same universal, which is tied in some way to that predicate.

According to the epistemic formulation, the problem is how we can correctly apply the same predicate to particulars that we have never encountered on the basis of what we have encountered. And the solution is that we can do this only if there are universals to which these predicates are referentially tied in some way, grasp of which enables us to do so. The metaphysical formulation may make no reference to language or to language users; but, given that we are thinking, language-using creatures and sometimes *correctly* apply predicates, there is a question of what makes for that correct application. The appearance, in thought and language, respectively, of general concepts, such as the concept *red*, and general terms and predicates, such as the predicate 'is red', which can be correctly applied to an indefinite number of distinct particulars, calls out for explanation.

Of course, if we were thought-less creatures, there would be no problems for us to solve, though the problems would still exist. But we can accept this, and with it the view that the existence of universals is independent of the existence of the phenomenon of generality in thought and language, while recognizing that the phenomenon itself calls out for explanation. The phenomenon may not be necessary, but it may be sufficient, to motivate an affirmative answer to the question: are there universals, entities whose existence explains how distinct particulars can be the same?

That there is generality in thought and language apparently commits us to the existence of universals – apparently, since ordinary discourse about objects, kinds, properties, etc., is just that. A metaphysical theory will need, starting with this, to attempt to uncover from such discourse its real ontological commitments. As we saw in chapter 1, the distinction between apparent and real commitments will be determined, in part, by our choice of semantic theory.

Suppose, for example, that we work with a theory that says that the occurrence of singular terms in true sentences commits its users to items in the world. Then one will immediately run into problems with sentences such as 'The round square does not exist' and with sentences like 'The average man has 2.4 children'. If we do not wish to be committed to such entities as the average man and non-existent round squares, then, we must abandon the semantic theory in favour of another that does not have this consequence.[2] If our choice of semantic theory puts us in the position of acknowledging the existence of items which, for other reasons, some pragmatic, some explanatory, some epistemic, we have no good reason to think do exist, then this may force the adoption of a different semantic theory.

In what follows we shall pursue the question whether there are universals, and argue that the answer to the question is yes, since their existence is required to explain how it is that we can think and speak *correctly* in general terms. This ability is a genuine cognitive achievement, whose explanation requires the positing of universals. The argument is thus a kind of explanatory argument for Realism (cf. Swoyer 1983, 1999).

The discussion to follow will harbour no preference for any view about the relation between thought and language. Specifically, it is uncommitted to any view about whether there are or could be thinking creatures who possess no language, and so whether thought is prior to language. We shall take it that the problem that the postulation of universals is meant to solve is that of explaining how the correct application of general terms and concepts is possible. So, in what follows, we take no stand on the priority of one of these over the other.

Our approach will be broadly Kantian. We shall set out to answer questions of the form: How is it possible that P?, where 'P' is a truth. In the case of the 'problem' of universals, 'P' is 'we think and speak correctly about generality'. The question cries out for an answer, because it assumes that the world is, by and large, the way we think it to be (distinct things are alike), and that cannot amount to what it seems to, namely, that things that are alike are both the same and not the same, since that is a contradiction. So we need an answer to the question of how distinct things can be qualitatively the same, in order to answer the question of how we can think and speak correctly about generality.

The Issue

We have now circumscribed the phenomenon whose explanation may require commitment to universals: the ability to speak and think correctly in general terms. In the case of language, the phenomenon shows up in the correct predicative use of predicates and of general terms (e.g., 'red', 'square') that appear in subject position. Many predicates (though not all: consider 'is one of thirteen grapes' and 'is the positive square root of 4') are devices that are capable of grouping, collecting, or bringing under them or within their extensions an indefinitely large number of individual objects. Classic examples are colour and shape predicates, such as 'is red', and 'is square', and kind predicates, such as 'is a tiger' or 'is water'. (In the case of thought, generality emerges in the employment of general concepts such as characterizing concepts (e.g., concepts such as *red*, and *square*), kind concepts (e.g., concepts such as *tiger*, and *water*), and so on.)[3]

The claim is that universals are required in order to explain this capacity.[4] It is not that such entities are needed merely in order to explain how we can think and speak in general terms. It is that these entities are needed in order to explain how we can *correctly*, i.e., *truly*, apply predicates and general concepts to an indefinite number of particulars. In order for this to be possible, there must be something in the world that grounds, or makes for, that correct or true application. So, what forges the connection between semantic/epistemological concerns here and metaphysical ones is the concept of truth.

The issue between Realists with respect to universals, on the one hand, and Nominalists, on the other, then, is not (or not primarily) whether there are sentences and thoughts involving such generality, nor even whether at least some of these are true. The issue is whether this agreed-upon phenomenon is one whose explanation requires positing universals. What Realists and Nominalists disagree about is whether the devices in language (and thought) that capture the idea of generality are matched by real generality in the world spoken or thought of.

Roughly speaking, Nominalists maintain that all that exists in the world is particular and concrete. That is, all that exists are things that are wholly and completely in only one place at a given time (and so are particulars), and are such that no other thing of the same kind can be in the same place as them at the same time (and so are concrete).[5] Realists, in contrast, believe that there are also properties, at least some of which are universals, that are both universal and abstract. Unlike particulars, they are such that either (1) they can be wholly and completely in many places at the same time, or (2) they can be exemplified in many places at the same time. In either case, they are universal, and are what explains qualitative sameness between distinct particulars.[6] What is the same is the property, or attribute, that the different things possess. Realists take seriously the idea that there really is something the same (i.e., identical) when different things are truly said to be the same. Further, they hold that universals, unlike concrete things, are such that many of them can be either in the same place at the same time or exemplified in the same place at the same time (and so are abstract).[7]

Suppose that there are two blue cups on my desk. We can describe the agreement in colour of the two cups in either of the following two ways. We might say that the first blue cup is exactly like the second blue cup in colour. Or we might say that the first blue cup has or shares the same colour as the second blue cup.[8] The first way of describing the situation suggests that two blue cups, and a relation between them of likeness or resemblance, enter into it. This is the way a certain kind of Nominalist would describe the situation.[9] According to the Nominalist, 'x and y are both red' wears its metaphysical commitments 'on its sleeves'.

Realists, however, would describe the situation, not as one of colour resemblance, but as one of colour identity. According to them, 'x and y have the same colour' wears its metaphysical commitments 'on its sleeves', and there are in our imagined situation three things: two cups, and one universal, blueness, which is instantiated wholly and completely in each.

Nominalists have objected to Realism on a variety of grounds, one of which concerns theoretical simplicity, claiming that the positing of universals is unnecessary.[10] This objection appeals to a principle known as Ockham's razor (Campbell 1990). According to it, we should not accept more kinds of entities in a theory than is absolutely necessary. Realists, however, need not contest the importance of this principle in deciding between competing ontologies. What they can, and often do, deny is that the positing of universals is unnecessary for the explanation of our ability to correctly apply general terms and concepts to an indefinite number of particulars. So, much depends on whether Nominalists can make good their claim that the positing of universals is unnecessary to explain that phenomenon.

In the remaining sections of this chapter, we shall consider two issues. First, we'll consider whether Nominalists can explain the ability to correctly apply general terms and concepts to items we have never encountered before, and argue that they cannot account for the fact that this ability is a genuine cognitive achievement.[11] This clearly is not a decisive argument in favour of Realism by itself, since it leaves open the possibility that the positing of universals also fails, in the end, to provide an adequate explanation. So, second, we'll consider whether Realists can provide that explanation, and argue that they can.

Varieties of Nominalism

We have been speaking up to now as though there were only one position that falls under the name 'Nominalism'. But, as is so often the case in metaphysics, things are more complicated than this. It is possible to identify at least four different positions that deserve to go under that name. Two we classify as *extreme* Nominalist positions, and two we classify as *moderate* ones.[12] The argument will be that each position leaves out of the explanation the cognitive achievement involved in the ability to think and speak correctly in general terms. Again, by this it is not meant: what would the world have to be like in order to contain beings like us? The question is, what would the world have to be like if most of our beliefs about generality are true? None of the versions of Nominalism we shall consider provides an explanation of what the world would have to be like, and so none offers an adequate explanation of our true beliefs and speech.

Some Extreme Nominalist Positions

Let's begin, then, with an extreme version of Nominalism, one encapsulated in the work of Nelson Goodman (1951). To the question, 'What

do things that are called by the same name have in common?', the
response is, 'the name'. Goodman claims that there *is* no generality in
the world beyond language, that generality lies in language alone. What
all red things have in common is only our willingness to call them all
'red' (i.e., to apply the word 'red' to them), or only the fact that the word
'red' applies to them.[13]

This kind of position need not deny that a psychological story can be
told about how one acquires language, and with it the ability to correctly
use predicates in assertions. But it does deny that there is a problem here
that calls out for explanation; a fortiori, it denies that there is a problem
that requires any explanation in terms that involve commitment to universals. This is not to say that the position is committed to denying that
there are entities that make sentences of the form '*a* is *F*' true, and so to
denying that such sentences can be true or false. It simply maintains that
the only truth-makers for such sentences are individual concrete particular objects. That is the end of the story. Essentially the same response
is made with regard to the explanation of the ability to correctly employ
general concepts, or to think in general terms.

This position is more than just an expression of the view, in itself unex-
ceptionable, that explanation has to come to an end somewhere, and that
in this case here is where it ends.[14] It is a much stronger position. According to it, the ability to think and speak correctly in general terms is not
properly to be seen as the explanandum – the thing to be explained – of
any explanation. Rather, it is properly to be seen as the *explanans* – the
explainer – of the *appearance* (not: the existence) of generality in the
world. Of course there may be a psychological story to be told about this
phenomenon, but that is a psychological matter, not a semantic/meta-
physical one. It is not a matter of our predicative use of predicates being
anchored in features of the world, grasp of which explains, not language
acquisition, but our epistemic warrant or justification for that ability – of
why we are *right* to trust our inclinations to apply predicates in future
situations to new instances as we have done in the past.

However, that epistemic right or warrant is not purchased simply by
the fact that there is, as it happens, a reliable psychological mechanism
that leads us to correctly apply predicates predicatively and/or apply
general concepts. Appeal to psychological considerations alone cannot
deliver an answer to what is in effect a normative question; a question,
not about how we tend to apply our general terms and concepts, but
how we *ought* to apply them. So it will tell us only *how* we do it, not
what justifies us in our belief that we are doing it *correctly*. But being a
competent speaker of a language, a competent user of general concepts,
essentially involves appeal to adherence to norms of correctness.

This version of Nominalism frankly gives up on the possibility of explanation at the outset, because it doesn't begin to address the normative question that is raised by the ability we have to correctly think and speak in general terms. It takes the phenomenon as a brute fact, and appeals to that fact to explain another, apparent, fact about the objective – mind-independent – world. It may be that, after considering all other avenues of explanation, we will find ourselves forced to conclude that there is no explanation to be had. But this position does not even take seriously the need for explanation. It is not therefore a viable place at which to begin.

It may be that Predicate Nominalism is to be understood in the first of the two ways suggested above, as the view that what all things to which the same word (e.g., 'red') applies have in common is simply our willingness to apply the same word to them. If so, then, once it faces the fact that how we use language is a decision, up to us, it is committed to the idea that there is no *objective* fact about whether, say, this barn is red. But once the objectivity of our beliefs about the world is relinquished, there is nothing to explain. If my belief that the barn is red is true because we decide to use the word 'red' in such a way as to apply to the barn, then either there is nothing that makes my belief objectively true, or there is something in the world that obliges or requires us to use the word 'red' in this way. If it is the latter, then the problem of universals arises once again, and Predicate Nominalism is not a viable option.

One might agree with this, and nevertheless maintain that there is no problem here that needs addressing. This is the kind of position that is taken by extreme Nominalists of another kind.[15] These Nominalists are prepared to agree that there is, in a sense, an explanation to be given for the ability to correctly think and speak in general terms. Consider the predicative use of the predicate 'red'. Things are correctly called red, they will say, because they *are* red. There is some objective basis for this ability.

Further, they will maintain, the story doesn't end here. Physical theory can explain what it is for something to be red. Such an explanation will appeal to wave reflectance frequencies of surface colours of objects, or perhaps other physical properties that things that are red possess in virtue of which they are red. So, we can explain not only our ability to correctly apply predicates like 'is red' to things in the objective world in terms of the objective fact that they are red, but we can also explain what it is for something to be red. Crucially, however, we do not need to know that physical story about what it is for something to be red in order to be able to correctly apply 'red' predicatively to red things. On the contrary, the vast majority of competent thinkers and speakers of language correctly apply terms such as 'red' predicatively without knowing any physical story about what it is for something to be red.

As we have said, this less extreme form of extreme Nominalism departs from the more extreme one in conceding that there is a phenomenon that needs to be explained. What it aims to deny is that it is necessary to give a reductive explanation of that phenomenon in terms of another fact, *grasp* of which enables speakers to correctly apply predicates predicatively to items that they have never encountered before. It denies, that is, that we are able to correctly think and speak in general terms because of our grasp of something general in the world. There is this ability; and there is something general in the world. And that is the end of the story.

This is clearly an improvement on the first extreme Nominalist position. Nevertheless, it fails to come to terms with a crucial feature related to the ability to correctly speak and think in general terms. We do know when we get things right and when we do not. We correct ourselves and others when mistakes are made. We do so by pointing out facts using the terminology of ordinary discourse, the very predicates and concepts whose correct employment stands in need of explanation. Suppose, after glancing quickly at a stop light, I judge to myself, 'that's green' and continue to proceed toward the intersection, when in fact it is red, and my companion quickly tells me this. My companion is getting me to correct my initial judgement that here is an instance of green by getting me to *see* that this is a mistake, that here is an instance of red. In order for this to affect my attitudes and behaviour, I need not only to see an instance of red; I need to see it *as* an instance of red. On what basis do I see it *as* an instance of red?

This needs explaining, on pain of failing to account for the fact that we do know when we are getting things right that we are doing so, and when we are not, that we are not. This not only requires an objective basis; it requires *grasp* of that basis. The knowledge that grounds our appreciation of the difference between correct and incorrect application of general terms and concepts may not be evidence-based, nor based on inference. It may, in short, be epistemically immediate. But that knowledge is inseparable from the ability to correctly speak and think in general terms. It cannot be explained simply by reference to a physical story about what it is, say, for something to be red.

So this second form of extreme Nominalism, while being an improvement on the first, isn't up to the task of explaining our ability to correctly think and speak in general terms. It isn't, because it bypasses the question, 'how is it that we *know* that and when we are correctly applying general terms and concepts?', addressing instead the question 'what in the objective world grounds our correct application of general terms and concepts?'

The situation is, in fact, worse, since the position does not give a satisfactory answer even to the second of the two questions just raised. Divested of its epistemological connections, the objection is this. In the objective world, is what grounds the truth of our applications of 'red' to the red things, the *same* in each case? If it is not, we still have no explanation of why *all* red things are correctly called 'red'. If it is the same in each case, then we appear to have something universal on our hands, and we are driven to consider at least another version of Nominalism in order to show that we do not have something universal on our hands.

Some Moderate Nominalist Positions

Let us turn, then, to the more moderate forms of Nominalism. Of these there are at least two. The first, weaker form, Resemblance Nominalism, attempts to supplement the explanation given by the second extreme Nominalist by appealing to the fact that particular concrete things resemble one another in quite specific ways. The second is what we shall call 'Trope Nominalism' (Armstrong 1989; Campbell 1990; Rodriguez-Pereyra 2002; Hoffman and Rosenkrantz 2003).[16]

Resemblance Nominalists concede that there is more to the explanation of our ability, say, to correctly apply the term 'red' predicatively than that things are objectively red. However, they think that what more is required can be provided without compromising the Nominalist commitment to the existence of only particular concrete things. According to Resemblance Nominalists,

> When we have found a resemblance among several objects, that often occur to us, we apply the same name to all of them, whatever differences we may observe in the degrees of their quantity and quality, and whatever other differences may appear among them. (Hume 1967, I, I, vii, 'Of Abstract Ideas', p. 20)

Actually, this quotation from Hume doesn't get the Resemblance Nominalist position completely right. He says that we find 'a resemblance among several objects'; but, strictly speaking, all that Resemblance Nominalists are committed to saying is that particular objects resemble one another.[17] My red pen resembles my red clock, for instance, and my red clock resembles my red purse. All red things resemble each other. Still, we can extract from this an explanation for our ability to correctly apply general concepts and terms to objects that we have not encountered before. According to Resemblance Nominalism, this ability is due to the fact that the new ones and ones that we have encountered in the past resemble one another, and grasp of this enables us to correctly apply general concepts and terms to the new ones.

However, this by itself won't suffice to explain our ability to correctly speak and think in general terms. For many, if not all, of the concrete particular objects that we encounter resemble one another in many different ways. My blue book resembles my blue computer, but not my red computer (with respect to colour). My blue computer resembles my red computer, but not my red clock (with respect to being a computer). Further, these are things that we know when we apply such concepts as *red*, *blue*, *computer*, and *clock* and their linguistic correlates. So we need a way of accounting for the facts that (a) we know when and in what ways new objects resemble old ones, and (b) we know when and in what ways new objects do *not* resemble old ones.

However, this is exactly what Resemblance Nominalism cannot explain, at least not without begging questions, because it denies that things that fall under the same predicate do so because of any objective fact about sameness of kind. Instead, it hopes to get by with positing objective facts about resembling things. But what is it for an object to resemble another? And how does this help to explain our ability to correctly think and speak in general terms, in such a way as to make intelligible that we know when and in what ways newly encountered objects resemble old ones, and in what ways they do not?

The fact is that Resemblance Nominalists are in big trouble here. They might try to get away with speaking of 'natural' resemblance classes, and claim that many different predicates apply to the red computer because it is a member of many different resemblance classes (e.g., the red things, the things with silicon in them, the things that weigh more than 2 kg, etc.) But if they do try to handle matters in this way, they face at least two serious problems, which Goodman calls, respectively, the companionship difficulty and the problem of imperfect community. According to the companionship difficulty, there could be two different properties (say, red and round), which, as it happens, are possessed by all and only the same particulars. That is to say, the world could be such that all and only the red things are the round things. In a world like this we cannot distinguish the way in which those particulars resemble one another that matters to their falling under the term 'red' from the way in which those particulars resemble one another that matters to their falling under the term 'round', unless we appeal to respects with which things resemble one another.

According to the problem of imperfect community, constructing different resemblance groupings or classes cannot simply be a matter of selecting a particular object, O, and grouping everything that resembles O in any way whatever. For, without reference to different ways or respects with which things resemble one another, we will end up with a heterogeneous collection with nothing in common (as the example of the blue book, blue computer, red computer, and red clock illustrates). One way of attempting to do this without positing respect-specific resemblances might be to require, not just that all the members of the resemblance group or class resemble O, but that they all resemble one another. But while this is a necessary condition on things belonging to the same resemblance group or class, it is not sufficient. Consider a situation where we have four objects: object a has features A, B, and C, object b has features B, C, and D, object c has features C, D, and E, and object d has features D, E, and A. Although each of a through d resemble all of the others in the group, they do not all resemble one another in a single way that makes for them being in the same resemblance group.[18]

What Resemblance Nominalists seem forced to do in the face of these problems is to concede that there are particular, respect-specific ways in which some things resemble one another more closely than they do others (Armstrong 1978a speaks of paradigms). So a scarlet thing resembles a crimson thing in that they are similar with respect to redness but not with respect to blueness.

But now the problem with this kind of response is clear: in order to grasp the different ways that different things resemble one another, so as to be consistent with such facts as that we know that red things aren't blue things, we already need to know something further. We need to know the *ground* of such resemblances. We need to know that resembling with respect to redness is different from, and excludes, resembling with respect to blueness. But in virtue of what do we know this? Reverting to an explanation in terms of psychological mechanisms will not do the trick here, since that kind of explanation is not couched in epistemic terms. But we cannot simply help ourselves to knowledge that resembling with respect to redness is different from and excludes resembling with respect to blueness (or roundness, or whatever). To do so would be to presume knowledge of the very features that Resemblance Nominalists maintain we *construct* on the basis of noticing particular resemblance relations between particular things. This explanation of our ability to correctly speak and think in general terms presumes the very competence that it is meant to explain.

One might think that the Resemblance Nominalist can avoid the problem of imperfect community and the companionship difficulty by positing particular resemblance relations. According to this strategy, objects resemble one another because they bear particular resemblance *relations* to one another.[19] Noting the fact, mentioned above, that different objects resemble one another in different ways, however, the Resemblance Nominalist must have a rich ontology of particular resemblance relations. The particular resemblance relation that my blue book bears to my blue computer is a different relation from the particular resemblance relation that my blue computer bears to my red computer, which is different again from the particular resemblance relation that my red computer bears to my red clock.

Matters are yet more complicated. Consider the resemblance relations that hold between objects in virtue of each one's being a determinate colour, say, red. Each of these objects is a determinate shade of red, so some will resemble certain others more closely than they do the rest. Consider a particular, orangey shade of red. It may resemble objects that are orange more closely than it resembles many shades of red.

How do we capture not just the fact that particular resemblance relations must not only all be different ones (each being as particular as the particular objects that they relate), but also are different *ways* of relating the objects that they relate? A particular scarlet thing resembles more closely a particular crimson thing than a particular mauve thing, in a way that makes for them both being red. The way that the scarlet thing resembles more closely a particular crimson thing itself resembles more closely the way that a particular crimson thing resembles a particular magenta thing than the way that it resembles a particular mauve thing. What ways are these, and how do Resemblance Nominalists account for them without recourse to particular *respect-specific* resemblance relations?

It seems that Resemblance Nominalists can have no more success in accounting for this by appeal to particular resemblance relations than they can have by appeal to the mere fact that objects resemble one another.[20] But note that the problem here is different from another one that is sometimes thought to defeat Resemblance Nominalism, namely, a problem concerning an infinite regress. Russell, for example, argued that, once one posits particular resemblance relations, one must, in order to avoid an infinite vicious regress of particular resemblance relations, posit at least one universal, resemblance, of which all particular relations are instances (Russell 1911–12, 1912). The reason is that relations themselves are particulars, and so can only relate things in respect-specific ways if they themselves are related to one another in respect-specific ways, and so on.

It isn't clear, though, whether Russell's objection works. Resemblance Nominalists can claim that there is nothing wrong with (or vicious about) an infinite regress, so long as that infinity need not be grasped by those who think and speak correctly in general terms. Or they can claim that resemblance relations are brute, not further analysable in the sense that their being instantiated between any two or more things cannot be accounted for in virtue of anything else (the instantiation of any other resemblance relations included). If this is so, then the regress cannot get started. Rejecting the demand for analysis at the very first step, then, blocks the regress.[21]

In any case, a similar objection can be raised against Realism, so it cannot be one that favours Realism over Resemblance Nominalism. What does favour Realism is the inability of Resemblance Nominalism to account for the fact that we are not only able to correctly predicate predicatively, but that we are able to know that and when we are doing so. Again, this is quite a cognitive achievement, and Resemblance Nominalism cannot account for it in a way that doesn't already presuppose the very ability it is attempting to explain.

Before moving on, let's consider one further strategy, the sceptical response of the Wittgensteinian.[22] According to this, there is no solution to the problems raised here against Resemblance Nominalism. Whether things that are B, C, and D resemble things that are C, D, and K more than they resemble things that are A, B, and C is not a factual matter. It is a decision we make. Thus, we must return to Predicate Nominalism and its attendant rejection of the idea that there is anything in the world that makes our judgements objectively true or false. There is only our decision to use language in this way rather than in that way, and our non-objective decision to 'go on' in a particular way.

If the Wittgensteinian is right, then we are not back to our original problem, since the original problem never existed; it was spurious, since it tries to account for an objectivity that does not exist. However, if this is so, then we only *appear* to understand language, and that seems incredible. In view of it, the better path for the Resemblance Nominalist to pursue is to embrace the moderate Nominalist position that we have called 'Trope Nominalism'. Trope Nominalism has a long and distinguished history. It is thought that versions of this position were held by philosophers as diverse as Aristotle, Leibniz, Berkeley, Hume, Husserl and Stout (Mertz 1996). More recently versions of it have been held by Strawson (1959), Honderich (1988), Bennett (1988, 2002), Armstrong (1989), Heil (1992, 2003), Simons (1994), Campbell (1990), and Bacon (1995). Campbell's is a revival of the earlier foundational work of D. C. Williams (1953). Williams set forth the version of trope theory now regarded as the classic account.

The classic account is both a theory of the nature of particulars (as discussed in chapter 3) and a theory of the nature of resemblance capable of grounding an explanation of generality. However, it is possible to separate the two parts of the account. Since the theory of what it is to be a particular thing has problems of its own, which do not impinge on the theory of the nature of resemblance, we will restrict our attention to the latter theory here.[23]

Consider, for example, this pen on my desk. It has certain properties: it is red, has a particular shape and size, a certain spatial position, and so on. When I observe this pen, I observe its redness, its size, its shape, and its position on this desk. According to Trope Nominalism, these properties are particular properties of the pen. They are as particular as the pen itself. Just as the pen cannot be in more than one place at any given time – just as it is located all at once, wholly and completely, in the place it occupies at any given time – so too its redness, its shape, its size, cannot be in more than one place at any given time. For what I observe when I observe its redness is *this particular* redness of the pen, and similarly for the other properties it has.

What, according to Trope Nominalism, are properties? According to the classic account, they are classes or sets of exactly similar or resembling tropes. Redness, for example, is the class of exactly similar rednesses; similarly for blueness, roundness, and all other properties (property-types, let us say). Individual tropes that are members of the set of exactly resembling tropes with which a given property is identical are what we might call 'property-tokens', or 'particularized properties'. So, according to Trope Nominalists, there are no universals; there are only properties. Further, for a substance to have a property is for one of its tropes to exactly resemble all of the tropes that fall into the set that is that property (or, for those who endorse both parts of the classic account, for the tropes that fall into the set that is the individual substance to overlap the tropes that fall into the set that is the property).

Trope Nominalism *can* avoid the twin problems of imperfect community and companionship difficulty, at least in the form that poses a threat to Resemblance Nominalism. It can do so by pointing out that (1) since tropes are already respect-specific, 'foreign elements' cannot get into the wrong trope-class (the companionship difficulty), despite the fact that resemblance itself is primitive; and (2) since the basic or fundamental ('simple') tropes can only resemble each other in one respect, we cannot construct trope-classes where no single feature is common to all (the problem of imperfect community). So it is an improvement on Resemblance Nominalism.

Does the positing of tropes solve the problem of how different particulars can be the same? It seems not. Resemblance Nominalism says that the explanation for this is that these particulars resemble one another and resemble one another more closely than they do other particulars. The problem with it is that, short of positing respect-specific resemblances, it cannot account for the fact that we know that different particulars resemble one another in different ways, and that the ways some things resemble one another exclude their resembling one another in other ways. Trope Nominalism attempts to avoid this by positing tropes, where tropes just are particularized properties and so already, so to speak, respect-specific. But this doesn't by itself solve the original problem, since, supposing that there are tropes, the problem is how a group of resembling tropes can be of the same type, i.e., that they can resemble one another *in the same way*. And this problem is not settled simply by positing tropes.

Trope Nominalists are likely to respond to this challenge by denying that the fact that tropes resemble one another needs further explanation by reference to something that they have in common. That they resemble one another, it might be said, is at root *brute*, and so not further analysable or explicable. The problem with this response is that it cannot account for the fact that we know that different things resemble one another in different ways, and that we know that we are able to mark these ways correctly and incorrectly with the use of general terms. We know that and when we do it correctly; and this seems to be anchored in our appreciation of such facts as, for example, that the blueness-resembling ways are not the redness-resembling ways, and that they exclude one another. This cannot be explained simply by reference to the facts that tropes resemble one another in their very nature and that we notice these resemblances. We don't just see red things; we see them *as* red. And seeing them *as* red is essential to the ability to correctly use the general term 'red' predicatively.

Related to this is the fact that Trope Nominalism cannot handle its own version of the companionship difficulty. Recall that, according to that difficulty, a situation in which all and only the red things are the round things is one in which Resemblance Nominalism cannot account for the difference between the two features, red, and round. But intuitively we know that even if we were to be in such a situation, we would be able to distinguish these features from one another. Trope Nominalism hopes to get round this problem by appeal to the respect-specific nature of tropes. Particular objects resemble one another only insofar as they are constituted by tropes which, being respect-specific, resemble one another by virtue of their very natures. But in the situation envisaged, we cannot distinguish the resemblance trope-class of particular rednesses from the resemblance trope-class of particular roundnesses. All and only the particular rednesses are compresent with the particular roundnesses.

How then can we explain the fact that we are able to distinguish the feature, red, from the feature, round?

One way that Trope Nominalists might do this is by embracing what they sometimes call 'Meinongianism': by appealing to the view that the resembling tropes that resemble one another in the red way and the resembling tropes that resemble one another in the round way are distinct because, although *in fact* every particular redness is compresent with a particular roundness, there are possible redness tropes that are not compresent with possible roundness tropes (and vice versa) (Bacon 1995, 2002). However, even if Trope Nominalists are unconcerned about positing possible tropes (which many will be if they are Nominalistically inclined), the explanation is question-begging. It presumes knowledge of the very features that Trope Nominalists tell us we construct on the basis of noticing particular resembling tropes. It thus presumes the ability to distinguish different resemblance classes of tropes in the explanation of that very ability.

Of all the Nominalist solutions we have considered, Trope Nominalism is the only one that tries to solve the problem at issue by introducing entities. All of the others try to get by with concrete particulars and sets of them. Insofar as that is so, and the positing of tropes does not solve the problem, by the principle of Ockham's razor alluded to earlier in this chapter they ought not to be posited at all – certainly not in order to account for how the nature of resemblance affords an explanation of generality.

Two Conceptions of Universals

Recall that the issue between Realists and Nominalists set out at the beginning of the present chapter is not whether there is in thought and language something that corresponds to the idea of generality, but rather, whether the devices in language and thought that capture the idea of generality are matched by real generality in the world spoken or thought of. In a situation in which there are two objects that 'agree' in colour in that both are red, Realists, but not Nominalists, would describe the agreement in colour as one of colour identity. Realists maintain that when we correctly say that distinct particulars are in some sense, nevertheless the same, there really is something the same (i.e., identical). What is the same is the property, or attribute (in this case, red, or redness), that the different things possess. According to Realists, the postulation of universals is necessary for the explanation of what is the same in different particulars, and so to the explanation of the ability to correctly speak and think about generality.

Realism about attribute agreement might be the best strategy available to explain generality in thought and language, if in fact it is not incoherent. But if it is, then an 'inferior' explanatory theory (say, Trope Nominalism) might have to be adopted. Given the strangeness of abstract universals, the coherence of Realism needs to be addressed and not presumed or ignored. It is not enough to show that, *if* coherent, it does the explanatory work better than its rivals. So part of our job in the remaining sections of this chapter will be to establish that Realism is coherent.

There are two main conceptions of universals, the Platonic one and the Aristotelian one. Both share the basic conception of realism, that when distinct particulars are in some sense the same, what is the same is the property or attribute that they possess. The difference between the Platonist and the Aristotelian concerns whether universals have spatio-temporal location. According to the Platonic conception, universals do not have spatio-temporal location. According to the Aristotelian conception, however, they do.

Both the Aristotelian conception and the Platonic one have suffered from charges of incoherence. The Aristotelian conception is said to be incoherent because, one way or another, it violates the so-called laws of thinghood that govern particulars. According to these,

(i) one thing cannot be wholly present at different places at the same time

and

(ii) two things cannot occupy the same place at the same time.

Aristotelian universals are said to violate these 'laws' because, traditionally understood, they can be 'wholly and completely' in many places at the same time. Being spatio-temporal, Aristotelian universals are literally in particulars. Oliver puts the point succinctly:

one might begin to wonder whether Aristotelian universals are really preferable to Platonic universals. True, the former conception conforms to our belief that properties are *in* their instances, but at the cost of quite puzzling claims about location and parthood. (Oliver 1996, pp. 27–8)

He continues:

How important is this belief? Not very, I suggest. The strongest interpretation it can plausibly bear is that it is just a different way of saying that the instances *instantiate* the properties. If I am right we might return to the Platonic conception of universals and start to look for reasons why it ought to be preferred to the Aristotelian conception. The Aristotelian conception aims to find a spatio-temporal location for universals by locating them in their instances. This yields two reasons to find this conception wanting. First, uninstantiated properties and relations may do some useful philosophical work. On the Aristotelian conception, however, uninstantiated universals do not exist because universals are present in their instances: no instances, no universal. Second, properties and relations of abstract objects may need to be acknowledged. But such objects have no spatio-temporal location and so they cannot instantiate Aristotelian universals, there being nowhere for such universals to be. (Oliver 1996, p. 28)

As Oliver sees it, the problem with Aristotelian Realism is not just that it seems to suffer from a kind of incoherence. It may be, for example, that it could avoid the charge by maintaining that these 'laws' are ones that apply to particulars, and universals are not particulars.[24] Or one might accept that Aristotelian universals violate the so-called laws of thinghood, but insist that this does not entail that the view is incoherent, only false. However, Oliver's point is that there are other disadvantages to the Aristotelian view, even if one were to accept that it isn't incoherent.

One way of getting round this charge of incoherence while conceding that the laws of thinghood apply to universals and that they are true would be to say that different parts of each universal are in each of many different particulars.[25] This treats universals as 'scattered objects', spread out amongst the particulars they are in. But this is not how Aristotelians regard the relation between universals and particulars. They claim that universals are wholly and completely in each particular that they are in.

It might be thought that a more promising strategy for avoiding the charge would be to view concrete particular things (e.g., material substances) as constituted by bundles of tropes, where tropes are 'particularized properties', such as this redness, this roundness, and so on: properties that are as particular as the particular things that they constitute. The trope view evidently can make sense of the Aristotelian idea that universals are universals-in-things. But there is a residual problem with this suggestion. If the Aristotelian view is to be a version of Realism, and not Nominalism, something must be said about how different tropes, such as different rednesses, or different roundnesses, relate to one another, for Realism is committed to the view that universals are the *commonalities* in different particulars. According to it, universals are what is the *same* in distinct particulars, not merely what is resembling, or makes for resemblances, between *different* particulars. And it is difficult to see how an explanation of this can be given that doesn't once again treat universals as scattered objects.

Let us put the Aristotelian conception to one side, then, and consider the Platonic one.[26] According to this, universals are not literally in concrete particulars and so are not spatio-temporal things. Rather, they are exemplified or instantiated in particulars, and they bear some kind of relation to those particulars.[27] This being so, Platonic universals do not breach the so-called laws of thinghood: although they are instantiated in many places at the same time, they are not literally in their instances. That is to say, their instances (i.e., concrete particulars), considered collectively, are in many places at the same time, though, individually, no instance (concrete thing) is in more than one place at a given time.[28]

If Platonic universals do not breach the laws of thinghood, then the Platonic conception cannot suffer from the same charge of incoherence that attaches to the Aristotelian view. But it does suffer from another. Critics claim that the conception can only work to explain what is the same in distinct particulars, and, by this means, explain the phenomenon of generality in thought and language, if it can explain the relation between universals and their instances; and it cannot do this without generating a vicious infinite regress.[29] In the remaining sections of this chapter we shall consider the charge and two ways of attempting to avoid it that are unsatisfactory. We'll finish by considering and defending a third way of avoiding it.

The Regress Charge and
Two Unsuccessful Attempts to Meet It

The problem that proponents of Platonic Realism are thought to face is often put in the form of a dilemma. Either universals are *other* than their instances (e.g., redness is other than all the red things), or they are not (e.g., redness is itself a red thing). If they are not other than their instances, but are one of them, then we are left with a many, which again need unification, and an infinite regress results. We never reach a point where the many are unified, and so no explanation of what is the same in distinct particulars is possible. Opting for this disjunct is thus subject to one version of what is called the 'third man argument'. The regress here is thought to be vicious, because at no stage in the process of positing a universal in order to unify its instances is the unification effected. So no explanation of what makes for sameness in distinct particulars is forthcoming; and consequently no explanation is forthcoming of how we can correctly think and speak about generality. For an explanation of the latter to be effected, one must reach a stage in the process where grasp of the unifier and its relation to its instances enables one to apply general concepts and terms to an indefinite number of particulars. But no such stage can be reached.

In the light of this, it is common for proponents of the Platonic position to opt for the first disjunct, and this is the strategy on which we shall concentrate for the remainder of our discussion. According to it, universals *are* other than their instances: they are not one of the many (redness is not itself red, squareness is not itself square, etc.), but rather, are the one *over* the many. This gives rise to the 'one over many' problem: how can universals unify their instances if they are wholly other than them? The Platonic Realist's answer is that universals bear a 'suitable relation' to their instances. Plato himself took that relation to be one of participation, but also talked of imitation.[30] Both of these are asymmetric relations, and both are problematic, as is well known. Contemporary discussions of the Platonic position take the relation to be one of instantiation, or exemplification (as the quotation by Oliver mentioned on pp. 237–8 indicates). This gives rise to a different charge of incoherence. Critics claim that this explanation generates a relational regress, an infinite regress of relational entities, and that the regress is vicious.

One way of formulating the regress charge is this. Consider a particular individual thing, a, and a property, F, and suppose that a has F. According to the Platonic position, a's having F just is a's instantiating the property, F (or F-ness). That is to say, a and F enter into a relation of instantiation R. Now this relation can only 'tie' F to a, and explain what it is for a to be F, if this relation itself bears a suitable relation to a and to F. Call this relation, 'instantiating the relation of instantiation' (R_1): a instantiates F by a and F instantiating the relation of instantiation. But now we have a further relation, R_1, whose relation to a, F, and R needs to be forged in order for a to be 'tied' to F and explain what it is for a to be F. Call this relation 'instantiating the relation of instantiating the relation of instantiation' (R_2). It is clear that in order for this relation to forge a tie between a, F, R, and R_1, we shall need to posit yet a further relation (R_3), and so on, ad infinitum. The charge is that this leads to incoherence because it leads to an infinite regress of relational entities and that the regress is vicious, since it is logically impossible for the positing of universals to explain how a given particular (a) can have a property (F). This being so, it is logically impossible for it to explain how distinct particulars can have the same property (F); how they can be qualitatively the same. Consequently, the positing of universals cannot explain how we can think and speak correctly about generality, since, in order for it to do so, we would have to be aware of or grasp an infinite number of universals, which task it is impossible to complete.

We can try to avoid this charge of incoherence in either of two ways. The first is to acknowledge the regress but deny that it is vicious. Here the claim will be that some regresses are vicious and some are not; and only if the regress involved in this case is vicious need we accept the charge of incoherence. In this case, the reason why the regress is not vicious is that the ability to correctly apply a general term to a particular, and to correctly apply the same term to distinct particulars, does not require awareness, or grasp, of an infinite number of relational entities.

Let's consider a couple of cases where this might seem plausible. Here is one: Frege's (1892) explanation of why substitution of co-referring terms fails to preserve the truth-value of sentences in oblique contexts (ones that are apparently non-extensional).[31] Frege argues that, whereas in ordinary contexts, terms such as proper names express a sense (e.g, an individual concept) and refer to an individual (e.g., a human being), when the same terms occur in oblique contexts, they take on as their reference their customary sense (i.e., their sense in ordinary contexts), and acquire a new (second-level) sense. So, for example, whereas 'Ben Franklin', in 'Ben Franklin invented bifocals', refers to the man, Ben Franklin, and has as its customary sense something expressible by the description, 'the first postmaster general of the United States', in a context like 'Joe believes that Ben Franklin invented bifocals', the same name 'Ben Franklin' refers to the sense of 'the first postmaster general of the United States' and acquires a new sense. For Frege, the new sense is not something that is a function of its customary sense, so one must effectively learn a new rule in order to grasp it. Since expressions such as 'Joe believes that' can be iterated an indefinite – in principle, an infinite – number of times, generating new oblique contexts from old ones, the result is that one and the same term can have an infinite number of senses or meanings. Frege's solution to the substitution problem thus leads to the generation of an infinite number of meanings for a term (Davidson 1965).

Is this regress vicious? Arguably not, because at each stage, one does not need to grasp the infinite number of new senses that an embedding further along the process generates in order to grasp the sense of the original expression in the new sentence. At each stage, one needs to grasp exactly one new sense; that is all.

Is this case similar in nature to the Platonist's case? According to the Platonist, the ability to correctly apply a general term or concept to a single particular is explained by an awareness or grasp of that particular's instantiating a universal. Further, the ability to correctly apply a general term or concept to an indefinite number of distinct particulars is explained by a grasp of qualitative sameness in these particulars. This, it is said, is explained by our grasp of each of these particulars' instantiating one and the same universal. In order for us to do this, we need both to grasp the instances (i.e., the particulars), and also to grasp the property instantiated and the relation of instantiation into which these instances and the universal enter.

Unfortunately, this does not seem like Frege's case, for the following reason. For Frege, each level n of senses can generate a level of senses $n + 1$, when level n senses become level $n + 1$ referents. But grasp of senses at levels higher than $n + 1$ is not required in order to grasp senses at level $n + 1$. Things apparently stand otherwise for the relational entities generated by the Platonist explanation of our ability to correctly apply general concepts and terms to an indefinite number of distinct particulars. The infinity of relational entities is required in order to effect the 'tie' between a universal and its instances at level 1, the very *first* level, and so for universals to unify their instances at all. Without it, the positing of universals cannot explain what is the same in distinct particulars and so cannot explain the ability to apply general concepts and terms to an indefinite number of distinct particulars.

Consider, then, another case where it might be plausible to say that an infinite regress is generated but where it is not, and should not be, worrying; a case concerning lower-level and higher-level properties. Suppose that a particular, a, has the property of being 2 inches long. Then, in virtue of having that property, it also has the property of being less than 3 inches long. It also has, in virtue of having that property, the property of being less than 4 inches long, and so on into infinity. It seems that a's having the property of being 2 inches long guarantees that a has an infinite number of other properties. Is it a necessary condition on a's having the property of being 2 inches long that a has these (infinite number of) other properties? Arguably so. Do we need to be aware of, or grasp, this infinity in order to correctly think or say that a has the property of being 2 inches long? Arguably not.

It might be claimed that one cannot be said to understand the concept expressed by '2 inches long' unless one also understands the concept 'less than 3 inches long'. Can one really understand what the number 2 is and not understand that it is less than three? If not, then an infinite number of things must be understood in order to understand what it is for something to be 2 inches long; and the regress looks vicious.

But this line of reasoning would lead to the conclusion that we cannot grasp the concept of being 2 inches long! And this is plainly unacceptable. The example is instructive, since it shows that the problem in the Platonist's case is not just that there is a regress, nor even that the regress is infinite. It has to do with the nature or type of regress involved. In the number case, the regress is not vicious because we don't have to be aware of or grasp an infinity of properties in order to think, say, that a has the property of being 2 inches long, even though being the number 2 does require that it be a member of an infinite set. The fact that a counting process cannot, even in principle, be completed does not show that we cannot count. But the Realist's account of how universals and their instances are related at level 1 requires not only that there be an infinite number of higher-level relations, but also that the infinity be completed. If it cannot in principle be completed, the 'tie' between universals and their instances at level 1 cannot be effected at all. And if not, there is no explanation of the ability to think and speak correctly about generality.

So there really is a problem here for Platonists to address, one that resists treatment by arguing that the regress is infinite but not vicious. In the face of it, Platonists might and often do attempt to avoid the charge of incoherence in the second way alluded to above. They attempt to block the regress altogether by maintaining that the relation of instantiation is 'brute', 'not further analysable'. Armstrong, for example, when discussing how it is possible for distinct particulars to be the same, explicitly takes this route out of the problem, saying:

> we must just stick with this proposition: different particulars may have the same property. . . . Different particulars may be (wholly or partially) identical in nature. Such identity in nature is literally inexplicable, in the sense that it cannot be further explained. But that does not make it incoherent. Identity in nature entails that the universe is unified in a way that the Nominalist finds unintuitive. But I take that to be simply the fault of the Nominalist's intuitions. We simply have to accept that different particulars may have the same property or be related by the same relation. (1978a, pp. 108–9)

The regress issue arises out of the Realist's account of what it is for a particular, a, to be F. If one takes the view that a and F are related by the relation of instantiation, then one is apparently forced to say that whenever things are related, there is a relation that relates them. One way of avoiding the resulting regress is to deny that this is so, by claiming that the relation of instantiation is 'brute', in the sense of being unanalysable, or inexplicable. In this case, what is meant is that the instantiation relation is not a universal *whose instantiation requires the instantiation of any further universal*. This strategy can then be applied to the account of what it is for two particulars, a and b, to be F. The Realist insists that for two (or more) particulars to both be F is for them each to bear the relation of instantiation to the universal F, or F-ness, where the relation of instantiation is brute. The view expressed by

Armstrong is not that a's being F (and correspondingly, a's being F and b's being F) *isn't* a's instantiating F or F-ness (and correspondingly, a's and b's both instantiating F or F-ness. It is that although what it is for a to be F or for a and b to both be F requires the relation of instantiation, nothing further can be said about what instantiation is.

Lewis points out one of the problems with this view: not only is it open to the Platonist to appeal to it in order to avoid charges of vicious infinite regress, it is also open to the Nominalist (Lewis 1983b, pp. 173–4). If so, and if Nominalism postulates fewer entities than does Platonism, then it may well be that Nominalism has the upper hand, or at least, not as bad a hand, in providing a satisfactory explanation of the ability to think and speak correctly about generality.

Lewis objects to Armstrong's handling of the Nominalist's position precisely because he fails to see this:

> There is to be no unanalysed predication. Time and again, Armstrong wields his requirement against rival theories. One theory after another falls victim to the 'relation regress': in the course of analysing other predications, the theory has resort to a new predicate that cannot, on pain of circularity, be analysed along with the rest. So falls Class Nominalism . . . : it employs predications of class membership, which predications it cannot without circularity analyse in terms of class membership. So falls Resemblance Nominalism: it fails to analyse predications of resemblance. So fall various other, less deserving Nominalisms. . . . How does Armstrong himself do without primitive predication? – He doesn't. Consider the predicate 'instantiates' (or 'has'), as in 'particular a instantiates the universal F' or 'this electron has unit charge'. No one-off analysis applies to this specific predicate. 'Such identity in nature [as results from the having of one universal in many particulars] is literally inexplicable, in the sense that it cannot be further explained' (*Universals*, I, p. 109) (Lewis 1983b, pp. 173–4)

Lewis here is talking about primitive predication; but it is clear that he intends his complaint to attach to the metaphysical version of the so-called problem of universals, for he continues:

> Let us dump the project of getting rid of primitive predication, and return to the sensible – though not compulsory – project of analysing . . . facts of apparent sameness of type. Now does the relation regress serve Armstrong better? I think not. It does make better sense within the more sensible project, but it still bites Armstrong and his rivals with equal force. Let the Nominalist say 'These donkeys resemble each other, so likewise do those stars, and there analysis ends.' Let the Platonist say 'This statue participates in the Form of beauty, likewise that lecture participates in the Form

of truth, and there analysis ends.' Let Armstrong say 'This electron instantiates unit charge, likewise that proton instantiates tripartiteness, and there analysis ends.' It is possible to complain in each case that a fact of sameness of type has gone unanalysed, the types being respectively resemblance, participation, and instantiation. (Lewis 1983b, p. 174)

Lewis's point is precisely that if the strategy of blocking regresses works to save the Platonist, it also works to save the Nominalist, and that just goes to show that appeal to the bruteness, or unanalysability, of the instantiation relation will not favour Platonism over Nominalism, which can appeal to the bruteness of the resemblance relation.

However, Lewis is also disparaging about rejecting a theory that appeals to primitive predication or primitive relations merely because it appeals to such primitives. In his view, trying to do away with all primitive predication is not an attainable aim, and so no theory should be criticized for failing to do it. If he is right about this, then, far from this constituting a reason to reject Platonism (or Nominalism), it is not a reason to reject any theory. Are Platonism and Nominalism on an equal footing, then, given that in both cases regress objections can be blocked by appeal to primitive relations? No, Lewis says, since a theory

> may be faulted for its overabundant primitive predications, or for unduly mysterious ones, or for unduly complicated ones. These are not fatal faults, however. They are to be counted against a theory, along with its faults of overly generous ontology or of disagreement with . . . commonsensical opinions. Rival philosophical theories have their prices, which we seek to measure. But it's all too clear that for philosophers, at least, there ain't no such thing as a free lunch. (Lewis 1983b, p. 173)

On these criteria, however, Nominalism would seem to win over Platonism, since it makes do with entities of one kind rather than two (although they may be as mysterious as, or even more mysterious than, universals). The moral is that if Platonism is to discharge its claim to provide a better explanation than Nominalism of how distinct particulars can be the same, and so of how we can apply general concepts correctly to an indefinite number of distinct particulars, it had better not appeal to the bruteness of the instantiation relation.

An Alternative

How, then, is Platonism to discharge its explanatory commitment while avoiding the charge of incoherence? One suggestion is to further develop

Armstrong's claim that the 'relation' between a universal and its instances is a not a dyadic (2-place) relation. Indeed, he suggests, it isn't a relation at all. Here is what he says:

> I am . . . simply trying to emphasize the inseparability of particularity and universality. I am not suggesting that '*Fa*' is an indivisible semantic unit, in the way that Quine once suggested that 'believes-that-p' is an indivisible semantic unit (1960, p. 216). Obviously, we can and must distinguish between the particularity of a particular, on the one hand, and its properties (and relations), on the other. But it is a distinction without relation. (Armstrong 1978a, p. 111)

Lewis describes the position articulated by Armstrong a 'non-relational Realism'; and he points out that Armstrong's view is that nothing more can be said about the non-relational 'tie' that binds instances of universals with the universals they instantiate.

Armstrong is on to the right way of dealing with the regress problem that dogs Platonism (even if he himself rejects that position in favour of Aristotelian Realism). But something more *can* and *must* be said about this so-called non-relational tie if Platonism is to have a chance of discharging its claim to have provided an explanation of how distinct particulars can be the same, and so of how we can think and speak correctly about generality.

The suggestion to be developed here is that talk of the kind of non-relational tie that binds instances of universals with the universals they instantiate can be better understood as veiled talk of internal relations. Specifically, the claim is that instances of universals (i.e., particular things, such as red birds) are internally related to the universals of which they are instances. This instance of red, e.g., this red bird, is internally related to the universal, redness.

There are many versions of the so-called doctrine of internal relations. Leibniz (1998) endorsed some version of the doctrine, claiming that each monad 'contains within it everything that it was, is, and shall be'. The doctrine is perhaps most familiar from the work of the British idealist Bradley (1969), but it also surfaces in the work of the early Wittgenstein (1961) and in his transitional and later work, although in a different form. Our use of it here, in furthering the kind of position favoured by Armstrong, is independent of its development of idealism by Bradley. Bradley claimed that 'Relation presupposes quality, and quality relation. Each can be something neither together with, nor apart from, the other' (1969, p. 20). His view was that all relations are internal relations. Thus, he says,

[Relations] . . . are nothing intelligible, either with or without their qualities. In the first place, a relation without terms seems mere verbiage; and
terms appear, therefore, to be something beyond their relation. At least,
for myself, a relation which somehow precipitates terms which were not
there before, or a relation which can get on somehow without terms, and
with no differences beyond the mere ends of a line of connexion, is really
a phrase without meaning.

But how the relation can stand to the qualities is, on the other side,
unintelligible. If it is nothing to the qualities, then they are not related at
all; and, if so, as we saw, they have ceased to be qualities, and their relation is a nonentity. But if it is to be something to them, then clearly we
now shall require a *new* connecting relation. . . . And, being something
itself, if it does not itself bear a relation to the terms, in what intelligible
way will it succeed in being anything to them? But here again we are
hurried off into the eddy of a hopeless process, since we are forced to go
on finding new relations without end. The links are united by a link, and
this bond of union is a link which also has two ends; and these require
each a fresh link to connect them with the old. (Bradley 1969, pp. 27–8)

In this passage, Bradley argues that although our usual way of thinking of (dyadic, or 2-place) relations is to think of them as 'something
added' to the things related, this is an illusion. If one does think of them
in this way, one is forced into an infinite regress of relations, and this is
what our Platonist is faced with. So one must think of them as not adding
something to the items related. But then, Bradley says, aren't we forced
to think of relations as genuine nonentities?

Well, in a sense they are. Armstrong agrees: he denies that there is a
genuine relation obtaining between a universal and its instance. But by
'genuine relation' he clearly means, not 'internal relation', but 'dyadic
relation', 'something added' to the universal, and its instance, to bind
them together in some way. Thus, Armstrong's position leaves space
within which to develop a strategy that invokes internal relations.

What, then, is the doctrine of internal relations, and how do we articulate it in such a way as to help explain the so-called relation between universals and their instances? Hymers (1996) articulates the doctrine thus:

An object, *a*, is internally related to another object, *b*, if and only if *a*
is related to *b* in virtue of *a*'s possessing some property, *P*. (Hymers 1996,
p. 591)

However, this formulation of the doctrine is not very helpful in the
present context. Applied to universals and their instances (particular
things), it amounts to saying that an instance of a given universal, *F*, is
internally related to *F* if and only if it is related to *F* in virtue of instan-

tiating some property, *P*. So, suppose that the red bird is an instance of red, or redness. On the present account, the red bird is internally related to redness if and only if it is related to redness in virtue of instantiating some property *P*. What could that property be? If it is *F* (redness) itself, then we have simply reiterated our problem, the solution of which was intended to be given by appeal to universals. For, it amounts to saying that the instance of *F* is internally related to *F* if and only if it is related to *F* in virtue of instantiating property *F*. In the case of our red bird, it amounts to saying that the red bird is internally related to redness if and only if it is related to redness in virtue of instantiating the property, redness. But what we wanted an account of was what it is for something to instantiate the property *F*, and appeal to the doctrine of internal relations was intended to provide that, not presuppose it. Does an instance of redness instantiate the property, redness? Yes, of course. Does this explain the relation that holds between the instance and the universal? No.

Nor is it plausible to suppose that *P* might be some other property than *F*. For one thing, supposing this would still presuppose rather than explain what it is for an instance (i.e., a particular thing) to instantiate a property. For another, it supposes that an instance of a property instantiates it in virtue of being related to some other, distinct, property. How could it be, for example, that an instance of redness is internally related to the universal, *redness*, by being related to redness by instantiating some *other* property? Finally, and relatedly, it looks as though this attempt will generate exactly the kind of vicious regress that the appeal to internal relations was intended to circumvent.

Here is another possibility. Russell (1966a, p. 139) described internal relations as ones that are 'grounded in the natures of the related terms', although he disparaged the doctrine of internal relations, at least as it was articulated by Bradley. Is this formulation of the doctrine any more helpful than the previous one? It seems so. Consider redness and its instance, the red thing. The instance is an instance of redness, and it is arguable that it is in the nature of the instance to be an instance of the universal of which it is fact an instance. And the universal is the universal it is because it *is* redness. So it looks like an instance of redness is internally related to redness, since its relation to redness is 'grounded in the natures of the related terms'.

This might appear to be the view that each instance of redness is essentially an instance of redness, which might well be true if an instance of redness were to be a red trope. But on the standard Realist view, an instance of a universal is the particular thing, not a trope of that universal. Further, on the standard view, a particular thing has a property by being an instance of it. If the view of internal relations is the view that each instance of redness is essentially an instance of redness, it is the view that each red thing is essentially red.

But this is not the view being advanced here. Rather, the view is that each thing that *happens* to be red is internally related to redness. Recall that, in chapter 3, a property exemplification account of material substances was advanced. According to it, where $s = [x, P, t]$, and where x is a place, P an atomic substance-kind, and t a time, s is the exemplification at x of P at t. Material substances are essentially exemplifications of atomic substance-kind properties in places at times. It follows from the account that each material substance is essentially an exemplification of the atomic substance-kind of which it is in fact an exemplification. On the assumption that *bird* is an atomic material substance-kind, it follows that the red bird is essentially a bird.

But it does not follow that the red bird is essentially red, even given the doctrine of internal relations. Remember that the property exemplification account works with the distinction between constitutive and characterizing properties of things, and we have seen that this distinction amounts to the distinction between essential and accidental properties of them. In particular, it amounts to the distinction between properties that are kind-determining essences of things that form a metaphysical kind, like substances, and properties, some of which they merely have or possess. The red bird possesses the property of being red, but this is not a kind-determining essence of the bird, so is a property that the bird has only contingently. It is a not a property whose exemplification just is the bird, but is, rather, a property exemplified *by* the bird, and contingently so, as it is not a property that the bird has in virtue of being an exemplification of the (constitutive) property, *bird*. So, although it is true that, necessarily, the red bird is red, it is not true that the red bird is essentially (necessarily) red.

None of this shows that the red bird is not internally related to redness. Given that the bird *is* (contingently) red, it could not be a red bird unless it is an instance of redness. We can put the point another way. The relation, say, of being taller than, is an external relation, since it relates two independent material substances. But the relation of instantiation or exemplification is internal, in that it relates a material substance with a property. This is a legitimate distinction between exemplification and being taller than; and exemplification relates material substances to both essential and accidental properties.

To think otherwise is to retreat to something like a trope view of instances of universals. The trope view encourages one to suppose that instances of properties can be essentially characterized *as* instances, without reference to the properties (i.e., property-types) of which they are instances. If that were so, one might view the relation that holds between a particular redness trope and the property-type as a genuine relation, a dyadic relation, whose holding makes 'the instance is essentially an instance of redness' true. But, on the Realist's view, instances are not tropes; they are particular things, like birds, or other material substances. So, given Realism and given the property exemplification account of substances, although it is false that the red bird is essentially red, it is true that the red bird is red (and that, necessarily, the red bird is red), where its being red just is its being an instantiation or exemplification of redness.

Wittgenstein never advanced the Bradleyan view that all relations are internal relations, but he did advance some such doctrine of internal relations. It shows up in his picture theory of meaning (Wittgenstein 1961). Here he formulates the doctrine, not in purely metaphysical terms, as Russell does, but in epistemic ones. He claims that

> A property is internal if it is unthinkable that its object does not possess it. (Wittgenstein 1961, 4.12)

But he gives metaphysical bite to the claim. Wittgenstein takes such unthinkability to be an indication of what is possible (3.02); so his view seems to be that an internal property is one that an object could not exist without, i.e., it is an essential property of the object. In this sense of 'internal property', we might say that the kind-determining essences of substances, on the property exemplification account, are internal properties of them. However, Wittgenstein extends this account to relations, and says, of two shades of blue, related as brighter to darker that 'It is unthinkable that *these* two objects should not stand in this relation' (Wittgenstein 1961, 4.123). It is unthinkable because neither could exist without standing in this relation.

Wittgenstein's doctrine of internal relations needs careful handling. On the basis of what he says, it might be thought that the doctrine requires that all of the properties that a particular thing has are essential to them; but it is not compulsory to read Wittgenstein in this way. His claim that 'it is unthinkable that *these* two objects should fail to stand in this relation' permits another, weaker, reading. According to it, internal relations hold between universals and things, *given* their determinate properties, irrespective of whether these properties are accidental or essential to them.

The doctrine of internal relations seems to be what the Platonist needs to make sense of the relation between instances of universals and the universals of which they are instances. The red bird is contingently red, but, given that it is red, it is not possible for it not to stand in a relation to redness. Indeed, its being red just is its being an instance of redness, and its being an instance just is its being an exemplification of redness. The relation of exemplification is internal because it relates the red bird to its properties, rather than to some other substance from which it is independent. Here we have a metaphysical doctrine that seems capable of being used to explain how it is that distinct particulars can be qualitatively the same without generating a relational regress. It also has an epistemological pay-off, which can help to explain the ability to think and speak correctly in general terms.

Consider once again the red bird, and the universal, redness. The suggestion on behalf of the Platonist is that the red bird is internally related to the universal, redness, in the sense that it is not possible that *these* two objects should exist without standing in that relation. Why is it not possible? It's not possible because this bird's being red just is its standing in an internal relation to redness. The two 'terms' of this relation are not terms that are independent of one another, in the sense that each could exist without the other. Nor is the relation dyadic, although it is true that there are two things, the red bird and the universal, redness. It is not dyadic because the red bird is not red in virtue of being composed of a red trope. It is red in virtue of being (i.e., being identical with) an instance of redness. Although redness could exist without this instance, this instance (this red bird) could not exist without being an instance of redness. Their being related to one another partly consists in their being the terms that they are, one, a red bird, the other, redness.

One consequence of viewing things in this way is that it is a mistake to suppose that the instance of redness is (a) an instance, and (b) of redness, where these are contingently related. Since its being this instance just is its being this instance *of* redness, awareness or grasp of this instance just is awareness or grasp of it *as* an instance of redness. To see an instance of redness is to see it *as* an instance of redness. And this can help to explain the ability to think and speak correctly in general terms. This just is to have the ability to be aware of, or grasp, instances of universals as instances of those universals and bring them under general concepts and terms. The explanation here is not reductive; we do not first do one thing and then do the other. The reason why is that one can only be aware of an instance *as* an instance of redness (or of squareness, roundness, triangularity, and so on) if one is capable of recognizing another instance as of the same property – as the same again – and this means that the notion of 'grasping as' is intensional. In order to be aware of or grasp an instance as an instance of redness, one must have the concept of redness.

So awareness of an instance as an instance of a universal requires having the concept of that universal. It cannot be, then, that we are able to apply the concept, *red* (or *redness*), to red things by first being aware of instances of redness in those things. Our ability to apply that concept to red things consists in our being aware of instances of redness in those things as instances of redness. This may not be a reductive explanation, but it is an explanation nonetheless.

Notes

1 I owe this way of putting things to Larry Lombard.
2 As Oliver puts it:

> To suppose that there is no distinction between the apparent and real commitments of a sentence is to suppose that we all have the correct semantic theory for the whole corpus of English sentences. But this is absurd. The apparent semantic theory of the ordinary man is a hazy and ill thought out beast which needs to be developed and modified by the philosopher. And philosophers disagree among themselves about the apparent commitments of sentences, because these commitments are precisely determined by applying a semantic theory, a theory whose merits will inevitably be debatable. Do not say that the apparent semantic theory is simply the claim that a sentence is committed to whatever it explicitly mentions. That would be to make the mistake of thinking that the notion of 'explicit mention' is theory-neutral. But it is not. How would you argue against someone who said that 'the average man has 2.4 children' is apparently committed to the average man on the grounds that it explicitly mentions him? (Oliver 1996, p. 59)

3 These are items that meet what Evans (1982) calls The Generality Constraint, which it is plausible to think is a condition on an item's being a concept at all. Peacocke expresses the principle thus:

> If a thinker can entertain the thought Fa and also possess the singular mode of presentation b, which refers to something in the range of objects of which the concept F is true or false, then the thinker has the conceptual capacity for propositional attitudes containing the content Fb. (Peacocke 1992, p. 1)

If there are any general principles governing concepts, this seems to be one of them. For it is true, not only of general concepts involved in simple cases of first-order, monadic predication, but also of singular concepts. Thus, it is true not only that, if a thinker is capable of entertaining thoughts of the form Fa and possesses the singular concept b, then she is capable of entertaining thoughts of the form Fb; but also that, if a thinker is capable of entertaining thoughts of the form Fa and possesses the concept G, then she is capable of entertaining thoughts of the form Ga.

4   Some Realists maintain that universals and abstract objects like numbers are *indispensable* to science (see, for example, Putnam (1969, 1971), Quine (1964e), and Sober (1981, 1993)). It may be that the explanatory motivation that is grounded in the phenomenon of generality in thought and language is a version of an indispensability argument for Realism.

5   They do often make a concession to classes or sets, however, in their attempt to explain the phenomenon of generality in thought and language. See, for example, Quine (1960, 1964a). These are deemed acceptable because, although they are abstract objects, they are particulars rather than universals.

6   Whether universals are multiply located (wherever the things that exemplify them are, as (1) suggests), or are non-spatial (as (2) suggests) depends on whether one endorses the Aristotelian conception or the Platonic conception. We discuss the differences between these conceptions in chapter 6, pp. 236–9.

7   This way of expressing the difference between Realists and Nominalists (and Tropists) is due to Loux (1978). Strictly speaking, Nominalists may recognize the existence of properties, where these are viewed as classes or sets of concrete particulars. However, these classes will themselves typically be viewed as constructions on individual concrete particular things, not as irreducible kinds of things that exist in the world alongside particular concrete things. So, for example, Campbell says:

> Some writers use the label 'Nominalist' for every denial of universals, but this blurs a crucial distinction: ordinary Nominalisms, in denying universals, deny the existence of properties, except perhaps as shadows of predicates of classifications. They recognise only concrete particulars and sets. (Campbell 1990, p. 27)

A recent exception to this is Rodriguez-Pereyra (2002), whose Resemblance Nominalism requires resemblances between both actual and possible particulars.

8   Actually, there is a third way: the two cups are both blue. This is the way that a particular kind of Nominalist would prefer to describe the situation, what we later describe as a Predicate Nominalist (see note 9).

9   We might call this kind of Nominalist a *moderate* Nominalist because such a person is prepared to say that there is an objective basis in reality for the application of the same predicate, such as 'is red', to a number of particular things, namely, particular resemblance relations that hold between them. This contrasts with the more extreme view, which Armstrong (1978a) calls 'Predicate Nominalism', that things that are called by the same name have nothing more in common than that they are called by the same name.

10   For a useful recent survey of arguments for and against Nominalism, see Szabó (2003).

11   One way in which Nominalists have attempted to defend some version of the position is by appeal to the notion of a paraphrase. According to this

defence, sentences whose truth appears to require commitment to universals can be paraphrased, or replaced by near synonyms of them, in such a way as to avoid any such commitment. In what follows we steer clear of the issue of paraphrase altogether, principally because it is very unclear what can be established by its means (Alston 1958, Szabó 2003). Even if some unambiguous conditions for sentence replacement by paraphrase could be given, there is the question of what the truth of either the paraphrased sentence or the paraphrase requires commitment to. As Szabó (citing Alston 1958) puts the point,

> even if we grant that (2) [It will most likely snow tomorrow] is an adequate semantic paraphrase of (1) [There is a good chance that it will snow tomorrow] in any context, and that consequently the intuitions that (1) entails the existence of a chance and that (2) does not both cannot be correct, we still don't know which one to jettison. Why interpret the alleged equivalence in a deflationary rather than an inflationary way; why assume that neither of them entails the existence of changes, rather than that both of them do? (Szabo 2003, pp. 22–3)

Szabó suggests that it might appear more promising to invoke a pragmatic notion of paraphrase instead of a semantic one, but then the problem for Nominalists is to come up with a story of just when paraphrase is applicable and when it is not, and this is none too easy a thing to do. For discussion of various Nominalist attempts at semantic paraphrase, see Loux (2002).

12 Armstrong (1978a) distinguishes six versions of Nominalism: Predicate Nominalism, Concept Nominalism, Class Nominalism, Mereological Nominalism, Resemblance Nominalism, and Ostrich Nominalism. According to Predicate Nominalism, for any sentence of the form, 'a is F', 'a is F' is true if and only if members of our linguistic community apply the predicate 'F' to. According to Resemblance Nominalism for any sentence of the form 'a is F', 'a is F' is true if and only if a resembles other F things, or some paradigm of an F thing. According to Ostrich Nominalism, for any sentence of the form 'a is F', 'a is F' is true if and only if a is F. Ostrich Nominalism takes sentences of the form 'a is F' to be incapable of reductive analysis. Ostrich Nominalists are 'those philosophers who refuse to countenance universals but who at the same time see no need for any reductive analyses of the sort just outlined. There are no universals but the proposition that a is F is perfectly all right as it is' (1978a, p. 16) Predicate Nominalism and Ostrich Nominalism, respectively, are what are here taken to be the two extreme Nominalist positions, whereas Resemblance Nominalism covers both of the moderate Nominalisms that we will discuss.

13 As noted, Armstrong (1978a) calls this Predicate Nominalism. Which formulation one uses here ('only our willingness to call them all "red"' vs. 'only the fact that the word "red" applies to them') depends on how much one wants to emphasize the idea that Predicate Nominalism purchases ontological economy at the price of the objectivity of our judgements.

14 Note here that the second part of this claim, 'and in this case here is where it ends' is not what the second, less extreme of the two extreme Nominalist positions discussed here maintains, although it does maintain the first part. This second position is what Armstrong calls 'Ostrich Nominalism' and he associates it, as we do, with the kind of position Quine (1960, 1964a, 1964b) holds.

15 This is the position Armstrong (1978a) dubs 'Ostrich Nominalism'. One might take the following to be an expression of this view:

> One may admit that there are red houses, roses, and sunsets, but deny, except as a popular and misleading manner of speaking, that they have anything in common. The words 'houses', 'roses', and sunsets' are true of sundry individual entities which are houses and roses and sunsets, and the word 'red' or 'red object' is true of each of sundry individual entities which are red houses, red roses, red sunsets; but there is not, in addition, any entity whatever, individual or otherwise, which is named by the word 'redness', nor, for that matter, by the word 'household', 'rosehood', 'sunsethood'. (Quine 1964a, p. 10)

But note that Quine calls himself a Platonist because he is committed to classes or sets as well as to concrete particulars, and does not construe classes as mere aggregates of particulars. This difference between his position and that of the extreme Nominalist under discussion may put him more squarely in the camp Armstrong classifies as 'Class Nominalism'. We will not discuss that view here.

16 This term is used by a number of philosophers: see, for example, Campbell (1990) and Armstrong (1989). Though many philosophers think of Trope Nominalism as a version of Nominalism, it is not. All real forms of Nominalism should hold that the only objects relevant to the explanation of generality are concrete particulars, words (i.e, word tokens, not types), and perhaps sets. Tropes, however, are abstract particulars. We have discussed them in chapter 3 when considering theories of material substances, and will discuss them further below, this time as a way of accounting for what it is for a concrete particular to have a property, i.e., as a theory of properties, rather than as a theory of concrete particulars. Of course, a trope account of the relation between particulars and their properties has ramifications for an account of the nature of concrete particulars, and many who endorse the former endorse a trope account of the latter.

17 Thus, Rodriguez-Pereyra (2003, p. 229) says, 'the truthmakers of "a and b resemble each other" are just a and b. The truthmakers of a sentence are those entities in virtue of which the sentence is true.' But note that his particulars are not ordinary concrete particulars, like tomatoes and birds. They are temporal slices of actual particulars and their possible-world counterparts (conceived as Lewis (1986) conceives of them), as well as ordered pairs, facts, and classes of such.

18 See Goodman (1951). Goodman's objections are to Carnap's (1928) attempt to construct an account of properties using the minimal resources of

phenomenalistic particulars, momentary experiences. Carnap's strategy is to attempt to construct quality classes on the basis of resemblance relations between their members, these phenomenalistic particulars. The companionship difficulty is articulated as follows. Suppose that colour classes are classes that satisfy the following two requirements: (a) of the members of any such class, each pair is 'colour akin', i.e., each pair is on the list of pairs for which that relation holds; and (b) every such class is the greatest possible class satisfying (a), i.e., no thing outside the class may be colour akin to all things in the class. And suppose that there are six items on the basis of which to construct the colour classes: br, b, bg, g, r and bgr. The problem is to determine, solely on the basis of (a) and (b), colour classes. {b, bg, bgr} works because each element paired with another element in the class appears on the list, and nothing not in the class is paired in the list with every member of the class. Intuitively, it is the colour class for b. The classes, {br, r, bgr}, and {bg, g, bgr}, also work and satisfy both (a) and (b). Intuitively, these are the colour classes for r and g, respectively. But suppose now that the items on the basis of which to construct the colour classes are not the above six, but rather, the following five: br, b, bg, b and bgr. Here, on the basis of (a) and (b) we can construct the class {br, b, bg, bgr}, as seems right, since, intuitively, this is the colour class for b. We should also be able to get the class {br, bgr}, since it is the colour class for r. But we can't, because b is paired in the table with both br and also bgr, and so, according to the requirement (b), b cannot be excluded from the class. The same is true of bg, so we end up once again with the class for b {br, b, bg, bgr}. The problem here is that if qualities exist only as companions with others, and never on their own, quality classes for them cannot be constructed in accordance with requirements (a) and (b).

The problem of imperfect community is different, since it arises in situations in which quality classes can be constructed whose members do not all resemble one another in a single way. Goodman articulates it as follows. Suppose we have the items br, b, bg, g, r, and bgr. Then we can construct a class {br, b, bg, bgr} that meets the requirements (a) and (b) because each element paired with each other element in the class appears on the list (a) and nothing not in the class is paired in the list with every member of the class. Intuitively, this is the quality class for b. The classes, {br, r, bgr}, and {bg, b, bgr}, also work, and satisfy both (a) and (b), which also seems right, since, intuitively, these are the quality classes for r and g, respectively. But suppose instead that there are the following items: bg, rg, br, r, b, and g. In this situation, the companionship difficulty does not arise, because no colour exists only as a companion with others. But a colour class can be constructed in accordance with (a) and (b) whose members have nothing in common: the class {bg, rg, br}. Both of these problems dog not only Resemblance Nominalism, but also Trope Nominalism, as we shall see.

19 See for example H. H. Price (1953). Note that here is where the strategy parts company with other versions of Resemblance Nominalism, and invites

Russell's objection, viz. that once one posits resemblance one must, in order to avoid an infinite regress of particular resemblances, posit at least one universal, resemblance (Russell 1911–12, 1912, chapter 6). There are many problems with this version of Nominalism, but Russell's objection is itself problematic, as we've noted in the text. Most obviously, there is the response that there is nothing wrong with an infinite regress, so long as that infinity need not be grasped by those who think and speak in general terms (which it need not).

20 Not, at least, without making use of rich ideological and ontological resources of the kind appealed to by Rodriguez-Pereyra (2002); see note 17. Given these resources, Resemblance Nominalists can avoid the objection voiced here by saying, as Rodriguez-Pereyra does, both that 'a particular that is F and G is F in virtue of resembling all the F particulars and G by virtue of resembling all the G particulars' (2002, p. 96) and that 'what makes a particular F is that it resembles all *possible* particulars' (2002, p. 99). But many Nominalists may well think that the ontological and ideological commitments of this approach are not worth the price; and many Realists will consider these commitments to be a disadvantage rather than a virtue of the position. Possible worlds and possible particulars are certainly no less abstract and are (at least) as mysterious as universals. Further, if, using Ockham's razor, we count both the numbers and kinds of entities required by the approach, Resemblance Nominalism does not come out as more economical than Realism.

21 There is also the point, made by Van Cleve (1994), that Russell's charge assumes that if two particulars resemble each other there is some entity, a *resemblance*, which relates them. But, as noted in the text, strictly speaking, Resemblance Nominalism requires only that particular things resemble one another, not that there are resemblances. Of course, we've seen that this version is unsatisfactory.

22 This is the kind of response that many think is to be found in some form in Wittgenstein (1968).

23 Further, as Heil (2003) points out, it is possible to hold one part of the classic account without holding the other. He himself endorses a trope account of the explanation of generality (or of what it is for a particular to have a property), but rejects a trope account of the nature of particulars.

24 In fact, if what we have argued in chapter 5 is correct, then at least one of these 'laws' is false, viz. the one that says 'Two things cannot occur in the same place at the same time', since two events can occur in the same place at the same time.

25 Plato considers this possibility in *Parmenides* 131 (in Taylor (ed.) 1934).

26 Note that it is not being assumed here that Plato himself held a Platonic conception of universals. It is not entirely clear that Plato held that there are universals, since understanding Aristotle's criticisms (that the world of forms reduplicates the problems that Plato had with the world of physical objects, and the third man argument, which rests on the assumption that

each Form is a perfect exemplar of itself – that, e.g., the Form of Man is a man, that Justice is perfectly just) might require reading Plato as a Nominalist. Thanks here to Larry Lombard.

27 Oliver (1996) speaks of the Platonic view as the view that universals have instances that are in particulars and bear some kind of relation to their instances. But this cannot be right, since on the Realist understanding of universals, an instance of a universal just is the thing that has it, i.e., a particular concrete object. Thus, for example, an instance of the property, red, just is the red bird. Oliver's talk encourages the view that instances of universals are tropes, but this is not the Realist understanding of 'instance'. On the Platonic view, there are no 'property instances' that mediate between particular and form, or universal.

28 One could (as D. C. Williams (1953) did) combine Platonic Realism about universals with trope theory. However, the usual way of developing the Platonic view does not appeal to trope theory. Talk of instances of universals being related in some way (talk that Oliver, for example, engages in), such as instantiation, to universals, encourages a trope understanding of particulars, where these stand in some kind of relation (e.g., compresence – see chapter 3) to such instances, now understood as tropes, which in turn instantiate universals. We follow the standard Realist view, in which particulars, and not tropes, instantiate universals.

29 This is sometimes known as Bradley's regress concerning the construal of exemplification as a real relation (Bradley 1969). The claim is that there is a need to posit another relation to relate, say, the bird, redness, and the relation of exemplification.

30 See Plato (1934). Note that the latter (imitation) and possibly the former (participation) are capable of a Nominalistic construal of Plato's views. See note 26.

31 Apparently non-extensional in that the terms in such contexts do not appear to be functioning in the normal referential way. See chapter 2 for a discussion of extensionality.

Suggested Further Reading

Armstrong, D. (1978a): *Universals and Scientific Realism, Vol. I Nominalism and Realism*. Cambridge: Cambridge University Press.

Armstrong, D. (1978b): *Universals and Scientific Realism, Vol. II A Theory of Universals*. Cambridge: Cambridge University Press.

Armstrong, D. (1989): *Universals: An Opinionated Introduction*. Boulder: Westview Press.

Hoffman, J. and Rosenkrantz, G. (2003): *Platonistic Theories of Universals*. In Loux and Zimmerman (eds) 2003, pp. 46–74.

Laurence, S. and Macdonald, C. (eds) (1998): *Contemporary Readings in the Foundations of Metaphysics*. Oxford: Blackwell.

Lewis, D. (1983b): 'New Work for a Theory of Universals'. In *Australasian Journal of Philosophy* 61, 343–77. Reprinted in Laurence and Macdonald (eds) 1998, pp. 163–97.

Loux, M. (ed.) (1970): *Universals and Particulars*. New York: Doubleday and Company, Inc.

Loux, M. (1978): *Substance and Attribute*. Dordrecht: D. Reidel Publishing Company. Part I, chapters 1–5.

Loux, M. (2002): *Metaphysics: A Contemporary Introduction*. 2nd edn. London: Routledge, chapters 1 and 2.

Marsh, R. (ed.) (1956): *Logic and Knowledge*. London: Macmillan.

Oliver, A. (1996): 'The Metaphysics of Properties'. In *Mind* 105, 1–80.

Plato (1934): *Parmenides*. In *Plato*. Transl. A. E. Taylor. Oxford: Clarendon Press.

Putnam, H. (1969): 'On Properties'. In Rescher (ed.) 1969, pp. 235–54. Reprinted in Putnam 1972, pp. 305–22.

Quine, W. V. O. (1964a): 'On What There Is'. In Quine 1964f, pp. 1–19.

Quine, W. V. O. (1964f): *From a Logical Point of View*. 2nd edn. Cambridge, Mass.: Harvard University Press.

Rescher, N. (ed.) (1969): *Essays in Honor of Carl G. Hempel*. Dordrecht: D. Reidel.

Rodriguez-Pereyra, G. (2002): *Resemblance Nominalism – A Solution to the Problem of Universals*. Oxford: Clarendon Press.

Russell, B. (1911–12): 'On the Relations of Universals and Particulars'. In *Proceedings of the Aristotelian Society* 12, 1–24. Reprinted in Marsh (ed.) 1956, pp. 105–24.

Sober, E. (1981): 'Evolutionary Theory and the Ontological Status of Properties'. In *Philosophical Studies* 40, 147–76.

Swoyer, C. (1999): 'How Ontology Might be Possible: Explanation and Inference in Metaphysics'. In P. A. French and H. K. Wettstein (eds), *Midwest Studies in Philosophy* 23, 100–31.

Szabó, Z. (2003): 'Nominalism'. In Loux and Zimmerman (eds) 2003, pp. 11–45.

Van Cleve, J. (1994): 'Predication without Universals? A Fling with Ostrich Nominalism'. In *Philosophy and Phenomenological Research* 54, 577–90.

Bibliography

Alston, W. (1958): 'Ontological Commitments'. In *Philosophical Studies* 9, 8–17. Reprinted in Laurence and Macdonald (eds) 1998, pp. 46–54.

Armstrong, D. (1978a): *Universals and Scientific Realism, Vol. I Nominalism and Realism*. Cambridge: Cambridge University Press.

Armstrong, D. (1978b): *Universals and Scientific Realism, Vol. II A Theory of Universals*. Cambridge: Cambridge University Press.

Armstrong, D. (1980): 'Identity Through Time'. In van Inwagen (ed.) 1980, pp. 67–78.

Armstrong, D. (1989): *Universals: An Opinionated Introduction*. Boulder: Westview Press.

Aune, B. (1986): *Metaphysics: The Elements*. Oxford: Blackwell.

Ayer, A. J. (1953): 'The Identity of Indiscernibles'. In *Proceedings of the XI International Congress of Philosophy*, vol. III. Amsterdam: North Holland Publishing Company. Reprinted in Ayer 1954.

Ayer, A. J. (1954): *Philosophical Essays*. London: Macmillan.

Ayer, A. J. (1990): *Language, Truth, and Logic*. London: Penguin. First published by Victor Gollancz (1936).

Bacon, J. (1995): *Universals and Property Instances: The Alphabet of Being*. Oxford: Blackwell.

Bacon, J. (2002): 'Tropes'. In Zalta, E. (ed.), *The Stanford Encyclopedia of Philosophy* (Fall 2002 edn). URL = <http://plato.stanford.edu/archives/fall2002/entries/tropes/>.

Baker, L. (2000): *Persons and Bodies: A Constitution View*. Cambridge: Cambridge University Press.

Baker, L. (2001a): 'Précis'. Symposium on *Persons and Bodies. A Field Guide to Philosophy of Mind* (Spring 2001). URL = <http://www.uniroma3.it/kant/field/bakersymp_precis.htm>

Baker, L. (2001b): 'Reply to Olson'. Symposium on *Persons and Bodies. A Field Guide to Philosophy of Mind* (Spring 2001) URL = http://www.uniroma3.it/kant/field/bakersymp_replytoolson.htm

Barnes, J. (ed.) (1984): *The Complete Works of Aristotle*. Princeton, NJ: Princeton University Press.

Barresi, J. and Martin, R. (eds) (2003): *Personal Identity*. Malden, Mass.: Blackwell.

Beck, L. W. (transl.) (1950): *Prolegomena to Any Future Metaphysics*. Indianapolis: Bobbs-Merrill.

Benardete, J. (1989): *Metaphysics: The Logical Approach*. Oxford: Oxford University Press.

Bennett, J. (1988): *Events and Their Names*. Cambridge: Cambridge University Press.

Bennett, J. (1996): 'What Events Are'. In Casati and Varzi (eds) 1996, pp. 137–51.

Bennett, J. (2002): 'What Events Are' (expanded version). In Gale (ed.) 2002, pp. 43–65.

Bergmann, G. (1964): *Logic and Reality*. Madison: University of Wisconsin Press.

Bergmann, G. (1967): *Realism: A Critique of Brentano and Meinong*. Madison: University of Wisconsin Press.

Berkeley, G. (1996): *Principles of Human Knowledge; and Three Dialogues*. Ed. by H. Robinson. New York: Oxford University Press.

Black, M. (1952): 'The Identity of Indiscernibles'. In *Mind* 61, 153–64. Reprinted in Loux (ed.) 1970, pp. 250–62.

Bradley, F. H. (1969): *Appearance and Reality*. 2nd edn. Oxford: Oxford University Press.

Brand, M. (1976): 'Particulars, Events, and Actions'. In Brand and Walton (eds) 1976, pp. 133–57.

Brand, M. (1977): 'Identity Conditions for Events'. In *American Philosophical Quarterly* 14, 329–37. Reprinted in Casati and Varzi (eds) 1996, pp. 363–71.

Brand, M. and Walton, D. (eds) (1976): *Action Theory*. Dordrecht: D. Reidel.

Brown, S. (ed.) (1974): *Philosophy of Psychology*. London: Macmillan.

Burge, T. (1986): 'Intellectual Norms and the Foundations of Mind'. In *Journal of Philosophy* 83, 697–720.

Burtt, E. A. (1963): 'Descriptive Metaphysics'. In *Mind* 72, 18–39.

Campbell, K. (1976): *Metaphysics: An Introduction*. Encino, Calif.: Dickenson.

Campbell, K. (1990): *Abstract Particulars*. Oxford: Blackwell.

Carnap, R. (1928): *Der logische Aufbau der Welt*. Berlin: Benary. English transl. R. George (1967): *The Logical Structure of the World*. 2nd edn. London: Routledge & Kegan Paul.

Carnap, R. (1950): 'Empiricism, Semantics, and Ontology'. In *Revue Internationale de Philosophie* 4, 20–40. Revised and reprinted in Carnap 1956.

Carnap, R. (1956): *Meaning and Necessity*. 2nd edn. Chicago: University of Chicago Press.

Cartwright, R. (1971): 'Identity and Substitutivity'. In Munitz 1971, pp. 119–33.

Casati, R. and Varzi, A. (eds) (1996): *Events*. Aldershot: Dartmouth.

Casati, R. and Varzi, A. (2002): 'Events'. In Zalta, E. (ed.), *The Stanford Encyclopedia of Philosophy* (Fall 2002 edn). URL = <http://plato.stanford.edu/archives/fall2002/entries/events/>.

Castañeda, H. (1974): 'Thinking and the Structure of the World'. In *Philosophia* 4, 3–40.

Causey, R. (1977): *Unity of Science*. Dordrecht: D. Reidel.

Chisholm, R. (ed.) (1960): *Realism and the Background to Phenomenology*. Illinois: Free Press of Glencoe.

Clark, R. (1970): 'Concerning the Logic of Predicate Modifiers', In *Nous* 4, 311–35.

Cleland, C. (1991): 'On the Individuation of Events'. In *Synthese* 86, 229–54. Reprinted in Casati and Varzi (eds) 1996, pp. 373–400.

Cohen, S. M. (2003): 'Aristotle's Metaphysics'. In Zalta, E. (ed.), *The Stanford Encyclopedia of Philosophy* (Winter 2003 edn). URL = <http://plato.stanford.edu/archives/win2003/entries/aristotle-metaphysics/>.

Collingwood, R. G. (1940): *An Essay on Metaphysics*. Oxford: Oxford University Press.

Crisp, T. (2003): 'Presentism'. In van Inwagen and Zimmerman (eds) 2003, pp. 211–45.

Davidson, D. (1963): 'Actions, Reasons, and Causes'. In *Journal of Philosophy* 60, 685–700. Reprinted in Davidson 1984, pp. 3–20.

Davidson, D. (1965): 'Theories of Meaning and Learnable Languages'. In Bar-Hillel, Y. (ed.) 1965: *Proceedings of the 1964 International Congress for Logic, Methodology, and Philosophy of Science*. Amsterdam: North Holland Publishing Company. Reprinted in Davidson 1984b, pp. 3–15.

Davidson, D. (1966): 'The Logical Form of Action Sentences'. In Rescher (ed.) 1966, pp. 81–95. Reprinted in Davidson 1984, pp. 105–21.

Davidson, D. (1967): 'Causal Relations'. *Journal of Philosophy* 64, 691–703. Reprinted in Davidson 1984, pp. 149–62.

Davidson, D. (1969): 'The Individuation of Events'. In Rescher (ed.) 1969, pp. 216–34. Reprinted in Davidson 1984, pp. 163–80.

Davidson, D. (1970a): 'Mental Events'. In Foster and Swanson (eds) 1970, pp. 79–101. Reprinted (with Appendix 'Emeroses by Other Names'), in Davidson 1984, pp. 207–27.

Davidson, D. (1970b): 'Events as Particulars'. In *Nous* 4, 25–32. Reprinted in Davidson 1984, pp. 181–9.

Davidson, D. (1974): 'Psychology as Philosophy'. In Brown (ed.) 1974, pp. 41–52. Reprinted (with 'Comments and Replies') in Davidson 1984, pp. 229–44.

Davidson, D. (1984a): *Essays on Actions and Events*. Oxford: Clarendon Press.

Davidson, D. (1984b): *Inquiries into Truth and Interpretation*. Oxford: Clarendon Press.

Davidson, D. (1985): 'Reply to Quine on Events'. In LePore and McLaughlin (eds) 1985, pp. 172–6.

Descartes, R. (1984): *Meditations on First Philosophy*. In *The Philosophical Works of Descartes*. Transl. J. Cottingham, R. Stoothoff, and D. Murdoch. Cambridge: Cambridge University Press.

Edwards, P. (ed.) 1967: *Encyclopedia of Philosophy*. New York: Macmillan Publishing Company.

Ehring, D. (1997): *Causation and Persistence: A Theory of Causation*. New York: Oxford University Press.

Elder, C. (2004): *Real Natures and Familiar Objects*. Cambridge, Mass.: MIT Press.

Evans, G. (1982): *Varieties of Reference*. Oxford: Clarendon Press.

Evans, G. and McDowell, J. (eds) (1976): *Truth and Meaning: Essays in Semantics*. Oxford: Clarendon Press.

Field, H. (1980): *Science Without Numbers*. Princeton: Princeton University Press.

Forrest, P. (2002): 'The Identity of Indiscernibles'. In Zalta, E. (ed.), *The Stanford Encyclopedia of Philosophy* (Summer 2002 edn), URL = http://plato.stanford.edu/archives/sum2002/entries/identity-indiscernible/.)

Foster, J. (1991): *The Immaterial Self: A Defense of the Cartesian Dualist Conception of the Mind*. London: Routledge.

Foster, L. and Swanson, J. W. (eds) (1970): *Experience and Theory*. Amherst: University of Massachusetts Press.

Frege, G. (1892): 'On Sense and Reference'. In *Zeitschrift fur Philosophie und philosophische Kritik* 100, pp. 25–50. Reprinted in Geach and Black (eds) 1970, pp. 56–78.

Gale, R. (ed.) (2002): *The Blackwell Guide to Metaphysics*. Oxford: Blackwell.

Garrett, B. (1998): *Personal Identity and Self-Consciousness*. London: Routledge.

Gazzinaga, M. S., Bogen, J. E., and Sperry, R. W. (1962): 'Some Functional Effects of Sectioning the Cerebral Commisures in Man'. In *Proceedings of the National Academy of Sciences* 48, pt. 2, p. 1765.

Geach, P. (1965): 'Some Problems about Time'. In *Proceedings of the British Academy* 51, 321–36. Oxford: Oxford University Press. Reprinted in Geach 1972, pp. 302–17.

Geach, P. (1972): *Logic Matters*. Oxford: Blackwell.

Geach, P. and Black, M. (eds) (1970): *Translations From the Writings of Gottlob Frege*. Oxford: Blackwell.

Gendler. T. (2000): *Thought Experiment: On the Power and Limits of Imaginary Cases*. New York: Garland Press.

Gill, C. (ed.) (1990): *The Person and the Human Mind*. Oxford: Clarendon Press.

Goldman, A. (1970): *A Theory of Human Action*. Englewood Cliffs, NJ: Prentice-Hall, Inc.

Goodman, N. (1951): *The Structure of Appearance*. Cambridge, Mass.: Harvard University Press.

Goodman, N. (1965): *Fact, Fiction, and Forecast*. 2nd edn. New York: Bobbs-Merrill Co.

Grice, H. P. (1941): 'Personal Identity'. In *Mind* 50, 330–50. Reprinted in Perry 1975, pp. 73–95.

Grier, M. (2002): 'Kant's Critique of Metaphysics'. In Zalta, E. (ed.), *The Stanford Encyclopedia of Philosophy* (Spring 2004 edn). URL = <http://plato.stanford.edu/archives/spr2004/entries/kant-metaphysics/>.

Guyer, P. (ed.) (1992): *The Cambridge Companion to Kant*. Cambridge: Cambridge University Press.

Guyer, P. and Wood, A. (transl. and eds) (1998): *The Cambridge Edition of the Works of Immanuel Kant: The Critique of Pure Reason*. Cambridge: Cambridge University Press.

Haack, S. (1976): 'Some Preliminaries to Ontology'. In *Journal of Philosophical Logic 5*, 457–74.

Haack, S. (1978): *The Philosophy of Logics*. Cambridge: Cambridge University Press.

Haack, S. (1979): 'Descriptive and Revisionary Metaphysics'. In *Philosophical Studies 35*, 361–71. Reprinted in Laurence and Macdonald (eds) 1998, pp. 22–31.

Haslinger, S. (2003): 'Persistence Through Time'. In van Inwagen and Zimmerman (eds) 2003, pp. 315–54.

Heil, J. (1992): *The Nature of True Minds*. Cambridge: Cambridge University Press.

Heil, J. (2003): *From an Ontological Point of View*. Oxford: Clarendon Press.

Heller, M. (1990): *The Ontology of Physical Objects: Four Dimensional Hunks of Matter*. Cambridge: Cambridge University Press.

Hoffman, J. and Rosenkrantz, G. (1994): *Substance Among Other Categories*. Cambridge, Mass.: Cambridge University Press.

Hoffman, J. and Rosenkrantz, G. (1996): *Substance: Its Nature and Existence*. London: Routledge.

Hoffman, J. and Rosenkrantz, G. (2003): *Platonistic Theories of Universals*. In Loux and Zimmerman (eds) 2003, pp. 46–74.

Honderich, T. (1981): 'Psychophysical Lawlike Connections and Their Problem', in *Inquiry* 24, 277–304.

Honderich, T. (1982): 'The Argument for Anomalous Monism', In *Analysis* 42, 59–64.

Honderich, T. (1988): *A Theory of Determinism*. Oxford: Oxford University Press.

Hookway, C. (1988): *Quine: Language, Experience and Reality*. Cambridge: Polity.

Hume, D. (1967): *A Treatise of Human Nature*. Ed. by L. Selby-Bigge. Oxford: Clarendon Press.

Hymers, M. (1996): 'Internal Relations and Analyticity: Wittgenstein and Quine'. In *Canadian Journal of Philosophy* 26, 591–612.

Irwin, T. (1988): *Aristotle's First Principles*. Oxford: Oxford University Press.

Ishiguro, H. (1998): *Leibniz's Philosophy of Logic and Language*. 2nd edn. Cambridge: Cambridge University Press.

Johnston, M. (1987): 'Human Beings'. In *Journal of Philosophy* 84, 59–83.

Kemeny, J. and Oppenheim, P. (1956): 'On Reduction'. In *Philosophical Studies* 7, 6–18.

Kim, J. (1969): 'Events and Their Descriptions: Some Considerations'. In Rescher (eds) 1969, pp. 198–215.

Kim, J. (1972): 'Phenomenal Properties, Psychophysical Laws, and the Identity Theory' In *Monist* 56, 177–92.

Kim, J. (1973): 'Causation, Nomic Subsumption, and the Concept of Event'. In *Journal of Philosophy* 70, 217–36.

Kim, J. (1976): 'Events as Property Exemplifications'. In Brand and Walton (eds) 1976, pp. 159–77.

Kim, J. (1985): 'Psychophysical Laws'. In LePore and McLaughlin (eds) 1985, pp. 369–86.

Kim, J. (1991): 'Events: Their Metaphysics and Semantics'. In *Philosophy and Phenomenological Research* 51, 641–6.

Kolak, D. and Martin, R. (eds) (1991): *Self and Identity: Contemporary Philosophical Issues*. New York: Macmillan.

Körner, S. (1974): *Categorial Frameworks*. Oxford: Blackwell.

Kripke, S. (1980): *Naming and Necessity*. Revised and enlarged edn. Oxford: Blackwell.

Laurence, S. and Macdonald, C. (eds) (1998): *Contemporary Readings in the Foundations of Metaphysics*. Oxford: Blackwell.

Leibniz, G. (1998): *Monadology*. In *Philosophical Texts*. Transl. R. Francks and R. S. Woolhouse. Oxford: Oxford University Press.

Lemmon, J. (1966): 'Comments on D. Davidson's "The Logical Form of Action Sentences"'. In Rescher (ed.) 1966, pp. 96–103.

LePore, E. and McLaughlin, B. (eds) (1985): *Actions and Events: Perspectives on the Philosophy of Donald Davidson*. Oxford: Blackwell.

Lewis, D. (1976): 'Survival and Identity'. In Rorty 1976, pp. 17–40. Reprinted with 'Postscripts to Identity' in Lewis 1983, pp. 55–77.

Lewis, D. (1983a): *Philosophical Papers*, vol. I. Oxford: Oxford University Press.

Lewis, D. (1983b): 'New Work for a Theory of Universals'. In *Australasian Journal of Philosophy* 61, 343–77. Reprinted in Laurence and Macdonald (eds) 1998, pp. 163–97.

Lewis, D. (1986): *On the Plurality of Worlds*. Oxford: Blackwell.

Lewis, D. (1988): 'Rearrangement of Particles: Reply to Lowe'. In *Analysis* 48, 65–72.

Locke, J. (1975): *An Essay Concerning Human Understanding*. Ed. by P. H. Nidditch. Oxford: Clarendon Press.

Lombard, L. (1979a): 'The Extensionality of Causal Contexts: Comments on Rosenberg and Martin'. In *Midwest Studies in Philosophy* 4, 409–15.

Lombard, L. (1979b): 'Events'. In *Canadian Journal of Philosophy* 9, 425–60. Reprinted in Casati and Varzi (eds) 1996, pp. 177–212.

Lombard, L. (1986): *Events: A Metaphysical Study*. London: Routledge & Kegan Paul.

Lombard, L. (1998): 'Ontologies of Events'. In Laurence and Macdonald (eds) 1998, pp. 277–94.

Loux, M. (ed.) (1970): *Universals and Particulars*. New York: Doubleday and Company, Inc.

Loux, M. (1978): *Substance and Attribute*. Dordrecht: D. Reidel Publishing Company.

Loux, M. (1998): 'Beyond Substrata and Bundles'. In Laurence and Macdonald (eds), pp. 233–47.

Loux, M. (2002): *Metaphysics: A Contemporary Introduction*. 2nd edn. London: Routledge.

Loux, M. and Zimmerman, D. (eds) (2003): *The Oxford Handbook to Metaphysics*. Oxford: Oxford University Press.

Lovibond, S. and Williams, S. (eds) (1996): *Identity, Truth and Value: Essays for David Wiggins*. Oxford: Blackwell.

Lowe, E. J. (1989a): *Kinds of Being: A Study of Individuation, Identity and the Logic of Sortal Terms*. Oxford: Blackwell.

Lowe, E. J. (1989b): 'What is a Criterion of Identity?'. In *Philosophical Quarterly* 39, 1–21.

Lowe, E. J. (1998): *The Possibility of Metaphysics*. Oxford: Oxford University Press.

Lowe, E. J. (2003): 'Individuation'. In van Inwagen and Zimmerman (eds) 2003.

Lycan, W. G. (1998): 'Possible Worlds and Possibilia'. In Laurence and Macdonald (eds) 1998, pp. 83–95.

Macdonald, C. (1989): *Mind–Body Identity Theories*. London: Routledge.

Macdonald, C. and Macdonald, G. (1995): 'How to be Psychologically Relevant'. In Macdonald and Macdonald (eds) 1995, pp. 60–77.

Macdonald, C. and Macdonald, G. (eds) (1995): *Philosophy of Psychology: Debates on Psychological Explanation*. Oxford: Blackwell.

Mackie, P. (1993): 'Ordinary Language and Metaphysical Commitment'. In *Analysis* 53, 243–51.

Marsh, R. (ed.) (1956): *Logic and Knowledge*. London: Macmillan.

Martin, C. B. (1980): 'Substance Substantiated'. In *Australasian Journal of Philosophy* 58, 3–10.

Martin, R. (1990): 'Identity, Transformation, and What Matters in Survival'. In *Logos*, 57–70. Reprinted in Kolak and Martin (eds) 1991, pp. 289–301.

Martin, R. (1998): *Self Concern*. Cambridge: Cambridge University Press.

McCulloch, G. (1999): 'From Quine to the Epistemological Real Distinction'. In *European Journal of Philosophy* 7, 30–46.

McDowell, J. (1997): 'Reductionism and the First Person'. In Dancy (ed.) 1997, pp. 230–50.

McKeon, R. (ed.) (1941): *The Basic Works of Aristotle*. New York: Random House.

Mei, Tsu-Lin (1961): 'Subject and Predicate: A Grammatical Preliminary'. In *Philosophical Review* 70, 153–75.

Meinong, A. (1904): 'The Theory of Objects'. In Chisholm (ed.) 1960, pp. 76–117.

Merricks, T. (1994): 'Endurance and Indiscernibility'. In *Journal of Philosophy* 91, 165–84

Merricks, T. (2001): *Objects and Persons*. Oxford: Oxford University Press.

Mertz, D. W. (1996): *Moderate Realism and its Logic*. New Haven: Yale University Press.

Munitz, M. (ed.) (1971): *Identity and Individuation*. New York: New York University Press.

Nagel, E. (1961): *The Structure of Science*. New York: Harcourt, Brace and World.

Noonan, H. (1989): *Personal Identity*. London: Routledge.

Nozick, R. (1981): *Philosophical Explanations*. Cambridge, Mass.: Harvard University Press.

Oliver, A. (1996): 'The Metaphysics of Properties'. In *Mind* 105, 1–80.

O'Leary-Hawthorne, J. (1995): 'The Bundle Theory of Substance and the Identity of Indiscernibles'. In *Analysis* 55, 191–6.

Olson, E. (1997): *The Human Animal*. Oxford: Oxford University Press.

Olson, E. (2002a): 'Personal Identity'. In Zalta, E. (ed.), The Stanford Encyclopedia of Philosophy *(Fall 2002 edn)*. URL = <http://plato.stanford.edu/archives/fall2002/entries/identity-personal/>

Olson, E. (2002b): 'An Argument for Animalism'. In Barresi and Martin (eds) 2002, pp. 318–34.

Parfit, D. (1971): 'Personal Identity'. In *Philosophical Review* 80, 3–27.

Parfit, D. (1984): *Reasons and Persons*. Oxford: Oxford University Press.

Peacocke, C. (1992): *A Study of Concepts*. Cambridge, Mass.: MIT Press.

Penelhum, T. (1970): *Survival and Disembodied Existence*. London: Routledge & Kegan Paul.

Perry, J. (ed.) (1975): *Personal Identity*. Berkeley, California: University of California Press.

Perry, J. (1976): 'The Importance of Being Identical'. In Rorty 1976, pp. 67–90.

Plantinga, A. (1970): 'World and Essence'. In *Philosophical Review* 79, 461–592. Reprinted in Loux (ed.) 1970.

Plato (1934): *Parmenides*. In *Plato*. Transl. A. E. Taylor. Oxford: Clarendon Press.

Pollock, J. (1989): *How to Build a Person*. Cambridge, Mass.: MIT Press.

Price, H. H. (1953): *Thinking and Experience*. London: Hutchinson's University Library.

Putnam, H. (1969): 'On Properties'. In Rescher (ed.) 1969, pp. 235–54. Reprinted in Putnam 1972, pp. 305–22.

Putnam, H. (1971): *Philosophy of Logic*. New York: Harper.

Putnam, H. (1972): *Mathematics, Matter and Method: Philosophical Papers*, vol. 1. New York: Cambridge University Press.

Putnam, H. (1981): *Reason, Truth, and History*. Cambridge: Cambridge University Press.

Putnam, H. (1987): *The Many Faces of Realism*. LaSalle, IL: Open Court.

Quine, W. V. O. (1960): *Word and Object*. Cambridge, Mass.: MIT Press

Quine, W. V. O. (1964a): 'On What There Is'. In Quine 1964f, pp. 1–19.

Quine, W. V. O. (1964b): 'Logic and the Reification of Universals'. In Quine 1964f, pp. 102–29.

Quine, W. V. O. (1964c): 'Reference and Modality'. In Quine 1964f, pp. 139–59.

Quine, W. V. O. (1964d): 'Identity, Ostension, and Hypostasis'. In Quine 1964f, pp. 65–79.

Quine, W. V. O. (1964e): 'Two Dogmas of Empiricism'. In Quine 1964f, pp. 20–6.

Quine, W. V. O. (1964f): *From a Logical Point of View*. 2nd edn. Cambridge, Mass.: Harvard University Press.

Quine, W. V. O. (1969a): 'Speaking of Objects'. In Quine 1969b, pp. 1–25.

Quine, W. V. O. (1969b): *Ontological Relativity and Other Essays*. New York: Columbia University Press.

Quine, W. V. O. (1970): 'On the Reasons for the Indeterminacy of Translation'. In *Journal of Philosophy* 67, 178–83.

Quine, W. V. O. (1981): *Theories and Things*. Cambridge, Mass.: Harvard University Press.

Quine, W. V. O. (1985): 'Events and Reification'. In LePore and McLaughlin (eds) 1985, pp. 162–71. Reprinted in Casati and Varzi (eds) 1996, pp. 107–16.

Quinton, A. (1962): 'The Soul'. In *Journal of Philosophy* 59, 393–409. Reprinted in Perry 1975, pp. 53–72.

Quinton, A. (1973): *The Nature of Things*. London: Routledge & Kegan Paul.

Rescher, N. (ed.) (1966): *The Logic of Decision and Action*. Pittsburgh: University of Pittsburgh Press.

Rescher, N. (ed.) (1969): *Essays in Honor of Carl G. Hempel*. Dordrecht: D. Reidel.

Rey, G. (1976): 'Survival'. In Rorty (ed.) 1976, pp. 41–66.

Robinson, H. (1989): 'A Dualist Account of Embodiment'. In Smythies and Beloff (eds) 1989, pp. 43–57.

Rodriguez-Pereyra, G. (2002): *Resemblance Nominalism – A Solution to the Problem of Universals*. Oxford: Clarendon Press.

Rodriguez-Pereyra, G. (2003): 'Resemblance Nominalism and Counterparts: Reply to Bird'. In *Analysis* 63, 229–37.

Rorty, A. (1976): *The Identities of Persons*. Berkeley, California: University of California Press.

Rovane, C. (1997): *The Bounds of Agency: An Essay in Revisionary Metaphysics*. Princeton: Princeton University Press.

Russell, B. (1905): 'On Denoting'. In *Mind*, 479–93. Reprinted in Marsh (ed.) 1956, pp. 39–56.

Russell, B. (1911–12): 'On the Relations of Universals and Particulars'. In *Proceedings of the Aristotelian Society* 12, 1–24. Reprinted in Marsh (ed.) 1956, pp. 105–24.

Russell, B. (1912): *The Problems of Philosophy*. London: Home University Library.

Russell, B. (1966a): 'The Monistic Theory of Truth'. In Russell 1966b, pp. 131–46.

Russell, B. (1966b): *Philosophical Essays*. Revised edn. London: Allen and Unwin.

Russell, B. and Whitehead, A. (1910): *Principia Mathematica*. Cambridge: Cambridge University Press.

Shoemaker, S. (1963): *Self-Knowledge and Self-Identity*. Ithaca, New York: Cornell University Press.

Shoemaker, S. (1970): 'Persons and their Pasts'. In *American Philosophical Quarterly* 7, 269–85. Reprinted in Shoemaker 2003, pp. 19–48.

Shoemaker, S. (1984): 'Personal Identity: A Materialist Account'. In Shoemaker and Swinburne 1984, chapter 2.

Shoemaker, S. (2003): *Identity, Cause, and Mind*. Expanded edn. Oxford: Clarendon Press.

Shoemaker, S. and Swinburne, R. (1984): *Personal Identity*. Oxford: Blackwell.

Sider, T. (1996): 'All the World's a Stage'. In *Australasian Journal of Philosophy* 74, 433–53.

Sider, T. (2001): *Four-Dimensionalism: An Ontology of Persistence and Time*. Oxford: Clarendon Press.

Simons, P. (1994): 'Particulars in Particular Clothing: Three Trope Theories of Substance'. In *Philosophy and Phenomenological Research* 54, 553–75. Reprinted in Laurence and Macdonald (eds) 1998.

Simons, P. (1997): 'Higher-Order Quantification and Ontological Commitment'. In *Dialectica* 51, 255–71.

Simons, P. (2003): 'Events'. In Loux and Zimmerman (eds) 2003, pp. 357–85.

Smythies, J. R., and Beloff, J. (eds) (1989): *The Case for Dualism*. Charlottesville: University Press of Virginia.

Snowdon, P. (1990): 'Persons, Animals, and Ourselves'. In Gill (ed.) 1990, pp. 83–107.

Snowdon, P. (1996): 'Persons and Personal Identity'. In Lovibond and Williams 1996, pp. 33–48.

Soames, S. (1999): 'The Indeterminacy of Translation and the Inscrutability of Reference'. In *Canadian Journal of Philosophy* 29, 321–70.

Sober, E. (1981): 'Evolutionary Theory and the Ontological Status of Properties'. In *Philosophical Studies* 40, 147–76.

Sober, E. (1993): 'Mathematics and Indispensability'. In *Philosophical Review* 102, 35–57.

Strawson, P. F. (1959): *Individuals: An Essay in Descriptive Metaphysics*. London: Methuen.

Strawson, P. F. (1974a): *Subject and Predicate in Logic and Grammar*. London: Methuen.

Strawson, P. F. (1974b): *Freedom and Resentment and Other Essays*. London: Methuen.

Strawson, P. F. (1976): 'On Understanding the Structure of One's Language'. In Strawson 1974b. Reprinted in Evans and McDowell (eds) 1976, pp. 189–98.

Swinburne, R. (1984): 'Personal Identity: The Dualist Theory'. In Shoemaker and Swinburne 1984, chapter 1.

Swinburne, R. (1997): *The Evolution of the Soul*. 2nd edn. Oxford: Oxford University Press.

Swoyer, C. (1983): 'Realism and Explanation'. In *Philosophical Inquiry* 5, 14–28.

Swoyer, C. (1999): 'How Ontology Might be Possible: Explanation and Inference in Metaphysics'. In P. A. French and H. K. Wettstein (eds), *Midwest Studies in Philosophy* 23, 100–31.

Szabó, Z. (2003): 'Nominalism'. In Loux and Zimmerman (eds) 2003, pp. 11–45.

Taylor, B. (1985): *Modes of Occurrence*. Oxford: Blackwell.

Thomson, J. J. (1971): 'Individuating Actions'. In *Journal of Philosophy* 68, 774–81.

Thomson, J. J. (1977): *Acts and Other Events*. Ithaca, New York: Cornell University Press.

Unger, P. (1990): *Identity, Consciousness, and Value*. Oxford: Oxford University Press.

Van Cleve, J. (1985): 'Three Versions of the Bundle Theory'. In *Philosophical Studies* 47, 95–107. Reprinted in Laurence and Macdonald (eds) 1998.

Van Cleve, J. (1994): 'Predication without Universals? A Fling with Ostrich Nominalism'. In *Philosophy and Phenomenological Research* 54, 577–90.

van Inwagen, P. (ed.) (1980): *Time and Cause*. Dordrecht: D. Reidel.

van Inwagen, P. (1990): *Material Beings*. Ithaca, New York: Cornell University Press.

van Inwagen, P. (1993): *Metaphysics*. Oxford: Oxford University Press.

van Inwagen, P. (1998a): 'The Nature of Metaphysics'. In Laurence and Macdonald (eds) 1998, pp. 12–21.

van Inwagen, P. (1998b): 'Introduction: What is Metaphysics?'. In van Inwagen and Zimmerman (eds) 1998, pp. 1–13.

van Inwagen, P. (2003): 'Existence, Ontological Commitment, and Fictional Entities'. In van Inwagen and Zimmerman (eds) 2003, pp. 131–57.

van Inwagen, P. and Zimmerman, D. (eds) (1998): *Metaphysics: The Big Questions*. Oxford: Blackwell.

van Inwagen, P. and Zimmerman, D. (eds) (2003): *The Oxford Handbook to Metaphysics*. Oxford: Oxford University Press.

Walsh, W. H. (1967): 'Metaphysics, Nature of'. In Edwards, P. (ed.) 1967, *Encyclopedia of Philosophy*. New York: Macmillan Publishing Company, pp. 300–7.

Whitehead, A. (1930): *The Concept of Nature*. Cambridge: Cambridge University Press.

Whorf, B. J. (1956): *Language, Thought & Reality*. Cambridge, Mass.: MIT Press.

Wiggins, D. (1967): *Identity and Spatio-Temporal Continuity*. Oxford: Blackwell.

Wiggins, D. (2001): *Sameness and Substance*. New edn. Cambridge: Cambridge University Press.

Wilkes, K. (1992): *Real People: Personal Identity Without Thought Experiments*. Oxford: Oxford University Press.

Williams, B. (1956–7): 'Personal Identity and Individuation'. In *Proceedings of the Aristotelian Society* 57. Reprinted in Williams 1973, pp. 1–18.

Williams, B. (1966): 'Imagination and the Self'. British Academy Annual Philosophical Lecture. Reprinted in Williams 1973, pp. 26–45.

Williams, B. (1970): 'The Self and the Future'. In *Philosophical Review* 79, 161–80. Reprinted in Williams 1973, pp. 46–63.

Williams, B. (1973): *Problems of the Self*. Cambridge: Cambridge University Press.

Williams, D. C. (1953): 'The Elements of Being'. In *Review of Metaphysics* 7, 3–18 and 171–92. Reprinted in Williams 1966, pp. 74–109.

Williams, D. C. (1966): *The Principles of Empirical Realism*. Springfield: Charles C. Thomas.

Wittgenstein, L. (1961): *Tractatus Logico-Philosophicus*. Transl. D. F. Pears and B. F. McGuinness. London: Routledge & Kegan Paul.

Wittgenstein, L. (1968): *Philosophical Investigations*. Transl. G. E. M. Anscombe. Oxford: Blackwell.

Wolterstorff, N. (1970): 'Bergmann's Constituent Ontology'. In *Nous* 4, 109–34.

Zimmerman, D. (1997): 'Distinct Indiscernibles and the Bundle Theory'. In *Mind* 106, 305–9.

Zimmerman, D. (2003): 'Material People'. In Loux and Zimmerman (eds) 2003, pp. 491–526.

Index

abstract/concrete distinction, 38, 62, 88–9, 94, 99–100, 115–16, 237–9
Alston, W., 254 n.11
a priori and a posteriori knowledge, distinction between, 5, 7–8, 11–13, 23, 33 n.11, 101
Aristotle, 4, 7, 8–14, 18, 23, 30 n.1, 31 n.5, 83, 89, 124 n.9, 233, 257 n.26
  conception of metaphysics, 7–14, 18
  conception of universals, 237–9
  doctrine of substance, 10, 124 n.9
  'Unmoved Mover', 10, 11
Armstrong, D., 123 n.2, 220, 229, 231, 233, 243–4, 246–7, 253 n.9, 254 nn.12–16
Aune, B., 25
Ayer, A. J., 63, 82–3

Bacon, J., 89, 126 nn.18–19, 233, 236
Baker, L., 136–8, 175 nn.3–4, 178 n.21
bare substratum theory, 64, 81, 95, 110–22, 181
  objections to, 113–15
Barnes, J., 89
Benardete, J., 25, 37
Bennett, J., 183, 209 n.14, 212 nn.24 and 26, 233

Bergmann, G., 64, 74 n.26, 125 n.10
Berkeley, G., 11, 24, 82, 125 n.10, 233
Black, M., 107, 128 n.34
Bogen, J. E., 176 n.12
bound variables, 43–5, 49–51, 58
Bradley, F. H., 246–8, 250, 258 n.29
brain in a vat, 147
branching, 142–5, 158–9, 162–8
  see also fission, reduplication argument
Brand, M., 189, 191–2
bundle theory, 63, 65, 81–115, 118–22, 142, 181
  objections to, 84–112
Burge, T., 127 nn.22–3
Burtt, E. A., 40

Campbell, K., 37, 74 n.14, 126 n.19, 220, 229, 233, 253 n.7, 255 n.16
Carnap, R., 15–17, 255 n.18
Cartwright, R., 63, 65, 75 n.28
Casati, R., 209 n.7
Castañeda, H., 126 n.19
causality, 12, 13
Causey, R., 123 n.5
Clark, R., 208 n.4
Cleland, C., 183, 209 n.14
Cohen, S. M., 9

Collingwood, R. G., 32 n.8
Crisp, T., 122 n.2
criteria
  for events, 69, 182–3, 186–94,
    198–200, 205–8; for persons,
    136–74; for substances, 79–81,
    117; of identity, 36, 63–70,
    79–80 *see also* identity
  of persistence for persons, *see*
    persons

Davidson, D., 140, 181, 183–7,
  191–2, 208 n.1, 209 nn.7, and
  10, 241
Descartes, R., 24, 83, 137, 175 n.4

Ehring, D., 183, 191
Elder, C., 80
empiricism, 3–14, 32 n.11, 84, 124
  n.10, 203
endurantism, 80
essences
  kind-determining, 68, 75 n.30,
    120, 131 n.51, 196, 198, 200–1,
    205, 211
Evans, G., 252 n.3
events, 28, 61, 62, 67, 69–70, 79,
  119, 181–208
  and dynamic and static properties,
    201–2, 204–6
  as changes, 182, 186, 193, 208,
    209 n.14
  as dated particulars, 181
  as structured particulars, 194–5
  atomic and non-atomic events,
    203–7
  criteria of event identity, 69,
    182–3, 186–94, 198–200,
    205–8; causal criterion, 186–93;
    de facto spatio-temporal
    coincidence, 186–91; necessary
    spatio-temporal coincidence,
    186–91; spatio-temporal
    criterion, 186–91
  event/state distinction, 199, 201,
    208

event/substance distinction, 59–60,
  66–7, 80, 104, 131 n.50, 186,
  189–91, 199–200, 208
existence condition, 194–5
generic events, 194, 198–9
identity condition for, 194
property exemplification account of
  (PEE), 119, 187, 191, 193–201,
  205, 208
trope theory of, 182–3
exemplifications/exemplifyings
  distinction, 200–1
extensionality, 46, 58, 65
  Axiom of, 65
extensional language, 46–50, 52, 56

Field, H., 33 n.18
fission, 142–5, 150, 154–8, 160,
  164, 166–71, 177 nn.9 and 13,
  192
  and events, 192
  see also branching, reduplication
  argument
Forrest, P., 128 n.34
Foster, L., 137
Frege, G., 241–2

Garrett, B., 140, 151, 156
Gazzinaga, M. S., 176 n.12
Geach, P., 22
Gendler, T., 174 n.2
Goldman, A., 209 n.7, 212 n.27
Goodman, N., 213 n.32, 225–6, 230,
  255 n.18

Haack, S., 15–17, 19–23, 30, 74
  n.13
Haslinger, S., 80
Heil, J., 89, 233, 257 nn.22–3
Hoffman, J., 128 n.37, 129 n.42,
  229
Honderich, T., 126 n.18, 233
Hookway, C., 31 n.4
Hume D., 11, 15, 32 n.11, 63, 82–4,
  229, 233
Hymers, M., 248

identity
  and the Principle of the Identity of
    Indiscernibles, 63–5, 81–4,
    106–11, 121–2
  and the Principle of the
    Indiscernibility of Identicals,
    63–5, 68, 81, 87, 91, 102–3,
    111, 121
  condition for events, 194
  conditions for objects, 59–67
  conditions for persons, 136–8,
    173
  conditions for substances, 117–18,
    122, 136, 190
  of objects, 36, 56–8, 65
  see also criteria of identity
individuation conditions, 59–63
  for objects, 59–66
infinite regress, 232–3, 239–48,
    251
Irwin, T., 7, 10
Ishiguro, H., 127 n.22

Johnston, M., 174 n.2

Kant, I., 4, 8, 11–15, 18, 23, 31
    n.5
  conception of metaphysics, 8,
    11–15, 18
Kemeny, J., 123 n.5
Kim, J., 119, 129 n.44, 131 n.48,
    140, 194–201, 209 n.14, 210
    nn.15–16 and nn.18–24
kinds, 6, 14, 59–60, 66–70, 120,
    181, 199
  substance kinds, 60, 68, 116–18,
    120–1, 181
  see also properties
Körner, S., 32 n.8
Kripke, S., 127 n.25

Leibniz, G. W., 24, 63, 82–3, 127
    n.22, 233, 246
Leibniz's Law, 31 n.2, 63–7, 69–70
Lemmon, J., 187
LePore, E., 209 n.7

Lewis, D., 123 n.2, 140, 163, 174
    n.2, 244–6, 255 n.17
Locke, J., 11, 64, 74 n.26, 83, 124
    n.8, 140, 174 nn.1–2, 175 n.7
Logical Positivists, 15, 32 n.11
Lombard, L., 25, 63, 68, 74 nn.20
    and 23, 120, 127 n.27, 129
    n.44, 130 nn.45 and 47, 131
    n.50, 176 n.11, 177 n.16, 191,
    194, 196, 201–4, 206, 208 n.2,
    209 n.14, 211 nn.20–2, 213
    nn.32–3, 252 n.1
Loux, M., 7, 25, 31 n.3, 32 n.8, 74
    n.19, 75 n.32, 103, 116, 123
    n.2, 124 nn.6 and 9, 125 nn.10
    and 13, 127 nn.28 and 30, 128
    nn.38 and 41–2, 129 n.44, 132
    n.52–3, 220–1, 253 n.7, 254
    n.11
Lowe, E. J., 33 n.15, 63, 73 n.11, 74
    nn.18–19, 80, 126 n.18
Lycan, W. G., 86

McCulloch, G., 31 n.4
Macdonald, C., 187, 193, 211 n.21
Macdonald, G., 211 n.21
McDowell, J., 176 n.7
Mackie, P., 37
McLaughlin, B., 209 n.7
Martin, C. B., 89
Martin, R., 157, 161
Mei, Tsu-Lin, 40
Meinong, A., 27, 33 n.17
Merricks, T., 123 n.2
Mertz, D. W., 233
metaphysics
  Aristotle's conception of, 7–14,
    18
  derivation of term, 30 n.1
  descriptive and revisionary
    metaphysics, distinction between,
    17–24, 30
  Kant's conception of, 8, 11–15,
    18
  Methodology of, 4–8
  nature of, 3–4, 7, 14–30

Nagel, E., 123 n.5
Nominalism, 224–38, 244–5
  Ostrich Nominalism, 254 n.12,
    255 n.14
  Predicate Nominalism, 225–7,
    233
  Resemblance Nominalism, 229–35;
    and the companionship difficulty,
    230–1, 234; and the problem of
    imperfect community, 230–1,
    234
  Trope Nominalism, 90, 127 n.26,
    229, 233–7; Meinongianism, 236
Nominalism/Realism debate, 123 n.4,
    224–5, 236–9, 244–5
  Nominalism–Platonism debate,
    244–5
Noonan, H., 140, 160, 163, 176
    n.7
Nozick, R., 151, 160

objects, 59–70
  identity conditions for, 59–67
Ockham's Razor, 225, 236, 257
    n.20
O'Leary-Hawthorne, J., 128 n.33
Oliver, A., 237–8, 240, 252 n.2, 258
    n.27
Olson, E., 136–7, 175 n.5
ontological commitment, 36–58
  criteria of, 25–7, 29, 36–56
  Quine's criterion, 42–5, 47–56, 79
  Strawson's criterion, 38–44, 53–6
  to events, 182–6
  to material substances, 79–81
  to persons, 135–8
ontology, 15, 63
Oppenheim, P., 123 n.5

Parfit, D., 140, 155–61, 163, 174
    n.2, 175 n.7
particulars, 38–40, 42, 60–2, 79,
    220–2
  abstract particulars, 38, 61–2
  concrete particulars, 38, 61–2,
    181

events as, 135
identification of, 39–40
particular/property distinction, 57,
    62
particular/universal distinction, 38,
    181, 238–9
persons as, 135–6
Peacocke, C., 252 n.3
Penelhum, T., 175 n.7
perdurantism, 80, 104
Perry, J., 140, 174 n.2
persistence through time
  of persons, 136–74
  of substances, 80–1, 102, 104–6,
    112–13, 121–2
persons, 135–74
  as substances, 135, 181
  existence condition for, 173
  identity condition for, 173
  persistence, criteria for, 136–74;
    Closest Continuer Theory,
    150–7; continuity criterion,
    144–5, 149–51, 156, 162, 164,
    166–70; memory/psychological
    criterion, 138–46; multiple
    occupancy thesis, 162–4;
    physical criterion, 145–50
  property exemplification account of
    (PEP), 173–4
  reduplication argument, 138, 142,
    145, 149–50, 152–5, 163, 165,
    169–70, 174 n.2; see also
    branching, fission
  theories of the nature of, 137–8,
    171–4
Plantinga, A., 125 n.14
Plato, 240, 257 nn.25–6
Platonic Realism, 237–52
  Platonism/Nominalism debate,
    244–5
Plato's Beard problem, 43, 71 n.7
Pollock, J., 175 n.4
possible worlds, 86–7, 125 n.14
predicate calculus, 37, 44–7, 49–51,
    53–4
Price, H. H., 256 n.19

Principle
  of Acquaintance, 110, 124 n.10
  of the Identity of Indiscernibles,
    63–5, 81–4, 106–11, 121–2
  of the Indiscernibility of Identicals,
    63–5, 68, 81, 87, 91, 102–3,
    111, 121
  see also criteria of identity
properties
  and the Principle of the Identity of
    Indiscernibles, 63–5, 81–4,
    106–11, 121–2
  and the Principle of the
    Indiscernibility of Identicals,
    63–5, 68, 81, 87, 91 102–3,
    111, 121
  and quality spaces, 202–4, 206,
    208
  as abstract universals and as
    tropes, distinction between,
    99–100
  as kind-determining essences, 120,
    200, 249
  as tropes, 89–90, 94, 99, 234–6,
    249–50; see also tropes
  as universals, 88–9, 99, 115–16,
    224
  dynamic and static properties, 130
    nn.45–47, 201–2, 204–6; see
    also events
  essential and accidental properties,
    67–9, 114, 119–22, 200, 249
  impure properties, 106, 109–10,
    115–16, 121
  positional properties, 107–10
  property/particular distinction, 57,
    62
  property/substance distinction, 59,
    66, 85
  pure and impure properties,
    distinction between, 106,
    114–16
  pure properties, 107–8, 110, 114,
    115–16
  relation to substances, 80–122,
    200–3

substance-kind properties, 116–18,
  120, 122, 169–70; atomic and
  non-atomic, 117–18, 121–2,
  130, 131 n.47, 132 nn.54 and
  55, 136, 170, 177 n.15; see also
  substance kinds
property exemplification account of
  events (PEE), 119, 187, 191,
  193–201, 205, 208
  persons (PEP), 173–4
  substances (PES), 116–17, 119,
  122, 194, 249
Putnam, H., 32 n.8, 253 n.4

quantification, 43–6, 51–3, 56, 58
  first-order quantification theory,
    37, 43–4, 208 n.4
  second-order quantification, 53
quantifiers, 43–5, 53
  existential quantifiers, 43, 45–6
  universal quantifiers, 43, 45
Quine, W. V. O., 25, 31 n.4, 37,
  42–5, 47–56, 57, 75 n.28, 79,
  123 n.2, 127 n.22, 130 n.47,
  192, 202, 253 nn.4–5, 255
  nn.14–15
Quinton, A., 74 n.18, 129 n.42, 174
  n.2

Realism, 219, 224, 233, 236–52
  Aristotelian Realism, 237–9, 246
  Platonic Realism, 237–52
Realism–Nominalism debate, 123
  n.4, 224–5, 236–9, 244–5
reduction, 82, 123 n.5
reduplication argument, 138, 142,
  145, 149–50, 152–5, 163, 165,
  169–70, 174 n.2
  see also branching, fission
relations
  internal relations, doctrine of,
    246–52
Rey, G., 176 n.12
Robinson, H., 137
Rodriguez-Pereyra, G., 229, 253 n.7,
  255 n.17, 257 n.20

Rosenkrantz, G., 128 n.37, 129 n.42, 229
Rovane, C., 174 n.2
Russell, B., 27, 33 n.17, 37, 71 n.7, 126 n.19, 232, 248, 250, 256 n.19

semantic ascent, 50–1
Shoemaker, S., 138, 140, 146, 151, 156–7, 161, 174 n.2, 175 n.7
Sider, T., 123 n.2
Simons, P., 37, 89, 126 n.18, 208 n.2, 233
Snowdon, P., 137
Soames, S., 31 n.4
Sober, E., 253 n.4
Sperry, R. W., 176 n.12
Strawson, P., 17–22, 24, 25, 30, 32 n.8, 37–44, 53–6, 126 n.18, 233
subject/predicate distinction, 37–42, 53–4
substances, material
    and atomic/non-atomic properties, see properties
    and bare substratum theory, 64, 81, 95, 110–22, 181
    and bundle theory, 63, 65, 81–115, 118–22, 142, 181
    and essentialist theory, 81, 114–22
    dynamic and static properties of, 201–2
    existence condition for, 82, 117–18
    identity condition for, 82, 117–18
    in relation to properties, 80–122, 200–3; see also properties
    kind-determining essences of, 120, 200–1, 249
    persistence through time and change, 80–1, 102–6, 110, 112–13, 121–2
    property exemplification account of (PES), 116–17, 119, 122, 194, 249

substance kinds, 60, 68, 116–18, 120–1, 181
substance/event distinction, 59–60, 66–7, 80, 104, 131 n.50, 186, 189–91, 199–200, 208
substance/property distinction, 59, 66, 85
Substitution Principle, 64–5
Swinburne, R., 137, 174 n.2
Swoyer, C., 222
Szabó, Z., 253 nn.10–11

Taylor, B., 208 n.4
Thomson, J. J., 198, 209 n.7
Trope Nominalism, 90, 127 n.26, 229, 233–7
tropes, 89–90, 94, 99, 100
    as particularized properties, 89, 99, 234–5, classic trope theory, 233–4, 258 n.28
    trope theory of events, 182–3

Unger, P., 140, 151, 156, 174 n.2
universals, 38, 100, 219–52
    abstract universals, 88, 94, 99, 115, 181
    Aristotelian conception of, 237–9
    infinite regress problem, 232–3, 239–48, 251
    internal relations, doctrine of, 246–52
    particular/universal distinction, 38, 62, 88–9, 94, 99–100, 115–16, 181, 237–9
    Platonic conception of, 237–9
    problem of, 219–21
    and properties, 38; [and so many more], 88–9
    Realism–Nominalism debate, 123 n.4, 224–5, 244–5
    Realist theory of, 221–2, 248

Van Cleve, J., 127 n.24, 257 n.21
van Inwagen, P., 25, 31 n.3, 37, 72–3 n.10, 127 n.21, 174 n.2
Varzi, A., 209 n.7

Walsh, W. H., 31 n.3
Whitehead, A., 17, 33 n.17
Whorf, B. J., 40–2
Wiggins, D., 63, 74 nn.18, 19 and 25, 116, 136, 138, 151, 156, 174 n.2
Wilkes, K., 174 n.2
Williams, B., 141–7, 174 n.2

Williams, D. C., 126 n.19, 233, 258 n.28
Wittgenstein, L., 233, 246, 250, 257 n.22
Wolterstorff, N., 128 n.40

Zimmerman, D., 128 n.33, 174 n.2